# ROWLAND BROOMHEAD
## 1751–1820

# Rowland Broomhead
# 1751–1820

## Apostle of the North

Peter Francis Lupton

GRACEWING

First published in England in 2015
by
Gracewing
2 Southern Avenue
Leominster
Herefordshire HR6 0QF
United Kingdom
www.gracewing.co.uk

ISBN 978 085244 850 2

Typeset by Gracewing

Cover design by Bernardita Peña Hurtado

Front cover image: The Reverend Rowland Broomhead by Joseph
William Allen © Salford Museum & Art Gallery.

*Dedicated to Olive my wife;*
*James & Anne-Marie my children*
*and my family and friends.*

# CONTENTS

# FOREWORD

THE SUBJECT OF this study is described in the Preface as 'a forgotten priest'. He deserves to be known otherwise. The funeral of the Reverend Rowland Broomhead was witnessed by thousands of people who, lining the streets of Manchester in respectful silence, wished to pay their homage to a man who was 'to the poor a kind and inspiring benefactor'. So well-known was he in his day that a portrait of him is to be found among the great and the good at the National Portrait Library. The 'discovery' of Broomhead is owed in part to serendipity.

Peter Lupton, during the course of his introducing pupils to the history of the parishes of Manchester, came across archival sources in which Broomhead was clearly an important figure and one that deserved to be recognised for the part he played in the life of the Church in Manchester and its environs. Thanks to the author's careful and painstaking research this important figure from the early days of Catholicism in Manchester is at last beginning to emerge from the shadows of time. It is clear that in being introduced to Broomhead the reader will also come to know better the joys and the sorrows, the woes and the triumphs of the Catholic Church and its history in the north-west of England.

The figure portrayed in this study comes across as a man in the spirit of St Francis de Sales, the one-time bishop of Geneva, whose watchword was 'you will catch more flies with a drop of honey than with a barrel of vinegar'. Broomhead was equally a citizen, an educationalist and not least a churchman. We might say that he operated in these spheres as if they were concentric circles, whilst respecting the distinctiveness of each he succeeded in integrating all three in his service to the city, to the people and to religion.

Fr Martin John Broadley

# PREFACE

F R ROWLAND BROOMHEAD came to my attention when I introduced children to the history of their parishes through collections of archival material that were gathered from Manchester Central Library. The parishes were those of St Chad; St Patrick; St Edmund; Corpus Christi; St Malachy; Our Lady of Mount Carmel; St Anne; St Clare; St Dunstan; St John Bosco and St Thomas of Canterbury. It was the material for St Chad's which introduced me to a forgotten priest, who had worked in Manchester and its environs in the period 1778 to 1820. The material was a panegyric by Fr. Joseph Curr and a poem by Michael Gaffey and both of these documents gave a brief but a useful synopsis of Broomhead's life.

Within the Catholic community very few priests or laity were aware of Fr Rowland Broomhead, who was known by Catholics in his day as 'Good Father Broomhead' and by the non-Catholic community as 'The Poor Man's Friend' and portraits of him are held by the National Portrait Gallery; Manchester Art Gallery; Salford Art Gallery; Salford Cathedral; St. Mary's Mulberry Street and St. Chad's, Cheetham Hill Road. The Manchester Mission was delineated by the geographical shape made by Bolton, Rochdale, Stockport, Glossop, and Macclesfield and back to Bolton, with Manchester in the centre.

The decision to write a book about the life and times of Rowland Broomhead came to fruition when the sources I read suggested a man of great quality whose life should have been part of both the history of Catholicism in the many parts of the Manchester mission and part of the general histories of the area. Although it is a study of a leader of a local church, it is not restricted to the field of local history or to denominational history, for it explores the life and times of Rowland Broomhead from the perspectives of citizen, educationalist and churchman. I have tried to write a book as close to his personal life as possible but at the same time attempting to introduce the importance of his background and the world in which he was moving.

Broomhead's early years were formed in his recusant Catholic family in Sheffield, which was influenced by the Jesuits and the secular priests working in that area. His schooling continued for a short time in Sedgley Park Hall before moving on in 1765 to the English College in Rome where he spent the next ten years. Here he was influenced for the most part by Jesuit priests. Broomhead was in Rome at the time of the suppression of the Jesuits by the pope and observed the imprisonment of the General of the Jesuits in the English College. He was appointed to Sheffield in 1775 and then to Manchester in 1778.

The international backdrop to Rowland Broomhead's life, 1751 to 1820, was the British at war in Europe, especially with France; problems in Ireland and the difficulty of fighting a war in America all of which touched the life of Broomhead and the lives of the people in Manchester. Difficulties with the supply of food and their increasing costs and the breaking up of machinery regularly led to riotous behaviour in the town. The need for more troops for fighting in the colonies, Europe and Ireland led to government discussions about an oath, in recognition of the King, that could be taken by Catholic men which would allow them to become soldiers. In the same year 1778, the government passed the First Catholic Relief Act, which used the Irish oath of 1774, and which allowed a few reliefs, mainly the keeping of a Catholic school; ability to inherit land and property, and informers could no longer claim a bounty.

The agrarian revolution, which saw the demise of ancient methods of strip farming and open fields system and the beginning of the enclosure movement, the latter of which developed quickly from the middle of the eighteenth century and whilst some might say it was justifiable action many small farmers and cottagers were ruined and many were forced to look for work elsewhere. Industrial and social developments that commenced in south-east Lancashire with Manchester at the centre saw developments from about 1530 continuing to increase till in the late eighteenth century the cottage industry was in decline as the new machinery was invented, leading to the huge building programme for establishing the cotton mills. Population growth, fuelled by migrants from within the country including Ireland, gave rise to the building of shoddy houses to meet this population increase; wages that were poor and failing harvests added to their poverty.

The so-called 'Age of Enlightenment' led to revolutionary ideas which came to a head in the French Revolution of 1789 which led to war and the arrival in England of émigré clergy and laity, who escaped from the atrocities being meted out to them. Revolutionary activities in Manchester resulted in the so-called 'Peterloo Massacre'.

For his first nine years in Manchester, Broomhead was involved in the wider mission of Manchester but in 1787 he was placed in charge at Rook Street Chapel and as more priests were allocated to the mission this allowed him time to establish himself in the civic affairs of the town, which were mainly involved with charitable hospitals and serving the poor. The second Relief Act of 1791 allowed Catholics the liberty to practise their religion under certain conditions and they were freed from some of the disabilities under which they had laboured, in effect freeing them from penal laws.

Rowland Broomhead was deeply involved in his church of St. Chad at Rook Street and besides the everyday religious pattern of Mass, prayers and sacraments etc. he introduced 'Public Instructions' in order to listen, to question and to point the way forward to heaven and this exercise in reaching out to people of all faiths and none was hugely successful, which then led to the need to build churches to accommodate them all.

Rowland reached out to his fellow priests in Lancashire and succeeding Vicars Apostolic and deeply embraced their proceedings, especially those that involved Catholic Emancipation, the establishment of Ushaw College and looking after his church-students. He was involved in the overseeing of the Lancashire Infirm Secular Clergy Fund and was recognised for his work in the Manchester mission with his appointment as a member of the Old Chapter of England.

Broomhead was never a man to encourage isolationism. His works in Manchester transcended parochialism for he was open to all whom he encountered. He was a committee member of the non-denominational Sunday school movement and gave charity sermons to support them. The education of adults and children was realised in some of the Sunday school rooms and at his sermons but for the children he was constantly looking for ways to educate them, and the climax of his life was the opening of the church of St Augustine in Granby Row which not only provided for his many parishioners but made provision of a schoolroom underneath the church for one thousand pupils.

Whilst Broomhead was intellectually bright he was also a man of action and that is where his priorities lay. He was revered, highly respected and esteemed, the definition of 'venerable'.

# ACKNOWLEDGEMENTS

Y THANKS FOR all the help I have received in writing this book, especially from Dr John Cosgrove, who encouraged me over many years; Dr Ann Dillon who recognised the importance of my book and provided useful criticism and a great deal of support as did Rev Dr David Lannon of the Diocesan Archives of Salford; Rev Dr Martin John Broadley; Dr Peter Nockles and Mr M Monaghan. The nature of the work required many hours in libraries and archives and it was within these institutions that I received superlative support. It was in four archive collections that I found the majority of evidence for this biography: Chetham's Library (Dr Michael R. Powell et alia); Lancashire Record Office, Preston; Leeds Diocesan Archives (Mr Robert Finnigan) and Ushaw College Durham (Mr Matthew Watson).

I extend my gratitude to the personnel of the following institutions and archives: Archdiocese of Birmingham Archives (Rev Dr John Sharp);Archdiocese of Westminster Archives (Rev Nicholas Schofield);Bradfield Parish Archives (Mr Malcolm Nunn); the Catenian Association; Central Manchester and Manchester Children's University Hospital Trust Archives; Derbyshire Record Office, Matlock; Diocese of Hallam Archives(Deacon Bill Burleigh); Glossop Library (Derbyshire County Council); Greater Manchester County Record Office; John Ryland's Library (University of Manchester); Macclesfield Library (Cheshire East Council);Manchester Central Library Archives & Local Studies Departments; Old Brotherhood of the English Clergy, London (Mgr Ralph Brown and Mgr Anthony Stark); the Oratory House of St Chad, Manchester (the community of); Our Lady and the Apostles, Stockport (Fr Pat Munroe); Portico Library & Gallery,

Manchester (Emma Marigliano & Taylor Bishop who helped with the illustrations); Revell Grange (Martin Edwards); Rochdale Local Studies Library; St Vincent de Paul, Rochdale (Canon Paul Brindle); Salford Cathedral (Mgr Canon Anthony Kay VG BD and Fr Paul Carr); Sheffield Archives Shoreham Street; Sheffield Central Library Archives; Stannington research by Chris Wells and the Venerable English College Archives, Rome (Rev Mark Harold).

I wish to record my thanks, to Mrs M Knowles & Ricard Rodriguez for solving computer problems and other matters & to Mr Chris Langstone for his map work and to acknowledge those who read the script: Dr J C Cosgrove, Rev Dr J M Broadley, Dr A Dillon, Dr P Nockles and Miss K Mulheran.

I am especially grateful to the Chief Executive, Tom Longford and the Rev Dr Paul Haffner, Theological and Editorial Director, Monica Manwaring, publicity and all the staff of Gracewing who have been involved in bringing this book to fruition. Last and not least my thanks go to my wife and children who have been so supportive of my work.

# ABBREVIATIONS

| | |
|---|---|
| AAL: | Archives of the Archbishop of Liverpool |
| AAW: | Archives of the Archbishop of Westminster |
| AYVR: | Archbishop of York Visitation Returns |
| BAA: | Birmingham Archdiocesan Archives |
| BIY: | Borthwick Institute York |
| BPC: | Bradfield Parish Council, Sheffield |
| CLM: | Chetham's Library Manchester |
| CMUH: | Central Manchester University Hospitals |
| CRS: | Catholic Record Society |
| DDSC: 19/38 | The rules of the secular Clergy who are associated to the general Fund in the Counties of Lancaster, Westmorland, Cumberland and Chester. LRO: sometime between 1736 and 1820. |
| DRO: | Derbyshire Record Office |
| GMRO: | Greater Manchester Record Office |
| JRL: | John Ryland's Library |
| LISCF: | Lancashire Infirm Secular Clergy Fund |
| LDA: | Leeds Diocesan Archives |
| LRO: | Lancashire Record Office |
| MBH: | Manchester Board of Health |
| MBHM: | Manchester Board of Health Minutes |
| MCL: | Manchester Central Library |
| MG: | Bishop Matthew Gibson |
| MLH: | Manchester Lying-in Hospital |
| MM: | Manchester Mercury and Harrop's General Advertiser |

| | |
|---|---|
| MRIA: | Manchester Royal Infirmary Archives |
| MSLHA: | The Manchester & Salford Lock Hospital & Asylum |
| NAK: | National Archives Kew |
| NWCH: | North West Catholic History |
| RCCF: | Roman Catholic Clergy Fund at LRO (Name of the fund 'Lancashire Secular Clergy Fund). |
| SDA: | Salford Diocesan Archives |
| SCL: | Sheffield Central Library |
| UCA: | Ushaw College Archives |
| VEC: | Venerable English College Rome |
| WG: | Bishop William Gibson |
| WYAS: | West Yorkshire Archive Service |
| YAS: | Yorkshire Archaeological Society |

# ILLUSTRATIONS

# INTRODUCTION

## *Manchester in Mourning*

I T WAS 8 o'clock on Wednesday, 18 October 1820. There was an air of subdued expectation among the hundreds of people waiting outside the Roman Catholic Chapel in Rook Street, Manchester. Since the previous Wednesday the news of the death of the Reverend Rowland Broomhead had circulated through the town and had brought to the chapel thousands of people from all the different denominations represented in the emerging city, to pay their last respects to a man who had won the hearts of so many. By 9 o'clock the hundreds had swelled to thousands. The town had the appearance of a public holiday. Business ceased so that all who wished could accompany the body to St Augustine's, Granby Row. This church was built by Fr Broomhead and, despite his sickness had been present at the blessing and opening only three weeks previously.

The funeral procession was a very grand affair. It was led by four beadles of the town and four mutes, dressed in black and riding on sable horses. About one hundred gentlemen, drawn from the various religious groupings in the town, followed the hearse, which was drawn by six black horses. There were two mourning coaches and eleven private carriages. As the procession proceeded through the streets a large crowd followed it, drawn from every walk of life and from every age group. On arrival at St Augustine's the remains were carried into the Church by some of Broomhead's congregation. The key areas of the Church were draped in black, especially the altar. The officiating priests covered the coffin with the pall and then proceeded to the sanctuary singing the 'Miserere'. The solemn sung requiem was celebrated by Fr Thomas Lupton,[1] assisted by ten priests. Fr Joseph Curr gave the panegyric.[2] In his eulogy he called upon his fellow clerics to emulate the piety, zeal and virtues which this man had shown throughout his life. Broomhead was then laid to rest under the chancel.

Descriptions of the funeral and the recognition of Broomhead's virtues underline the respect that he had earned from the people of Manchester. Newspapers carried long articles about him and people wrote poetry to mark his life. Pamphlets of the Discourse at the funeral; a panegyric and memoirs, were printed and published in the town. The extract from the 'Exchange Herald' summed up how people felt:

> The tears now stream, deep sighs now heave the breast,
> And sorrow now bows down the drooping head,
> Because—no wonder the sad stroke opprest—
> Broomhead, the poor man's friend, is dead.[3]

## Notes

[1] Thomas Lupton: Born 27 March 1776 at Claughton, the estate of the Brockholes family who sent him to Douai College. Imprisoned at Dourlens during the French revolution but escaped 16 January 1794. Continued his education at Tudhoe and then Crook Hall and was ordained priest 3 April 1800. Missioner at Weld Bank, Chorley for a short time then transferred to St Chad's, Rook Street, Manchester, as an assistant to Rowland Broomhead. After nineteen years he suffered from ill health and was transferred to be chaplain at 'Old Garswood Hall', Ashton-in-Makerfield, Lancashire. Died 29 April 1843.

[2] J. A. Curr, *Discourse delivered at St Augustine's Chapel, Manchester, 18 October 1820 at the Funeral of the Rev Rowland Broomhead* (Manchester: Printed and Published by J. Robinson, Catholic Bookseller, 44 Deansgate, 1820). Joseph Curr was born in Sheffield circa 1773 and educated at Crook Hall, Durham. He was ordained circa 1808 and was appointed assistant to Rowland Broomhead at the chapel of St Chad's at Rook Street, Manchester and remained there until the opening of St Augustine, Granby Row. He was known for his publications, doctrinal and instructive, for the use of his

congregation and was also involved in controversy especial with the Protestant Bible Association.

3    M. Gaffey, *A Panegyric of the late Rev Rowland Broomhead, Forty-two years a Catholic Priest at Manchester* (Manchester: Printed and published by J. A. Robinson, 1822).

# 1 FORMATIVE YEARS 1751–1775

ROWLAND BROOMHEAD BORN 16 August 1751 at Revell Grange, Stannington, in the chapelry of Bradfield, parish of Ecclesfield, Sheffield was the third son of Richard Broomhead and Ann (née Revell). Rowland had two older brothers and two younger sisters and the eldest son Richard inherited his father's estates 17 August 1778.[1] Rowland and his brothers and sisters were brought up as Roman Catholics. Rowland's birth was entered in the margin of the register of Bradfield Parish Church (which entry was important for matters legal)[2] rather than the main body of the register which would suggests that his baptism was held at the family chapel at Revell Grange.

Ann Revell became sole heiress to the Revell estates on the death of her uncle Rowland Revell 23 May 1742, when her father Thomas succeeded to the estate of his bachelor brother and they moved from Nethergate Hall to Revell Grange. The inheritance of Thomas enhanced Ann's prospects enormously and the marriage to Richard Broomhead, the first son of Richard Broomhead and Ann (née Stead) took place within six months of the death of her uncle. After their marriage, 19 November 1742, Richard and Ann lived with Thomas at Revell Grange. On the death of her father, 15 November 1744, Ann inherited the estate.

The Revell and Broomhead families had lived in the Sheffield area since the fourteenth century.[3] During the period 1560 to 1616, George Talbot, 6th Earl and Gilbert Talbot, 7th Earl of Shrewsbury were successively Lords of the Manor of Sheffield and as Protestants and supporters of Elizabeth I, enforced the penal laws in Sheffield, which in consequence became a marked and dangerous locality to the poor Jesuit or seminary priest, who took care to leave behind, the fewest traces of his ministrations, which might have seriously compromised the friends who had sheltered him.[4]

Apart from the Lords of the Manor of Sheffield the Revells were the most influential family in the Stannington area. Nethergate Hall, their senior residence, was situated at the centre of a village divided in two by the names Upper-gate and Nether-gate, which later came to be known as Stannington. In the Bradfield area in 1672 the hearth tax was paid by those whose houses were worth more than twenty shillings a year and who contributed to the local church and poor rates. Mr Revell paid one shilling for each of his six hearths, the highest amount in Stannington, which gives an indication of the size of Nethergate Hall.[5] This Revell was the grandfather of Ann who inherited the Revell estates. Nethergate Hall was certainly a family home in the early part of the sixteenth, and it was still owned by the family in the early nineteenth century.

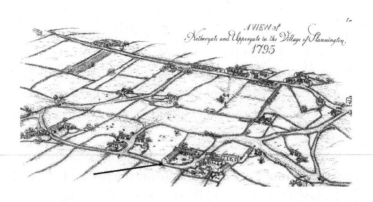

*1. Nethergate Hall*

To the west of the old village, about a mile away from Nethergate Hall, on Bingley Road, was the second house called Revell Grange. The hearth tax return for the Grange, Ladyday 1672, was only one shilling. The original house is believed to be dated from circa 1495 and was altered to its present appearance in the early eighteenth century.[6] The Revell's owned substantial land throughout the Stannington area and much of the land, in and around Revell Grange and Nethergate Hall, had been in their hands since the time of Gregory Revell in the sixteenth century.[7] Both houses were situated in fairly isolated areas of Hallamshire and they would have been difficult to reach on the poor roads, but their position on the side of the Rivelin Valley would have given them good notice of approaching pursuivants. The chapel of the Revell family was in Nethergate Hall until 1742 when a chapel was established at Revell Grange.

*2. Revell Grange, Stannington, Sheffield*

The Revell family became leaders of the underground church in the Sheffield area and were responsible for the ancient faith being retained, from the Reformation down into the twentieth century. The Revells had an unbroken affiliation to the 'Old Faith'. According to Hadfield:

> There is a well-founded tradition, that at Stannington, the seat of the Revells, Mass has been said all through the period we are considering, and that it had its chapel and priest.[8]

Establishing a chapel in their home was a very dangerous action, but the Revells not only established a chapel to take the place of the chapel of St Nicholas Bradfield, but also opened it for others who wished to maintain their ancient religion and it required much care to see that they were not apprehended, and it was important to have Roman Catholic employees who could be relied on for their secrecy and support.

Secret chapels set up in the homes of these Catholic gentry needed priests to say Mass and provide sacramental support and this need was supplied in the early years by those priests who had lost their livings:

> For the first sixteen years of the schism, from 1558 to 1574, (the maintenance of the Faith) was due to the priests, some regular, but mostly secular, ordained in the previous reigns ...[9]

Fr William Holt SJ, in a paper dated 1596, drawn up to show how the Catholic Faith had been maintained in England during more than a generation of persecution, asserted that there were still at that date between forty and fifty of the old Marian clergy labouring on the mission.[10] During the early years, Bolsterstone and Nethergate Hall relied on the Jesuit priests from Spinkhill, to the south-east of Sheffield, to serve these two Catholic houses.

The momentous decision of Rowland Broomhead's maternal ancestors was to reject the religious changes which had been consolidated in the Elizabethan Settlement of 1559; to refuse to attend services at the chapel of St Nicholas in Bradfield; to continue the observance of their ancient faith in their home in Stannington and to invite neighbours of Catholic persuasion to join them in their chapel at Nethergate Hall. Before the reign of Elizabeth there were no fines for non-attendance at chapel but there were after 1559. It was up to every succeeding generation of the family to reaffirm or reject the decision of their forefathers, but the evidence clearly supports their regular affirmation of the original decision.[11]

The ministering priests at the Chapel of St Nicholas were required to list those who did not attend their chapel at Bradfield and forward the information to the Archbishop of York. The town of Sheffield was too insecure for the establishment of a Catholic chapel because of strong Protestantism so some of the local Catholic gentry took it upon themselves to fill this gap and provide a place for Mass in their homes. Around the outlying areas of Sheffield, a network of missions or Mass-centres was established at Padley Hall (Fitzherbert), Hassop Hall (Eyre), Burghwallis Manor (Anne), and in the area closest to Sheffield there was Bolsterstone, Spink House, the home of the Blackburn's and later the Smith family; Spinkhill, the residence of the Pole family and Nethergate Hall and later Revell Grange in Stannington, homes of the Revell family.

There is no evidence of recusancy in Broomhead's family tree in the Bradfield chapelry, until 1742, and that was following on the marriage of Richard Broomhead and Ann Revell. In the Broomhead's family tree there is a reference to the death of Thomas Bromehead in 1587 'probably a priest at Stavely until the dissolution of the monasteries'.[12] This is supported by an entry of a burial of Thomas Bromehead 26 October 1587, in the Parish Church of Bradfield. This is the only reference to a priest in Broomhead's family tree until the ordination of Rowland Broomhead in 1775.[13] There is evidence in the records of the English College in Rome that Richard Broomhead, father of Rowland, was certainly a Catholic when Rowland entered the seminary, for the College recorded that his parents were both Roman Catholics.[14]

*3. Chapel of St Nicholas in Bradfield*

The Archbishop of York, Robert Hay Drummond (1761 to 1776) recorded in 1765 that 'A priest from Sheffield attends once a month at Mr Broomhead's at Stannington'.[15] This was the same year when Rowland Broomhead went to the English College in Rome.

The Returns of the Papists 1767 for Bradfield, in the parish of Ecclesfield, recorded eighty 'Papists' with only their initials, age, occupation and length of residency. Richard Broomhead, Rowland's father, who died 17 August 1778, would surely have been listed in that Papist Return of 1767.

A letter, written by Rowland to his nephew Richard Broomhead, who was then in possession of Revell Grange, referred to a sale by the Duke of Norfolk, of some of his estates in the Sheffield area. Rowland wrote from Rook Street, Manchester 14 July 1810:

> There can be little doubt, I think, of his selling you the storth,[16] and perhaps the old buildings in Stannington, which have been so long in the family, and was formerly the family residence,[17] and the priest formerly kept there was the chief cause of the Catholic religion being kept up at Sheffield and the neighbourhood, as well as at Stannington.[18]

Rowland was referring to the old house of Nethergate Hall.

Two secular priests came into Rowland Broomhead's life during his first thirteen years at Revell Grange, 1751 to 1764. The first was Christopher Gradwell, a priest, who came to Sheffield in 1736 and died there in 1758. He was described as 'a plain, sensible and pious man, a ripe scholar, and held in much esteem by all the people'.[19] During his twenty-two years in Sheffield he continued to serve both Nethergate Hall and after 1742 Revell Grange. For the last seven years of his life Gradwell was in contact with Rowland and his parents and tutored the children, often the secondary role of a priest, and may also have directed Rowland to a school. The second was John Lodge who, until 1764, was the sole occupant of the mission at Sheffield and continued to serve Stannington and influenced the young Broomhead's education when he visited Revell Grange.

In 1764 Broomhead was sent to Sedgley Park School. During the mid eighteenth century, Bishop Richard Challoner[20] and Rev William Errington rented Sedgley Park Hall, situated some two miles from Wolverhampton and assembled a school which they opened 25 March 1763. In the account book of the school[21] the arrival of Rowland Broomhead and his brother, Thomas was recorded, 25 September 1764:

> Master Thomas & Master Roland Broomhead came September 25th 1764 & brought with'em each 2 suits of cloths,

& dozen shirts, 8 pair of stockings, 2 pr of shoes, 2 hats, 8
Handkerchiefs, 6 night caps, 2 Gardens of the Soul & 2 daily
companions, 4 combs, 2 knives & 2 forks.

Underneath this entry is a section which appears to have been
crossed through, to show payment had been received:

they are prs[prices] for 4 pr of shoes 14s: 8d, 2 hats 4s: 3d,
2Sp. Books 2s, 2 brushes 4s & 2 spoons 6s[?] a box 3, for a
letter 4d, for carriage of a parcel 1s, for a letter 4d.Do[ditto]
4d, Do 9d; Do 41/2d: Do 41/2. apoth: 10s:6d'.

Rowland's date of birth was listed as 27 August 1751 but Thomas's
birth date was not entered and he did not appear on the family
pedigree.[22] Both brothers were recorded as 'parlour boarders'
which cost twenty pounds compared with twelve guineas paid by
the other students, but this extra payment allowed them to dine
with the Masters, which would have been in-keeping for pupils
coming from a gentry-family.

Church students and those destined for the trades and professions were educated there and the curriculum provided Classics,
French and Mathematics as optional subjects. It was difficult to
construct a timetable for students for there was no fixed time for
entering or leaving for those living locally, but most pupils did not
go home during their years there because of distance and cost, and
the School set down that:

No allowance will be made for absence in the vacation time;
and it is most earnestly wished, that parents would not often
call them home at those times.[23]

SEDGLEY PARK CHAPEL.

*4. Sedgley Park School Chapel*

The students had a variety of outside pursuits. Some worked in the local farms; others had little gardens to look after. They caught birds and tamed and caged them and they played marbles, tops and used skipping ropes.

A housekeeper looked after the boys and there was also a cobbler and a tailor to assist. Washing was done in the open air at a water pump. Anyone found transgressing rules was soundly whipped by the President and any breakages had to be paid for. A broken window cost 3d.

At the end of the academic year of 1765 Rowland went home to Stannington to see his parents and family before travelling to Rome to take up his studies at the English College. The fact that Broomhead only attended Sedgley Park for one year before being accepted for his preparation for the priesthood suggests that he already had the necessary rudiments of education. Gaffey recorded Rowland's transition to Rome:

> In early life this rev'rend champion trod
> The virtuous footsteps of a bleeding God:
> His Saviour call'd him—when he heard the call,
> He left his country, family, and all
> That he held dear, to follow him alone
> Who evidently mark'd him for his own.
> To Rome's fair city, where religion reigns
> In sacred splendour, free from error's stains;
> That seat of learning, that secure retreat
> Of every thing that's good, of all that's great.
> He bent his way, his studies to pursue,
> And daily greater in perfection grew.[24]

In 1765, having made his way by horse-drawn coach from Sheffield to London, Broomhead met up with Samuel Sayles from Yorkshire and William Casemore from Berkshire and travelled on to Rome together but there is no evidence of the journey.

The clue to their outward journey is to be found in the inward journey taken by Rowland Broomhead in 1775. He and his companion George Halsey, a fellow student and priest, chose to travel by sea and land. Halsey wrote a letter to: 'The Most Illustrious Lord and Most Cultured Patron the Lord Marco Magnani, Rector of the English College next to Piazza Farnese, Rome 6 September 1775'.[25] Halsey could not remember the date when he left the College except that it had been in April 1775 but according to John Kirk's diary, George Halsey and Rowland Broomhead departed towards England 28 April 1775.

The first day of the journey to Civitavecchia was fraught with difficulties:

> In the month of April (the actual day escapes my mind), I
> left your College with a companion and intended to travel

> to Civita Vecchia, and since we did not depart until after
> midday, half way there we spent the night at a tavern, the
> name of which I remember well, Castel Nuovo. It was a
> dreadful night, with a badly cooked supper. Even though
> the price was extortionate, the beds were hard, and what is
> worse, it was a den of thieves.

Before they left Castel Nuovo they were lucky enough to be able
to exchange some of their money with travellers on their way from
Corsica to Rome:

> Nevertheless, there was some consolation as there were
> some people who had come from Corsica and were clearly
> making their way to Rome for the Jubilee Year, with whom
> we made a mutually beneficial change of money.

On day two, 29 April 1775, they left the Castel Nuovo on their way
to Civitavecchia arriving there at midday and were lucky enough
to get a decent inn:

> On the following day we were on our way very quickly,
> reached the city by midday. By the fortunate intervention
> of a friend, we found a decent inn at no great cost.

Luckily for them it was a good inn, for they were to be marooned
there for nine days, but they had only travelled circa forty-four miles
from Rome:

> I do not doubt you are aware of our protracted delay there owing
> to misplaced trust in a French sea captain who, by an expressed
> promise, had proposed to sail to Marseilles on the second day
> after our arrival. In fact, we stayed there nine days …

Finally, on day ten of their journey, Sunday 7 May 1775, they
embarked, with Marseilles as their destination. They had to have
been relieved to be on their way after such a protracted wait,
unfortunately the journey at sea was dreadful and no doubt a very
frightening experience:

When at last we were travelling on the sea, we were tossed all over the place by dangerous waves. On the ninth day of sailing, just as we were happily about to reach the bay of Marseilles, an opposing wind detained us, which grew in strength that the ship barely escaped the jaws of the horrendous rocks. The blackest night was advancing with the very heavy storm. Finally, with the help of God, the wind ceased. The swelling subsided, and we carefully made our way into Marseilles harbour with great joy. Indeed we had suffered many things since the awful departure on account of the saltiness of the food, and we remained two days in Marseilles. We rested …

It was now day eighteen and the date was Monday 15 May 1775 and rest was surely needed:

On the third day we made the eight days' journey to ( … ) much afflicted by the cold wind and dust, we got as far as Lyons, a most famous city. There we hardly spent a night, for at three o'clock in the morning we left for Paris, which we reached on Whitson Eve. We went to the National College, where we were received by Mr. Howard the Rector with great charity and kindness … after six days in Paris we took up our journey to Douai, which we reached on the second day. We went to the very busy College, and were very generously received by the President… Mr Broomhead made for England a short time afterwards.

The National College he referred to was the English College in Paris. It appears from an analysis of the letter that it took twenty-nine days to reach Paris and another two days to reach Douai. There is no evidence of how long it took for Broomhead's journey from to Sheffield but it would have been at least seven days. There is no doubt that the journey was long, arduous, eventful and dangerous.

The establishment of the Venerable English College grew out of the pilgrim hospice established in January 1362 for the 'use of the poor, sick, needy and distressed people coming from England to the City'.[26] The action of William Allen in 1576, sending six students from the seminary at to the English hospice in Rome, because he had no room in Douai, established the beginnings of what eventually came to be known as the Venerable English College (VEC), which became home for Broomhead in 1765. The annals of the English College[27] recorded the arrival of Rowland Broomhead, 7 October 1765. They confirmed his Catholic parentage, his birth 27 August 1751, his baptism in England, his home town as Sheffield and his Confirmation in Rome. Pope Clement XIII (1758 to 1769) was the College Protector and the Rector was Rev Fr Booth.

Aspects of the historical events and decisions made across many years, formulated by both management and administration and the religious and academic life of the English College, casting light on matters which impacted on Broomhead's way of life during the period 1765 to 1775.

Broomhead and his fellow students were catapulted into a very different environment from that which they had been used to in England. Many of them had come from rural backgrounds. Most did not speak Italian; their food was very different; so was the climate and freedom from the rules and demands of their relations and neighbours. According to Fr Persons[28] it

> engendereth high spirits in them that are not well estab-
> lished in Almighty God's grace, for coming thither very
> young, and finding themselves presently placed and pro-
> vided for abundantly, and acquainted daily with sights and
> relations of popes, cardinals and princes' affairs, our youths
> that were bred up at home with much simplicity... forget-
> teth easily themselves and breaketh out to liberty.[29]

Person's reflections were still relevant in Broomhead's time.

The Council of Trent (1545 to 1563) had laid down that the diocese of a student attending a seminary was responsible for the financial upkeep of the student, and the bishop of the diocese given a right to be involved in decisions about the student. This was known as a Tridentine seminary. However, in the case of the English students, they had no diocese but were registered according to the county they came from, which in Broomhead's case was Eboracensis (Yorkshire), and the papacy financed the VEC but the English bishops had little say in what happened there.

The Bull of Foundation (1 May 1579) listed the rules under five headings: those pertinent to entry, piety, studies, domestic discipline and health. In a preamble to the document the Pope set out his motives and objectives for the English College

> he has seen its youth flying from persecution in their own
> country to seek instruction in Rome; and he has determined
> to assist them in their holy purpose, to provide for them the
> means of education and thus to qualify them for the arduous
> and important duty of declaring the truths of religion to
> their deluded countrymen.[30]

The motives and objectives as laid down by Gregory XIII (1572–1585) in 1579 were apposite for Broomhead for he was required on arrival to make an oath, swearing to obey the rules and be loyal to the Pope.

Pope Gregory XIII had given the new College a yearly grant and property which would realise an annual income of 3,000 ducats. The property, the Abbey of San Savino at Piacenza, was seized from the Jesuits by the Duke of Parma in 1768 and as a result, the College income reduced significantly. The response of the College authorities was to reduce the number of students and staff, which led to the appointment of Broomhead as a teacher of Italian and Latin for the younger students, despite the fact that he was still a student himself.

Unrest in the College (1579) had centred on a contention that the Jesuits were using the College as a means of recruitment for their Society, which had the potential to take students away to another mission than England. Fr Persons and Cardinal William Allen[31] drew up an oath that all students were required to take, for acceptance into the College. Broomhead took this same missionary oath which required him to 'lead a life befitting the clerical state and declare his readiness to return at the will of superiors to England and there labour for the good of souls'.[32]

The College was ruled by a rector, who was responsible to the Cardinal Protector, who in turn was responsible to the Pope. The rector of this secular College not only ruled the seminary but was also the prefect of the English Jesuit mission. Many problems over the years emanated from these arrangements. Students complained that 'the Jesuits were enticing scholars into the Society, especially through the Sodality'[33] set up in the College in 1581, which was concerned with apostolic work and personal piety. Students were selected before being allowed to belong to it, and Broomhead had joined the sodality.

As a result of quarrels at the College, William Allen advised the Pope, that an English Jesuit should be put in place, and this was accepted. However, by 1593, it was again under the stewardship of an Italian Jesuit. Troubles continued and the Pope sent in Cardinal Saga who prepared a report with recommendations. These were: that the Jesuits should continue to run the College; that the number of students should be reduced because of lack of finances; and dissidents unwilling to accept the discipline of the College should leave. From 1610 to 1773 English Jesuits were rectors of the College. The first eight years of Broomhead's education was in their hands.

Ecclesiastical, financial and political problems were considerable during the seventeenth and eighteenth centuries and they centred on the 'intrigues and jealousies' of the secular and regular clergy in England; the lack of priests being ordained for the English mission; lack of candidates being put forward from the English mission; opposition in

England to the Jesuits running a College for secular clergy and the loss of money and land especially in the eighteenth century.

The Jesuits continued to be a source of irritation, both for the Vicars Apostolic and the students. The English clergy lost interest in sending candidates to the English College in Rome and there was a subsequent decline in numbers. In 1737, Bishop Petre[34] wrote to Pope Clement XII for reforms to be instituted at Rome (and Valladolid). He asked, that the full income of the College should be spent on the education of the students; that only students submitted by the Vicars Apostolic should be admitted and that the course of studies 'be better adapted to the needs of the English Mission'.[35]

In answer to the concerns raised by Petre, decrees were issued that addressed matters of administration, accountancy, admissions, discipline and piety. The study of Sacred Scripture and modern controversies were set in place to answer the bishops' concerns about relevant preparation of English students for an English mission. Fr John Thorpe taught 'moral theology, and was aware of the need for a sound casuistry'.[36] He taught Broomhead until the suppression of the Jesuits. The new philosophies would also have been considered for there were fragments at the College of 'notes on the philosophy of John Locke'.[37] The key request for governance of the College to be handed over to English secular clergy was passed over and this resulted in lack of confidence in the College, and recruits difficult to find.

In 1753 the Pope (Benedict XIV) issued the Bull 'Apostolicum Ministerium' which 'regulated the jurisdiction of the Bishops over missions served by members of the Regular Orders'.[38] Consequently Dr Challoner decided to send three students to the English College under what he considered to be more favourable conditions. The agent of the English Bishops in Rome, Christopher Stoner, reported that this action had 'given great satisfaction'. Challoner, in response, said that the Bishops should do all in their power to find proper subjects. They should be at least fourteen years old, and know the rudiments of Latin.

Challoner wrote to Fr Booth, the rector of the College, 14 September 1764, telling him that he was sending him two young boys for rudiments. These were Samuel Shingler and George Goodman who arrived at the College ,2 December 1764, both from London.[39] In July 1765, George White arrived from Warwickshire and in the October, Rowland Broomhead and Samuel Sayles from Yorkshire, and William Casemore from Berkshire.

Throughout the history of the English College the problem of attracting students and the cost of keeping and educating them were perennial problems. The shortage of seminarians can clearly be seen in the numbers on the roll during the decade of Broomhead's residence at the College. The reduction of students during Broomhead's time led to the reduction of professors. In the first five years the average number of students per year was twenty-three and during the last five years was ten.[40]

Broomhead's life at the College can be divided into two periods; the Jesuit period from 7 October 1765 to August 1773 and the Italian secular clergy period from 1773 to 28 April 1775. The main resource for the earlier period is William Casemore's diary[41], which has suffered the ravages of time, and for the second period the diary of John Kirk which is better preserved. These two diaries are important for they are written by contemporaries of Broomhead. Casemore was a fellow traveller to Rome and both entered the College on the same day. Kirk[42] had known Broomhead only from June 1773 till 28 April 1775, although they were to know one another later when they were missioners in England and members of the Old Chapter of England. Some of Kirk's writing is based on his own experience, and some is also hearsay evidence from conversations he had at a later time. His interpretation of events might be coloured by his immaturity; having said that, it is valuable primary evidence. John Kirk, included Broomhead in a description of the early months of his life at the College just before the suppression:

> We were committed to the care of Rowland Broomhead, who was dean of the College & who was to instruct us in the Latin and Italian languages.

The lack of income and its effect on the College was described by Kirk:

> On account of our small income the Card. Protector Lante, rather than diminish our table & privileges had dismissed Repetitor, 3 lectors of morals, prefect of studies & as likewise most of the ordinary functions of the Church, (the summary of which may be seen in the Choir) were laid aside, but as yet the ancient custom of singing mass for the departed benefactors, as also for the scholars that died was retained. The custom of saying the beads & litanies in the sodality every day & of singing the litanies every Saturday in the same place was, as it was prescribed in rules at the last apostolic visitation, likewise retained.

> The authorities were so short of money that they dismissed many of the professors; reduced some of the ordinary functions of the Church hence Broomhead teaching languages.

According to Kirk the quality of meals was not reduced despite the shortage of income:

> Our table was always very good, these being as I have heard of, (for I forget at present) eight ounces for the boiled pittance & six for the other with different sort of fowls according to the different seasons. On the vacant days of the week we had a portion over & Parmesan Cheese or Butter for breakfast. The Minister always dined & supped with us, but the Rector & Confessor dined & supped at the second table, as likewise the sick & the lector (before the custom of reading all the time of table was taken away) on

the feasts of St Thomas, & the B. Trinity, Christmas, Easter,
St Ignatius & as likewise on the feast of some English saints.

In March 1773, Cardinal Andrea Corsini[43] was made Cardinal
Protector of the College. The news of his appointment seems to have
been welcomed, for he was 'congratulated by the four English Vicars
Apostolic and their Co-adjutors, and by the superiors of the English
seminaries at Douai, Paris and Valladolid.'[44] John Kirk only arrived
in the College 5 June 1773 which was three months after Corsini's
appointment and yet he entered in his diary the following:

> I had unto this time-viz. unto August 1773, lived a very
> happy & pleasant life, when all of a sudden fortune frus-
> trated all my hopes of a continuance, for on the 16th of the
> same month, the Jesuits having been destroyed, a cloud of
> troubles, not easily foreseen, began to hang over our heads
> & threaten us with sudden misfortunes: the thing in short
> was this:—Card. Lante dying March the 3rd 1773 the Clergy
> chose for their protector Card. Corsini as likewise of the
> Colleges:-and on the 23 of March in presence of the Schol-
> ars he received the office a little while after he came to the
> College & sealed up our archive & library with his own seal
> so that no one could enter.

Kirk was obviously relating what someone else had told him about
the events of 23 March 1773, referring to Broomhead's activities
as a librarian:

> The Higher School used to go into the library when they
> pleased & for that purpose had a key which was kept by the
> dean & used to write the books they took in a Book for that
> purpose in the library.

Broomhead was dean of the College and responsible for access to
the library that had been sealed by Corsini.

The latter reported to Foggini in early 1773 that the English
College was in disarray with only eight students, and archives that

were in chaos. Corsini immediately sealed the archives so that they could be reorganized and set about 'trying to remove financial control from the College staff and entrust it to a man of his own appointment'. He appealed to the Pope who granted 'all the necessary and appropriate powers for the administration of all the funds in existence both in Rome and throughout the Papal States'.[45]

The Jesuits were suppressed by Clement XIV (1769 to 1774) in his brief *Dominus ac Redemptor* dated 21 July 1773 and read in the English College by Pier Francesco Foggini. The Jesuit superiors were arrested and imprisoned in the College where they were interrogated about the financial affairs of the College and were released only when they were satisfied that the full information had been gathered. The College was then in the control of Foggini in the role of procurator; no rector was appointed but Giovanucci became vice-rector. Fr Lorenzo Ricci, General of the Jesuits, was brought to the College and was imprisoned there and later removed to the prison of Castel San Angelo. Broomhead was an observer of the events of that period which were recorded in the diaries of Kirk and Casemore.

With the Brief of Suppression, signed 8 June, but dated 21 July 1773, Corsini was able to establish full control over the English College. The suppression of the Jesuits and the control of the College by Corsini had an immediate effect on the students. According to Kirk the destruction of the Jesuits and the establishment of an Italian secular administration:

> very much displeased the Scholars (who were resolved not to part with their ancient liberties which now they plainly saw were going to be seized on) so shortly after they went to the Card(cardinal) for an English rector but he was deaf to their prayers. Seeing this (as I have been told by themselves) they went to the Pope (Clement XIV) who told 'em to go to the Card (Cardinal). But this was not all they had to suffer for F. (Foggini) was resolved with threats & promises to make 'em

go to confession in Italian which however they resisted manfully always remaining steadfast in that their resolution... all the privileges & indulgences which our Sodality enjoyed... all these indulgences I say were taken away & because there was no Confessor then in the house whose office it was to preside in the election of the prefect assistant no more general congregations were made. However the Scholars begged of the third rector, since the suppression (Magnani) a renovation of the indulgences possible, but to no purpose. Some few years after (about 6) a Prefect very familiar with the Superiors told a companion of mine F. (Foothead) that the reason for which we could not go into the garden any more was lest we should visit the Sodality of the B. V. which (he said) was forbidden by the Pope:—whether or not this reason was ever alleged by our Superiors I doubt.

Kirk described the incarceration of the Jesuit General, Ricci, in the College and the effect on the students, including Broomhead:

the day following the Suppression viz.-on the 17 of August, after supper, there came to our College, Ricci, general of the Jesuits accompanied by soldiers, who was placed in a Room over the Library, in which he was almost continually locked, he being served by a lay-brother (I believe) out of kitchen, though the Camera Pontificia paid afterwards all his expenses. The higher schools being then in the Divine's Gallery, it was pretended (whether true or not I can't say), that they had communication with the General (who was almost everyday examined by a Judge with his Scrivener) & so for this reason they were dislodged & sent into the Philosophers' Gallery where I & Fuller were with Broomhead, our prefect. Not long after, they were sent hence also. The assistant General of Germany & the General's secretary coming also to the College one of wh. was sent up into the lower School's Gallery, and the other into the Philosophers'. So part of us were sent into the infirmary- to wit Broomhead,

Shaw, Hurdy, Daniel, I (who was there already being sick)
& Fuller. Halsey was placed in the Confessor's room. (It
afterwards in 1776- was turned into a School for the Philosophers & painted & adorned with a pulpit, seats & benches
all of nut). Sayles was sent into the rector's sleeping room,
& Casemore into the room under that which was anciently
the shoe-makers or the first we meet going up stairs on the
left hand ( this room afterwards was made the Archive &
adorned with new shelves: the old one in the infirmary being
made a prison or dungeon- of which more hereafter).
Although all the boys moved, the prefect (Don Ignacio
Gomila) remained in his old room opposite to Guards'
room, or the wardrobe & the boys after ye country of the
same year were again placed in the same gallery: the General, the Assistant General of Germany & the General's
Secretary being gone to the Castle. It is to be observed that
during their abode or imprisonment here, there were always
soldiers with their muskets at the garden-door, & as one of
my companions has been told by a prefect, of whom I spoke
above, that the Divines' Gallery was full of soldiers.

The students in the latter part of Broomhead's time, 1773 to 1775
did not appear to be pleased with their new leaders for according
to Kirk they 'threaten us with sudden misfortunes' and a senior
group approached both their new masters and the Pope for they
were resolved not to part with their ancient liberties which now
they plainly saw were going to be seized but they were unsuccessful

Their new masters were congratulated by the four English Vicars
Apostolic and their Coadjutors and by the superiors of the English
seminaries at Douai, Paris and Valladolid. The Jesuits had difficulty
getting their income from the pope but Corsini was granted all the
necessary and appropriate powers.

In November 1773, Corsini wrote to Walmesley, Vicar Apostolic of the Western District:

> As regards the English College at Rome, I found it to a large
> extent deprived of the sources of income given to it by the
> Apostolic see, but I shall diligently ensure that it is reformed
> and if you have any youths who are not quarrelsome or
> fastidious but promising and obedient…I shall be glad to
> learn from you their names and situation.[46]

Broomhead is mentioned in both diaries but there is no evidence
of what he said or thought about the events of his decade in Rome
but we have the writings of Michael Gaffey written in 1820/21
whose writings suggest close knowledge of Broomhead's contemporaries in Rome, who remarked on his rapid progress, his modesty
and humility and 'of all the students he was thought the best, and
chosen as a model for the rest'.

Turning to the everyday matters of student life, their normal day
involved: preparation for prayer; mental prayer based on scripture;
Mass; rosary; a homily; litanies; examination of conscience and a
meditation.

Their meals had three courses: soup or salad, a main course and
a postpasto, which consisted of fruit or a little cheese. Beef was
served at dinner and veal at supper, but after Easter till the feast of
St John, mutton was served instead of beef. Antipasto was served
as an extra on Sunday, Monday, Tuesday and Friday but no portion
of meat was served at supper on Friday. On Wednesday there was
an extra antipastino. Breakfast consisted of a little bread and a glass
of wine. On the occasion of solemn feasts there might be two or
three antipasti and postpasti. Bread came fresh from the baker's
every morning and wine was bought in the market. The students
were allowed half a pint of wine per day. At meal times there were
readings from the lives of the saints or something from the writings
of Thomas a Kempis. After the reading, the students were allowed
to talk in low voices.

The following chart shows the structure of the everyday activities of the students but does not account for the changed structure for holidays and special feast days. Francis Shutt, writing in 1947, said: 'The picture one forms from the account of the Visitation of 1657 of the life of the English College was that men of that generation were curiously similar to the life of their modern counterparts'.[47] The chart below displays the daily life of the English College and separates winter time from the other three quarters.

Chart of Daily Life in the English College Rome

| NORMALLY | ACTIVITIES | WINTER |
|---|---|---|
| 8.00 | Rise | 12.00 |
| 8.00 - 8.30 | Wash, dress, preparation for prayer | 12.00 - 12.30 |
| 8.30 - 9.00 | Mental prayer based on a passage from Sacred Scripture | 12.30 - 13.00 |
| 9.00 - 9.30 | Mass | 13.00 - 13.30 |
| 9.30 - 11.30 | Study | 13.30 - 15.30 |
| 11.30 - 13.45 | Breakfast, set off for school at the Roman College with their companions saying the rosary on the way. Return to their own College in time for the first bell to ring for dinner. | 15.30 - 17.45 |
| 13.45 - 14.00 | Tidy or sweep their room | 17.45 - 18.00 |
| 14.00 - 14.30 | Dinner. Silence through the meal while one of the students reads some history or a homily of the Fathers of the Church | 18.00 - 18.30 |
| 14.30 - 15.30 | Recreation in common | 18.30 - 19.30 |
| 15.30 - 16.30 | Study and preparation for tutorials. These last for a whole hour, each class separately. When they are finished they return to their rooms for further study until they have to go to school between 19.00 - 20.00. | 19.30 - 20.30 |
| 19.00 - 20.00 | Students go to school at the Roman College | 23.00 - 24.00 |
| 22.15 - 22.30 | Return from school. Arrange beds and rooms | 2.15 - 2.30 |
| 22.30 - 23.00 | Supper | 2.30 - 3.00 |
| 23.00 - 24.00 | Recreation | 3.00 - 4.00 |
| 24.00 - 24.30 | Recite litanies and make an examination of conscience. Retire to bed as the prefect reads a meditation for the following day. | 4.00 - 4.30 |

*5. Chart of Daily Life in the English College, Rome*

Casemore[48] described a typical feast day, which did not follow the normal pattern of a weekday:

> On the feast of Corpus Christi, 30 May 1771, they rose at 9am and Mass was celebrated by the Minister at 9.30am. They took breakfast immediately after Mass and then joined the procession which began at 10.15am and finished about 12.30pm. The students came home at 1.15pm and studied till dinner ... common soup, a stew of capretto with 2 slices of fried bacon N.B. strawberries are marked in y' dispense book but as yet y' Minister said were too dear; roast lamb or rather boiled ... lamb, boiled beef exceeding bad, fruits 2 good apples and cherries with parmesan cheeses.

After dinner they had the Litanies and Benediction, and the prayers were longer than usual. This was the same for the Octave. Despite the longer time spent at prayer no extra sleep was added but the bell wasn't rung until fifteen minutes after normal time, so some of them slept on. After this the rosary was said and then they had an hour and a half recreation. They returned home at 11.20pm and supper was served at 12 o'clock. The menu was salad, cold roast ham, a very good tart but the usual bad cheese. He recorded that it was a fine day but too hot.

Despite the shortage of income the quality of meals was maintained:

> Our table was always very good, these being as I have heard of, (for I forget at present) eight ounces for the boiled pittance & six for the other with different sort of fowls according to the different seasons. On the vacant days of the week we had a portion over & Parmesan Cheese or Butter for breakfast The Minister always dined & supped with us, but the Rector & Confessor dined & supped at the second table, as likewise the sick & the lector (before the custom of reading all the time of table was taken away) on the feasts of St Thomas, & the B. Trinity, Christmas, Easter, St Ignatius & as likewise on the feast of some English saints.

Broomhead belonged to a camerata which was made up of five, four or three students. This organization dictated who they mixed with and they could also be chosen as a group to perform some activity. Each camerata was given a specific area and they were not allowed to mix with the members of another camerata. Recreation time was allocated for an hour, twice a day after dinner and after supper. Once a week (twice a week during vacations), they went to the vineyard or the garden near San Gregorio where they had free time all day. In addition, on a feast day, the students went for a walk after vespers until supper time. In the case of rain or excessive heat, when they could not go to the vineyard, they had recreation of an hour and a half before and after dinner and two hours before supper and an hour afterwards.

On arrival at the vineyard the students visited the chapel. They had to carefully put aside their overcoat, called 'toga superior', till they were leaving. They were also forbidden to pick fruit, break branches or cut up trees. When playing games they had to be modest and treat one another with peace and charity. Money wagers were not allowed.

Besides the 'toga superior' Broomhead had two sorts of dress, one of cloth called a 'panna' and one of fine wool called a 'saia'. When he travelled to and from the seminaries or travelled back to England he wore secular dress and carried a sword.

Students could not approach a pilgrim without permission, and should permission be given, they had to be careful not to divulge any information concerning another student, or information about the affairs of the College. This was to protect the students from the danger of spies who might seriously compromise their lives especially when they returned to England.

When the College finished lectures in July, the students remained in Rome, but were free every day from after the midday meal till supper time. There were two main holiday periods, July and August, called 'vacazioni minori' and September and October 'vacazioni grandi'. During these times the students had lectures only in the morning, but during the September period they were often sent to Monte Porzio, a summer retreat house, for the benefit of their health.

Every week, in addition to the lectures, repetitions and disputations at the Roman College, Broomhead and his fellow students met, normally on a Sunday or a free day especially in winter, to review the work of the past week with their superiors. At supper, one of the theologians would be asked to preach on the Gospel of the day. Later, at the end of recreation, one of the philosophers would give a short Latin composition known as a tone.

On the Monday following another philosopher would give an essay on some philosophical point which would be given in Latin. Every Friday, for one hour, in order to prepare the students for their missionary work in England, they were instructed in controversies with heretics. On a Sunday all students were instructed in Greek at home, but in second year theology, the students went to the Roman College for half an hour's tuition in Hebrew.

*6. The Martyrs Chapel, English College Rome*

Broomhead's first eight years at the English College were dominated by Jesuit teachers. The constitution of the Society of Jesus, conceived by Ignatius, had four strands: to go on the missions at the pope's bidding; to educate the youth of all classes; to instruct the ignorant and the poor; and to minister to the sick and prisoners.

Jesuits were held, both in great regard, and in great fear and were able protagonists in matters of religion. They were influential in many courts of Europe and abroad but more especially many of the popes and many of the curial officials had been educated by them. They could be relied upon for an uncompromising ideology. Any attack on the Church would be an attack on them and vice versa.

The revolutionary, political, philosophical, mathematical and scientific ideas of the early seventeenth on into the eighteenth century challenged the intellectual, religious and social bastions of society. Broomhead studied Aristotle and Aquinas and the work of these later scientists and philosophers in order to be able to respond to religious polemics. The authorities at the College had already separated theology from philosophy long before Broomhead's time. In the eighteenth century Locke was part of the students' work, for in the archives of the English College there is an essay of one of the student 'philosophers' on Locke, with the comments from one of the professors.[49]

John Kirk referred to examinations:

> Philosophers and first and second year theologians were examined at the end of the year to see how much they had gained in their studies. Top students, at each level, were appointed to give a religious paper to the students and staff.

Following in the footsteps of his fellow students Broomhead attended Mass, said the rosary, and practised mental prayer and the examination of his conscience. Communion was received on a Sunday at the community Mass. Confession on the preceding night took place instead of repetitions (rote learning). On the occasion of an important feast, Communion was also received at other times in the week, and confessions would be heard on the vigil. Every Sunday and every feast day, solemn High Mass and Vespers were sung by the students.

Michael Gaffey extolled the virtues that he had identified in Broomhead's priestly formation which in précis were: his religious zeal; modesty; humility; virtuosity; endurance of fasting and abstinence; God-like eloquence; piety; devotedness; sincerity; studious and a model to replicate.

> His rapid progress and religious zeal'
> Excited wonder, but the modest veil
> Which overspread his countenance, proclaim'd
> His heart to humble to be virtuous named.
> Of all the students he was thought the best,
> And chosen as a model for the rest
> Who could endure such fasts and abstinence?
> Who could display such god-like eloquence?
> Who could be so devout and so sincere?
> As BROOMHEAD, or full of holy fear?
> Who at his studies so intent as he?
> Or who so gifted with humility?
> None—there was not a single student there
> Who could with him in anything compare:
> For learning and for piety renown'd,
> He was the only one that could be found
> Most worthy to deliver an oration
> Before the Pope, at their examination;
> Which he went thro' with such a peerless grace
> As to astonish all within the place.
> Each own'd his merit, and were proud to raise
> Their voices in the young aspirant's praise.[50]

According to Kirk, a student was chosen annually to preach before the Pope and the Cardinals on St Stephen's day:

> … as the Cardinals were in the Conclave on the feast of St Stephen (1774) so no one preached this year tho' Casemore was to have made the discourse: the year before (1773) Broomhead preached; & Halsey in 1772, which pleased greatly many of the Cardinals who sent afterwards for a copy of it.

There was a petition from Rowland Broomhead, 23 March 1775, for special permission to be ordained as he was only twenty three years old. Michael Gaffey described (in verse) the relationship of Broomhead with Pope Clement XIV:

> The Pope, at all times ready to afford
> Assistance to the servants of the Lord,
> Esteem'd him much, became his warmest friend,
> And, for a priest, did strongly recommend
> The subject of my lay, as amply fit
> To preach the faith of Christ and practise it;
> But as the canons of the church required
> Those, who to that important charge aspired,
> Should not receive their orders, or engage
> (Unless full five and twenty years of age)
> In such a sacred office, it was thought
> That he must wait the twenty five years out;
> But mark the hand of Providence herein:
> The pious Clement thinking it a sin
> To keep him longer from his element.
> And rob the church of such an ornament,
> His Holiness, to set his favorite free,
> (Altho' but little more than twenty three)
> Granted a dispensation for his sake,
> And he with joy did quickly undertake
> The welcome office, longing to begin
> The sacred rites of his religion in

His native country, whither he was sent
To preach the faith and teach them to repent.[51]

It is evident from this piece of poetry written by Michael Gaffey
that he must have had inside information, probably from Broomhead's contemporaries. The Pope appears to have been a personal
friend of Broomhead and despite canon law cleared the way for him
to be ordained at the age of twenty-three.

According to Kirk:

> On the 16th of April, George Halsey & Roland Broomhead
> were ordained priests & on the 28th of the same month
> departed towards England, but Halsey stayed sometime at
> College.[52] He now is priest to Lord Pert at Whittle, &
> Broomhead is at Sheffield in Yorkshire, his own county.

## Notes

[1] Rowland's brothers and sisters were: Elizabeth born 10 January 1745;
Richard 7 October 1746; Revell 4 August 1748; and Mary 15 August 1753.
According to the records of Sedgley Park School there was a brother,
Thomas, who entered the School the same day as Rowland, but there is no
supporting evidence of his birth or death. Elizabeth did not marry and died,
1 February 1795, aged 49. She was buried in Bradfield Churchyard. The
other sister, Mary, married Henry Brown and had two children, Henry and
George. She died, 6 June 1784, aged 30 years. Richard, the son and heir, of
Richard and Ann, married Sarah Spooner of Crooks Moor, Sheffield. He
died about 1805. They had six children, five girls: Sarah; Mary-Anne;
Theresa; Anne; and Elizabeth and one son Richard. The latter did not
marry and when he died, 9 February 1835, the estate devolved to Theresa,
who firstly married Francis Wright and after his death Francis Sutton.

[2] *Bradfield Parish Church, Baptisms* (Bradfield Parish Council, Sheffield).

[3] The Revell family pedigree records the relocation of Thomas Revell and
Edward Revell, the first and second son of Sir Thomas Revell knighted in
1312, from Warwickshire to Stannington circa 1350. Knighthoods were
given to the Revell's down to the latter part of the fifteenth century but no

such rank was granted after that period. The Broomhead family, living in Bradfield was mentioned in a 'Quitclaim' of 1341.cf. Appendix One.

[4]   C. Hadfield, A *History of S. Marie's Mission and Church, Norfolk Row, Sheffield* (Sheffield, 1889), p. 4.

[5]   *South Yorkshire Hearth Tax Returns 1672* (Sheffield Archives).

[6]   Martin Edwards, present owner of Revell Grange, Stannington.

[7]   T. W. Hall, *The City of Sheffield, Descriptive Catalogue of Charters, Copy Court Rolls and Deeds* (Sheffield, J. W. Northend, 1920) p. 88–89:'According to an indenture of bargain and sale in 1580 Gregory Revell made a large purchase of land in the vicinity of Nethergate and Bingley Lane and sections of the court document pointed to large sections of land which he already owned, which abutted some of the new purchases'.

[8]   C. Hadfield, A *History of S. Marie's Mission and Church, Norfolk Row, Sheffield* (Sheffield, 1889).

[9]   H. N. Birt, *The Elizabethan Religious Settlement, A Study of Contemporary Documents* (London: George Bell & Sons, 1907) p. 30.1.

[10]   Birt, p. 301.

[11]   *The Recusancy of the Revell Family* (Appendix 1).

[12]   B. Broomhead, *Notes on the Broomhead Pedigree* (document hand written with no date in Sheffield City Archives) Ref. MD 1517/1a.

[13]   Cf. Appendix 1.

[14]   W. E. Kelly, et alia *Liber Ruber Venerabilis* (London: Catholic Record Society, MCMXL) p. 220, ref: 1447

[15]   Bishopthorpe, Ms. H. 2. 9.

[16]   Storth derives from the Old Norse word meaning a woody place but it is also defined as a small hamlet with a scattering of farms.

[17]   Nethergate Hall.

[18]   Hadfield, p. 12.

[19]   D. Evinson, *The Lord's House A History of Sheffield's Roman Catholic Buildings 1570-1990* (Sheffield: Academic Press, 1991), p. 33.

[20]   Richard Challoner, Bishop of Debra, Vicar Apostolic of the London District. Born 29 September 1691 of a Presbyterian father. His mother was housekeeper to the Catholic Gage family in Sussex and when he was thirteen he was converted to Catholicism. Richard entered the seminary at Douai 29 July 1705. Ordained 28 March 1719. Returned to London in 1730 and was known for his work among the poor and his prolific writings which included the 'Garden of the Soul' a prayer of devotion. Died 12

January 1781.

21  *Sedgley Park School, Account Book 1762 to 1766* (BAA).

22  J. Hunter, Rev. *Familiae Minorum Gentium.MS.170* (Sheffield: transcribed and printed for the Harlean Society 1894–6), ms.170, p. 387–390.

23  *Ordo, 1799* (BAA).

24  Gaffey (MCL: Ref. 922.2 B31).

25  G. Halsey: *Letter to Magnani at the VEC. 12 September 1775.* Translated from the Latin by Deacon Richard Bailey of the Manchester Oratory, October 2013. (VEC: Scritture (i) ref. 50.5.7).

26  Williams, p. 1. M. E. Williams, *The Venerable English College A History 1579–1979* (London: Associated Catholic Publications Ltd., 1979) p. 26.

27  VEC: *Liber Ruber* (London: CRS) vol.40; no. 1447; p. 220.

28  Fr Robert Persons, born at Nether Stowey, Somerset, 24 June 1546. Educated at St Mary's Hall, Oxford, 1574. Reconciled in the faith Persons became a student in Rome 1575. He became a Jesuit 3 July 1575. Drew up the 'Oath of the Missions' with William Allen. Missionary work in England, and France 1581. Founded a school at Eu(1582)which was transferred to St Omers in 1594, which led to Stonyhurst during the French Revolution. Much work in Spain: Founded the seminaries of Valladolid (1589), Seville (1592) and Madrid (1598); d. 15 April 1610.

29  Williams, p. 1.

30  F. A. Gasquet, *A History of the Venerable English College, Rome* (London: Longmans, Green and Co., 1920) p. 77.

31  William Allen was born 1532 at Rossall, Lancashire. Educated at Oxford 1547. Principal of St Mary's Hall 1556. Forced to resign and leave the country and crossed to Flanders taking refuge at the University of Louvain. Worked with a gathering of exiles that produced books in defence of the Catholic faith, which were smuggled into England. Holy orders 1565. Planned to establish a Catholic university at Douai. Students arrived from England 1575. Allen under the wing of the Pope was influential and powerful. Seminarians trained to teach and lead the people when they went back to England back to the Catholic faith. Dec 1575 Pope Gregory XIII founded the second seminary at Rome. 7 August 1587 created cardinal by Pope Sixtus V. Died 16 October 1594.

32  Gasquet, p. 78.

33  Williams, p. 14.

34  Francis Petre, Bishop of Amorium : Born into the Petre family of Ingatestone and West Horndon, Essex 2 October 1692; Educated at ;27 July 1750

Coadjutor to the Vicar Apostolic Dicconson of the Northern District; succeeded in 1752 and died in 1775.

[35]  Gasquet, p. 174.

[36]  Williams, p. 57.

[37]  Williams, p. 57.

[38]  Gasquet, p. 175.

[39]  VEC : *Liber Ruber:*(CRS. 37).

[40]  From the 'Liber Ruber' the numbers for each year extracted were: 26 (1765); 23 (1766); 20 (1767); 22 (1768); 21 (1769); 17 (1770); 12 (1771); 8 (1772); 10 (1773); 8 (1774); 11 (1775).

[41]  William Ignatius Casemore was born at Reading 13 September 1751. He travelled to Rome with Broomhead and produced a diary of his time at the English College. He was thrown out of the college and persuaded the Vicar Apostolic to support his application to become a Franciscan. He served Lower Hall at Samlesbury (St Mary's chapel which was dedicated to St Chad) from July 1798 till November 1802. He then became the first incumbent at Falmouth for the next thirteen years. He retired to the Convent of the Poor Clares at Plymouth where he died 29 September 1824.(The Registers of Samlesbury (Smith, J. P. (2013). pp. 312–3. *Lancashire Registers IV: Brindle and Samlesbury.* London: Forgotten Books. (Original work).

[42]  John Kirk: Born in Shropshire 13 April 1760. Educated at Sedgley Park School from 1770 to 1773 and then to the English College, Rome, 5 June 1773, a few months before the suppression of the Jesuits. Ordained priest 18 December 1784, he was placed in the Mission in Shropshire and became an antiquarian. Died 21 December 1851, aged 91.

[43]  Cardinal Andrea Corsini: Born 11 June 1735 in Florence. Great-nephew of Pope Clement XII. Elevated to Cardinal, 24 September1759, at the age of twenty-four. Ordained priest, 2 February 1769 and was appointed Cardinal-Priest and Cardinal Bishop of Sabina. Had immense power in the administration of the Church. Died January 1795.

[44]  A. Laird, *The English College, Rome, under Italian Secular Administration, 1773–1798.* (Recusant History: Journal of the CRS, Volume 14, No. 2. October 1977).

[45]  VEC. Scr. 50:3:14.

[46]  VEC. Scr. 45:2:15.

[47]  F. J. Shutt, *The Visitation of 1657* (VEC: May 1947, Vol. XIII. No.2).

48  W. Casemore, *The Diary of William Casemore* 1765–1775 (VEC: ref. Lib.
    Scr.50. 5. 6/50. 6/8).
49  VEC: Scritture (ii) 44. 19. 1
50  Gaffey.
51  Gaffey.
52  G. Halsey, *Letter to Magnani, Vice-Rector of the English College, Rome*, 6
    September 1775 (VEC: Scritture, 50. 5. 7).

# 2 SHEFFIELD

THE EARLS OF Shrewsbury, Lords of the Manor of Sheffield, were renowned for their Protestantism and it was out of the question to establish a Catholic chapel in the town. Catholics living in the town and the outer area relied on support for their religion from gentry-families of the same faith. From 1573 the Revell family of Nethergate Hall, Broomhead's maternal line, maintained a chapel, until Thomas Revell removed to Revell Grange in 1742, and established a chapel there. Jesuits, Marian priests and seminary priests served their missions.

The Jesuits had a long history in the Sheffield area at Spinkhill since 1580, initially as chaplains to the Pole family.[1] Many entries refer to Spinkhill, where the Jesuits lived and not the houses at which they served, but occasionally the entry for Stannington was given. As a result of the succession in 1651 of the Howards, Dukes of Norfolk, and Roman Catholics it was easier for Catholics in Sheffield to practise their faith, but a Catholic chapel was not built in the town until 1701.

In the period 1660 to 1739, various Jesuit priests were listed in the archives of the Society as working in the area known as the College of the Immaculate Conception, with its headquarters at Spinkhill, which area covered the counties of Derbyshire, Leicestershire, Nottinghamshire and Rutland.

The missionary priests continued to visit Nethergate Hall. Robert Percy SJ was recorded from 1685 till circa 1715, serving Stannington from Spinkhill. There is a gap in information, circa 1724 till circa 1733; then Ignatius Brooke SJ was to be found serving Stannington from Bolsterstone. The clergy at Bolsterstone often served the Revell family home at Nethergate Hall. From 1733 the first seminary priest in Sheffield, Edward Matthews, served Sheffield and Nethergate Hall till 1734. James Fox (alias Poole or Pole) SJ was at Bolsterstone from 1735 to 1739.

From this point on the Revell chapels were served by seminary priests. Thomas Holdford (alias Hunt), a seminary priest, was at Bolsterstone during 1735, for the Visitation Return sent to Lancelot Blackburn, Archbishop of York, from John Dossie, the Vicar of Sheffield, informed him that:

> There is a person called Mr Hunt who is suspected to be a popish Priest, he lives with Mr Blackburn mentioned before, and at whose house Mass is understood to be perform'd, and to which there is a resort of papists every Lord's day, or however very frequently.[2]

Holdford left Sheffield in 1735/1736 and was replaced in that same year by Thomas Gradwell, a priest, who was in Sheffield, serving not only the 'Lord's House' but Nethergate till 1742 and Revell Grange till his death 1758.

Early in 1758, John Lodge, a priest, arrived in Sheffield where he assisted Gradwell in what was to be the last year of the latter's life. According to the accounts of the Duke of Norfolk, Lodge appears as paid assistant to Gradwell. Thomas Shimmel and Charles Cordell were priests who assisted at Sheffield for which they received payments for travel from the ducal accounts. On the death of Gradwell, Lodge became priest-in-charge at Sheffield.[3] He was assisted by William Winter from 1764 to 1775. Rowland Broomhead, appointed to Sheffield 1 August 1775, according to a note of faculties given by Bishop Walton[4] was an assistant to John Lodge at the 'Lord's House' in the town. This was the chapel in which Broomhead served during the period 1775 to 1778 but he also served at the family home at Revell Grange then owned by Richard, his nephew. His stay in Sheffield was only short as he was transferred to Manchester in 1778. The third assistant was Samuel

Sayles who arrived in 1782 and was in Sheffield till 1787. When Lodge was transferred to Durham in 1786, Richard Rimmer, a Lancashire man, became priest-in-charge.

As the mission in Sheffield established itself, the need for a mission at Revell Grange began to recede. Rimmer 'was accustomed, once a month, to go over on a Sunday afternoon, to give devotions and instructions, hear confessions, and celebrate Mass and administer Holy Communion on Monday morning'.[5]

The shortage of priests and the death of Rimmer in 1828, reducing their number still further, brought about the closure of Revell Grange. The Vicar Apostolic of the Northern District, Thomas Smith, wrote to Richard Broomhead, Rowland's nephew:

> Durham, 17 February, 1828
>
> My very dear Sir,
>
> I received duly your favour of the 6th current. I beg to assure you that the convenience of yourself and family, the declining state of an old congregation, and your pious intentions in its behalf, not to mention the veneration I cherish for the memory of your late uncle, would all make me anxious to comply with your request, but I am under the painful necessity of stating my inability to do so at the present moment. Having no immediately disposable priest in the College, I cannot effect (sic) the indispensible object of having two efficient missionaries at Sheffield without an exchange of Mr McCartney with a missioner of some degree of maturity. I should hope, however, that this arrangement once effected, your situation at Stannington, will be somewhat bettered till Providence shall enable us to supply you with a suitable chaplain, which I beg to assure you shall not be lost sight of.
>
> In the meantime, with sincere respect,
>
> My dear Sir, Your obedient and humble Servant,
>
> (Signed) THOS. SMITH.[6]

In 1853, the promise of Bishop Smith was realised; the Vincentian Fathers of the Congregation of the Mission came to Sheffield and within a short time had decided to re-open the mission at Revell Grange in the person of Michael Burke.

*7. Revell Grange Chapel Entrance*

On the feast of the Assumption 1858, the Revell Grange chapel, which had been enlarged by Mr Sutton was reopened as a missionary chapel and from then until 1929 Mass was said there on Sundays and Holy Days of Obligation. Due to a change of ownership in 1929, the mission could no longer function there.[7]

The first Catholic chapel at Sheffield was built by Thomas Howard who succeeded his uncle as 8th Duke of Norfolk in 1701. He demolished most of the Manor House at Sheffield, which had been the home of the ducal agents, as the Duke's had removed to Worksop Manor. He relocated his agent, John Shireburn, in temporary accommodation in Coal Pit Lane, now known as Cambridge Street. This house allowed for a small Catholic chapel, 'the first post-Reformation Catholic chapel in the town of Sheffield'.[8] From 1701 the missionary priests began to include the chapel at Coal Pit Lane and from then on there was a permanent presence in the town. About 1711 the chapel at Coal Pit Lane was closed and the congregation relocated in a new building, situated in Fargate, at the corner of Norfolk Row:

> It had an elegant front, five bays wide and two storeys high, with a hipped roof. The central bays were stepped forward slightly and further accentuated by a triangular pediment. The central door had a semicircular pediment. The front was enclosed by a low segmental wall with a palisade. The garden stretched from the rear of the house, along Norfolk Row, as far as Norfolk Street.[9]

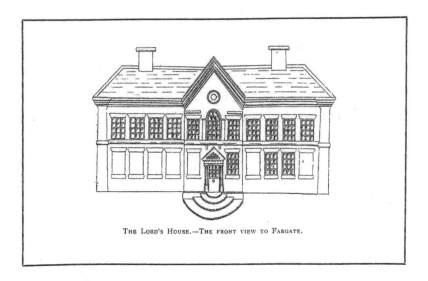

THE LORD'S HOUSE.—THE FRONT VIEW TO FARGATE.

*8. The 'Lord's House' Fargate, Sheffield*

This new house was variously called 'the Duke's House' or 'his Grace's House', but Hadfield coined the title 'The Lord's House' which became the accepted title. It looked like a domestic dwelling from the outside as all earlier chapels for the obvious reason that what went on there was certainly against the law and they did not want to bring attention to themselves.

It was entered at once from Norfolk Row through a lobby or porch, by a flight of steps, which gave access to the ground floor. At the Fargate end, opposite to the altar, was a gallery, reached by two flights of stairs, in which the Duke of Norfolk had a pew, approached from the mansion through an ante-room used as a vestry, with a window looking into the chapel and gallery.[10]

According to Hadfield, from information he had gathered from those who were old enough to have remembered the chapel:

It would appear that the old chapel was about 50 feet by 28 feet within, and with the gallery may have given accommodation to about 600 persons. It was entered at once from Norfolk Row through a lobby or porch, by a flight of steps, which gave access to the ground floor. At the Fargate end, opposite to the altar, was a gallery, reached by two flights of stairs, in which the Duke of Norfolk had a pew, approached from the mansion through an ante-room used as a vestry, with a window looking into the chapel and gallery.

Problems arose about the sale of the land, owned by the Duke of Norfolk, on which the present chapel was situated and a meeting of Sheffield Catholics was called and met at Fr Rimmer's house, 25 September 1813. A committee was formed of eleven gentlemen and one of them was Broomhead's nephew, Richard Broomhead. Rowland was also present at this first meeting. At a subsequent meeting it was agreed that the site for the new chapel should be in the town. At the same meeting the minute recorded: Mr Howard, Auditor to His Grace the Duke of Norfolk, having handsomely made an offer to the Congregation of the Dukes House premises adjoining in which the present Chapel is situated, the four first names of the Committee contracted for the purchase thereof.[11]

In a letter, dated 2 January 1814 to William Gibson[12] of the Northern District, six members of the committee advised the bishop on what had taken place, regarding the new chapel, and described the problems that they faced:

His Grace the Duke of Norfolk having offered his House & Offices in this Town for sale in which House we have been for many years accommodated with a Chapel, we have received notice … this must be taken from us at Lady Day next. To build a good and large Chapel at this time when materials & labour are so very expensive & money is so scarce among tradesmen of any description is not one of the easiest tasks. Nothing but the greatest unanimity of sentiment & good will can, under all the circumstances, carry us through these difficulties and we must beg every assistance in your Lordship's power to make us aware of the expense of the building and must rest upon ourselves, and it is our design when finished to place it in the hands of your Lordship, Bishop Smith and one or two of the Clergy, if your Lordship thinks proper, in trust for the Congregation of Sheffield ... At a General meeting of the Congregation held at the House of Rev Richard Rimmer on the 10th January 1814 the proceedings of the Committee were laid before them unanimously approved . After which it was resolved that a Subscription be immediately entered into, it being supposed that £2,500 will be required (immediately).[13]

The total collected was £2,737. 10. 0 and this included £25 from Richard Broomhead; Rev Mr Lupton, priest of Manchester, one guinea and Mr Broomhead of Manchester and his Congregation £47. 10. 0., on 5 May 1815. Broomhead had not forgotten his Sheffield people. The new church, known as St Mary's Norfolk Row, was opened in 1816.

## Notes

1    Evinson, p. 22.
2    G. Anstruther, *The Seminary Priests: A Dictionary of the Secular Clergy of England and Wales 1558–1850* (London, 1969), vol. IV, p. 141.
3    *Arundel Castle Manuscripts* (Sheffield City Library, Archives Division) S. 165.
4    Walton: faculties for Broomhead (LDA: 48).
5    Hadfield, p. 18.
6    Hadfield, p. 19.
7    Hadfield, p. 20.
8    Evinson, p. 23.
9    Evinson, p. 24.
10   Hadfield, p. 39–40.

11  Minutes: *Meeting of the Catholics of Sheffield with a view to building a new chapel 25 September 1813* (LDA: 834).
12  William Gibson
13  LDA: 834.

# 3 FROM SHEFFIELD TO MANCHESTER 1778

B ISHOP WALTON, in a letter dated 5 March 1778, to John Chadwick, Grand Vicar in Lancashire, wrote:

> I think of sending Mr Broomhead, from Sheffield to Manchester he is accustomed to a town & Mr Lodge thinks he will do. But I shall still be at a loss for a principal for the place.[1]

Many clergy would have had no experience of working in a town but Broomhead had the credentials that Walton was looking for, as he had worked as a priest in the rising industrial town of Sheffield. The affirmation of Broomhead for the Manchester position by Mr Lodge appears to have sealed the arrangement. John Lodge had been in Sheffield since 1758 and knew the family and the mission at Revell Grange, and Broomhead had been appointed to assist him in Sheffield in 1775 and was the natural person to be asked for his opinion.[2]

According to Michael Gaffey the people of the Sheffield mission had recognized something special about Broomhead:

> The people gloried in a man so good,
> And would have kept him with them if they could;
> But such a glorious light was meant to shine
> In places more in need of a divine.

His congregation was reluctant to see him leave because he practised what he preached and that, through his good example 'hosts of unbelievers join'd the elect'. This suggests that he was already using his 'Public Instructions', a method of conversion which he would later use to great success in Manchester.

Gaffey continued his reflections on Broomhead:

> The town of Manchester, that fertile spot,
> Where seeds of vice spring up, grow rank and rot,
> Was much in want of such a gardener
> As him, to weed, prune and embellish her;
> Nor could the place of more delay admit'
> For tares abundant choak'd and poison'd it.
> His flock entreated him with them to stay,
> But God had call'd, and he must obey.

## Notes

[1]   W. Walton: *Letter to Chadwick 5 March 1778* (UCA: President's Archives C 2).

[2]   Evinson, *The Lord's House A History of Sheffield's Roman Catholic Buildings 1570-1990*, p. 33.

# 4 THE MANCHESTER MISSION PRE-1778

I N THE PERIOD pre-1753 Manchester was part of the south-east
Lancashire mission which comprised the whole of the
Hundred of Salford as well as Macclesfield in Cheshire and
Glossop in Derbyshire. The missionary priests had no permanent
place to live in and relied on the good will of the Catholic gentry.
When Broomhead came to Manchester in 1778 he had a permanent
residence at Rook Street but he was sent out on the missionary
circuit and he had to rely on the goodwill of the Catholic gentry in
the other missions. His predecessors were the missionary priests
who had visited Manchester from 1661 to 1753.

The earliest proof that we have of missionary priests visiting the
Manchester Mission dates from the middle of the seventeenth
century. Thomas Weedon born in Worcestershire in 1637 studied
at Douai and was ordained in 1661 and came to the mission shortly
after his ordination. He became Dean of the Salford Hundred from
1704 till his death in 1719.[1] John Shepherd was born in Lancashire
in 1678, studied at Lisbon and was ordained in 1706 and came to
the Manchester mission in that year. George Kendal in 1734 came
to the Mission and according to John Kirk was at Manchester. In
the accounts for the Duke of Norfolk for his estate at Glossop, there
are two receipts signed by George Kendal for payments for his
service. He served Glossop and the wider mission, travelling every
so often to Manchester, to serve the needs of its growing congregation. His brother Henry was at Cottam for only a few years before
going to Manchester 'in or before 1741, in which year his name
appears in Bishop Dicconson's list'.[2]He died 29 October 1752.

There is no evidence that any of these priests lived in the Town but the close proximity of the Barlows, the Traffords and the Downes would certainly have been places of refuge.

We have no precise location of any early Mass centres. The map of 'Roman Catholic Places of Worship in Manchester, pre-1821' identifies the two possible locations of early Catholic worship pre 1753 and these were in order Smithy Door and Parsonage.

Deansgate, going east from the Roman area of the Town was not a straight thoroughfare as it is today for it bent round into Cateaton Street near the Collegiate Church (now Manchester Cathedral). To the right, as one turned into Cateaton Street, there was a small street on the right which bent its way through to Market Street Lane. This street can also be seen on the map of 1650, but it is unnamed. It was in this small street, called 'Smithy Door' that tradition has it that Roman Catholics first met in a room and secretly heard Mass.

Gillow records:

> There is a tradition that the chapel was a room near the old fruit market behind the Bay Horse and that during Mass a watchman had to be placed at the door to give warning of the approach of priest-hunters or other enemies. We don't know from what date this happened and we don't know when they moved to another location, said to be a dye house at 'Parsonage'.[3]

An examination of the title deeds of an area called the 'Parsonage' throws some light on the oral tradition of the use of a dye house as a chapel. There is no available plan or map to pinpoint the exact location of the various leases and sub-leases on this two acre site. Saintsbury's map of Manchester and Salford dated 1650[4] shows the land, not as yet called 'The Parsonage'. In 1650 it was still a field.

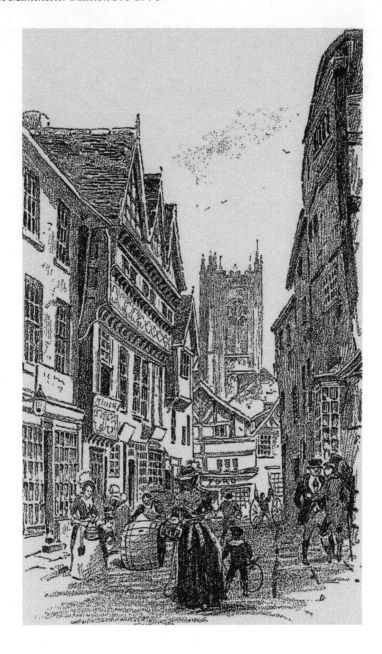

*9. Smithy Door, Manchester*

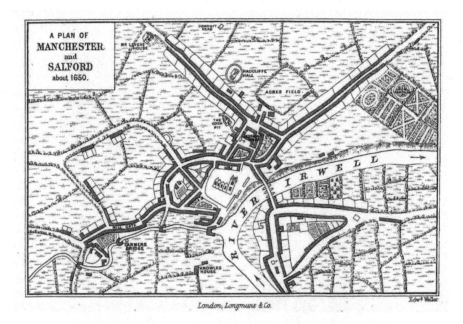

*10. Saintsbury's Map of Manchester, Dated 1650*

The first extant lease to the land called 'Parsonage' was given to William Bardsley by the Warden and Fellows of the College, 28 April 1668.[5] It had formerly been in the possession of Richard Howarth. The Lease stipulated that William Bardsley must 'maintain the hedges, ditches, gates, styles and fences at his own expense'. The land measured two acres. There were no buildings referred to in this lease. The conclusion is that it was a field just as it was in the 1650 map.

Some five years later a further lease, 12 April 1673, was described as a parcel of two acres of ground called 'Parsonage' in Manchester. The Lease from Nicholas Stratford, Warden, and Fellows of the College, confirmed the possession of William Bardsley and mentioned 'buildings lately erected thereon'. Some time, during those five years, the first buildings were erected on the site but again there is no mention of a dye house. However, it is evident from the deeds that from the late seventeenth century there was one dyehouse on the two acre site called the Parsonage. According to John Reilly: [6]

> The first chapel the Catholics had in Manchester, after the loss of the Collegiate Church, was a house in the Parsonage, where they met for worship about the year 1744, at which time the number of adult Catholics in the town was not more than fifteen.

There seems to be some problem with this order of chapels. The first lines of Reilly's extract has no support. Reilly's third line may well be true that the Catholics met for worship about the year 1744, and fits with the fact. Edward Helme moved his small community from the 'Parsonage' to 'Church Street' just after his arrival in Manchester in 1753. Reilly's fourth line has to be wrong, for the number of adult Catholics listed in the Papist Returns of 1767 for Manchester and Salford was 351.

The two possible chapels 'Smithy Door' and later 'Parsonage' were mentioned in a number of documents but their exact locations are difficult to detect. However, we are sure that priests were visiting the Town from 1661 onwards and they would certainly have needed a room that could be used as a temporary chapel and the evidence is dependable. Helme removed his congregation from 'Parsonage' to 'Church Street' in 1753. Blundell recorded the following:

> The first place mentioned as a 'meeting house' was an old building at 'Smithy Door' near to the present Victoria Station, probably one of the homes of the Catholic residents of the town; then we learn of their renting a building, formerly used as a dye-house, situated in the Parsonage, near to Blackfriars Bridge, which was then but a wooden structure over the Irwell, available for only foot-passengers. [7]

It was the work of these visiting missioners, who had supported a growing Catholic community, which eventually led to the establishment of the first independent chapel in 1753. The four earlier missionaries covered the period, 1661 to 1752, and after the death of Henry Kendal, 29 October 1752, Edward Helme was appointed to Manchester. He had entered Douai, 2 September 1737, and took the oath, 21 September 1743, and was ordained, 21 September 1748. In July 1753 he was sent to England and placed in charge of the Manchester mission and also with that of the surrounding villages within the Hundred of Salford and the adjuncts of part of Cheshire and Derbyshire. He spent twenty years on the Manchester Mission and died in Manchester, 16 October 1773.

During his years as a missioner at Manchester he was also responsible for looking after the congregation at Sutton near Macclesfield, where he had lived for a short period until moving to Manchester, purchasing premises at the corner of Church Street and High Street and removing his congregation there from the dye works (Parsonage) in 1753/54. 'Church Street' was the first permanent post-Reformation Roman Catholic chapel in Manchester and when Broomhead came to Manchester the building was still there and was important for its income and later its capital, which supported the mission for many years to come.

In 1753, the properties which Helme built or purchased were at the edge of the Town bordering on fields. High Street and Church Street were on the maps of the time but not the names of 'Roman Entry' or 'Roman Street' (one would hardly advertise a way to an illegal chapel). The numeration of High Street and Church Street was not present in earlier documents. The key documents that refer to this chapel use the title 'Church Street' to identify the place but Canon Wilding, who died in 1883, was believed to have used the title 'Old Roman Entry' which title was taken up, but reduced to 'Roman Entry'.

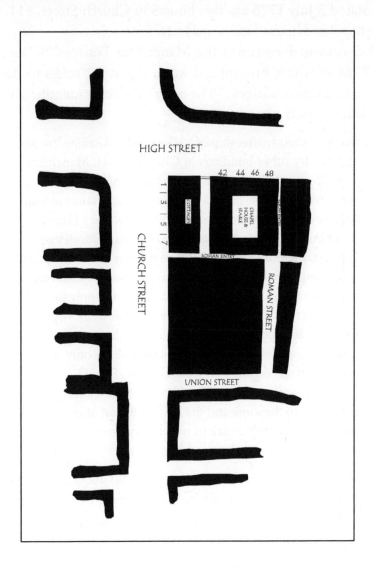

HIGH STREET

42 44 46 48

1 3 5 7

COTTAGE

CHAPEL HOUSE & STABLE

CHURCH STREET

ROMAN ENTRY

ROMAN STREET

UNION STREET

*11. 'Church Street', First Post-Reformation Catholic Chapel, Manchester*

The old chapel and property at 'Church Street' was rented out by the trustees of the Manchester & Salford mission when the new chapel of St Chad's Rook Street was opened in 1774. The income was stated 5 July 1776 as: 'two houses in Church Street, £11. 4s; old chapel and house (supposed) £16'.[8]

A document drawn up by the 'Manchester Trustees' 29 December 1784 of which Broomhead was a signatory, refers to 'Rook Street' and 'Church Street'.[9] The latter of which is identified in the following extract:

> declared their trusteeship of... the sundry dwelling houses and sundry other buildings in Church Street, Manchester as well as sundry sums of money now out at interest... acknowledge & declare to the Right Revd Father in God Matthew Gibson that the said Chapel Dwelling Houses & other buildings as well as said sum or sums of Money out at Interest, thereunto belonging; are held by not as Property pertaining or belonging to us or anyone else their executors administrators assigns, but in trust, solely and only towards supplying the said Town & vicinity with one or more priests to chose & appoint out of the Secular Clergy... Priest or Priests are to be appointed by him or them only for the purpose of serving the said Chapel (Rook Street)... enjoying the annual... rents of Buildings &c: in Church Street belonging to the same and the lawful interest of any sum or sums of money which are or may be committed in trust to us or any of us for such use and purpose.

The premises at 'Church Street' were sold to James Marshall November 1808. At the same time an indenture was drawn up and signed 30 November of the same year.[10] It recorded:

> Grant and Release of a yearly rent out of £54 issuing and arising out of land and buildings in Manchester in the County of Lancashire.

> Mr William Walton to the Reverend Rowland Broomhead and others.

The indenture referred to three separate sections of the land at Church Street. The first area of land and buildings on the map defined by the numbers 1, 3, 5 & 7 was the original position of the two dwellinghouses:

> All those two messuages[11] or dwellinghouses standing and being in and fronting a certain street in Manchester called Church Street sometime in the tenure or occupation of Anthony Jobling and Edward Helme.

According to this indenture, Helme was living in one of the two houses in Church Street which he owned, and received income from the other two houses which gave him financial support. Behind the house there were two buildings backing on to Elbow Entry, if that was the name of the thoroughfare at that time:

> And also all that other messuage or dwelling house standing and being at the back of the last mentioned messuages or dwellinghouses some time ago in the tenure or occupation of Thomas Johnson…

The third and final messuage which sat alongside the previous one was described as:

> All that other edifice or building standing also on the back of the two first above mentioned messuages or dwelling-houses thereby granted and released formerly used as a Chapel but later as a School… and in the tenure or occupation of the said William Medhurst.

The evidence shows that it was 'formerly used as a Chapel but later as a school'. This raises the possibility that pre-1808 (when the whole site of 'Church Street' was sold), a school had been in existence on this site. Knowing Broomhead's penchant for education, it raises the possibility that this old chapel may well have been used as a school house in the period from 1784 onwards, when the non-denominational Sunday schools had been established in the

Town. Furthermore Broomhead wrote from Rook Street to Brian Marsh, 27 February 1796:

> We are much in want of another Chapel here as the 2 we
> have are insufficient for the Congregation.[12]

Around the corner from Rook Street the mission still owned 'Church Street' so if they were short of accommodation space why did they not use the chapel space which also could have doubled up as a schoolroom? Broomhead did not manage to open a new church until 1820.

The rent charge or chief rent of £54 was payable to the trustees of the Manchester Mission which included Broomhead:

> The said Yearly Rent Charge was by a Release dated the
> Thirtieth day of November One Thousand Eight Hundred
> and Eight conveyed by William Walton, Thomas Whit-
> greave and Richard Kaye to the Reverend Rowland Broom-
> head the Reverend Thomas Lupton the Reverend Richard
> Thompson the Reverend James Blundell and the Reverend
> Edward Kenyon.

In a further document,[13] 26 July 1944, now using the title 'Roman Entry', the precise dimensions of the land were given and the street numbers of the premises involved:

> The land bounded by 1, 3, 5, & 7 Church Street on the south
> side has a frontage of 78 feet 4 inches and 42, 44, 46, 48 High
> Street on the west side a frontage of 100 feet 2 inches. It is
> bounded on the north side by Elbow Entry. The land
> measures 871 square yards. Roman Entry lies on the east
> side of the land.

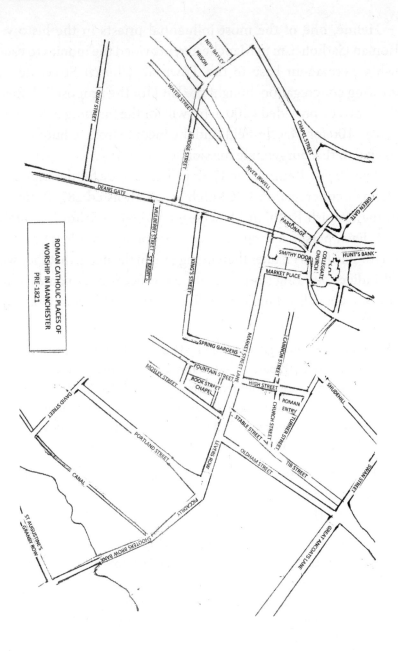

*12. Map: Roman Catholic Places of Worship in Manchester Pre-1821*

Helme, one of the most influential priests in the history of Roman Catholicism in Manchester, provided the monies to establish a permanent base in the Town at 'Church Street' for his growing congregation, bought the land for the proposed chapel at Rook Street, provided £200 in his will for the building of St Chad's and a £100 for Macclesfield, and the income from 'Church Street' so vital to this burgeoning mission.

The Papist Returns for 1767 provides a useful description of Helme's congregation at 'Church Street'. It listed 287 'Professors of the Romish Faith' in Manchester and 64 in Salford; a total of 351. Each person's name, age, occupation and resident years was listed. The family names therein suggest, in the main, that they were all indigenous English but there were occasional names which suggest a small number of Irish migrants. The enumerator for Salford prefaced his 'Papist Returns':

> The number is greater than I cd have wished tho' not more than a sixtieth part of ye Inhabitants; & perhaps may be in some measure accounted for from ye extensive Trade of this Country wch will naturally draw ye poor & needy of other Countries in order to find employment here. Rob Kenyon. Manchester 30 Sept. 1767.

The 1767 Papist Returns[14] shed some light on the Catholic families who were living in Manchester from the turn of the seventeenth and on into the eighteenth century:

> William Waters, a shoemaker, born in Manchester in 1689; John Bradshaw, a farmer and James Ashcroft, a shoemaker, in 1709; Abraham Walker, a shoemaker, in 1717; Michael Walton, a merchant, and James Bradshaw, a perukemaker, in 1718; Peter Hesketh, a woolcomber in 1720 and Warren Walker, a weaver, in 1721. William Walton, born, 9 December 1716, (the first Catholic from Manchester to become

Vicar Apostolic of the Northern District) lived in Market Street Lane, between High Street and Marsden Square.

Many of these family names were to be noted in the later history of the Manchester Mission.

John Orrell was entered as a student at Douai 15 October 1758 and was ordained in 1770. He remained at the College as general prefect from 1771 to 1773 before going to Manchester to run the Mission, after the death of Edward Helme October 1773. His residence at that time was 'Church Street'. A letter of contract dated 13 December 1775 by Rev John Orrell, Incumbent at Manchester, to the Right Reverend William Walton at York referred to the will of Helme:

> Rev Edw. Helme of Manchester bequeathed £300 the annual interest of £200 for assisting the Catholics at Manchester & the yearly interest of the remain £100 for assisting the Catholics at Sutton near Macclesfield, Cheshire. £300 was paid to (what were called) the Manchester Trustees who made their sign manual, have bound themselves & successors as Trustees to be accountable for said money & the interim faithfully to pay the respective annual interests in conformity with the Bequeather's Intention (dated) October 18 1775.

Attached to this document was a note:

> These two sums viz. of £200 and of £100 were compended (sic) in building a new chapel in Rook Street, Manchester. Notwithstanding the above mentioned Trustees engage by a paper signed by themselves & successors to pay four pounds ten shillings: yearly and every year for each respective hundred. Signed John Cook, William Moorhouse, William Walton, Benj. Wildsmith, Nath. Eyre, Thomas Whitgreave, Richard Kaye.

In conjunction with the 'Manchester Trustees' for the money left by Edward Helme for the benefit of the Manchester and Sutton

Catholics which was paid over, 18 October 1775, a decision was taken to erect a chapel at Rook Street, Manchester. John Orrell, within a short time of being appointed to Manchester, drew up the plans for the new church. Land, belonging to two spinster ladies named Alexander had been conveyed in 1772 to Samuel Tennant who then conveyed it to the 'Manchester Trustees'. The date of 1772, the year before Helme's death, supports a view that he already had plans afoot to build a new Manchester chapel.

The land purchased by the Manchester Trustees was in Rook Street, off Fountain Street, behind the Royal Hotel, which was situated on the corner of Mosley Street and Market Street Lane. It is described in the deeds as:

> Part of certain gardens... theretofore a meadow, commonly called or known by the name of Bank House Meadow... Situate near, unto and on the most southerly side of a certain street called Market Street Lane.

The dimensions of the whole plot of land, including the Chapel, a dwelling-house under part of it and the yard were stated to be, on the east side (or Back Mosley Street) 38 yards; on the west (or Rook Street) side 56 yards; its area 881 superficial yards. On the east side the deeds go on to describe the plot; it was 'bounded by a small piece of land of nine inches in breadth, being the bank of the River Tib'.[15]

There is no available picture of the chapel but it is possible to construct in one's mind something of the design and structure of the building from an article in the 'Manchester Guardian' of 1845:

> If a stranger were to pass from one end of Rook Street to the other, he would not discover the chapel, and certainly could find no entrance to it, even if he were fortunate enough to guess aright as to the building. Let anyone turn from Fountain Street down Meal Street, he will find, nearly opposite to one of the most elegant edifices for a warehouse in the town (and

certainly its architectural beauties are wasted on the desert of a narrow back street ), a similar small street on the right, striking off at right angles, with a low building at the corner a public house, by its sign as the Fountain Inn, denoting that once there existed in that neighbourhood a refreshing fountain for the good folks of old Manchester. This street is Rook Street; and about halfway down on the left side is a building a little higher than its neighbours, the ground floor occupied as warehouses and by Mr A. Birchall, Sharebroker, and others. Above are large casement windows like those of a cottage or the upper rooms formerly occupied as loom shops. Anything more unlike the exterior of a chapel we never saw; yet these are the windows of St Chad's. There is no entrance to the chapel from Rook Street; and if the stranger determined to find some means of ingress, wends round to Back Mosley Street, he will find only a low wall, with a large and small door in it opening into a yard, with an old dwelling facing the door. Entering this door, however, he will find in a corner of the yard, almost hidden from view—and the building itself quite shut in by a lofty pile of modern warehouses a flight of stone steps which lead up to the chapel. Entering it the stranger will find himself in a small chapel with a gallery supported by eight iron columns; in the low roof of which several openings have been made for the sake of ventilation and light. Still it is a dark and gloomy place and is apparently attended by a very poor class of Catholics.[16]

A description of the Rook Street Chapel interior has also been compiled from a number of sources:

The building consisted of a number of ground floor rooms which served as a residence for the priests. The actual chapel was on the first floor and had galleries on three sides. Such a structure initially made good use of all the space available, yet because it did not look like a chapel it provided a degree of anonymity and security against possible anti-Catholic reaction. The exterior resembled a dwelling house, having 'an aspect of an exaggerated three storey brick building of the old-fashioned type'. The building stood a little higher than its neighbours in Rook Street and was larger than most Dissenting chapels. Above the ground floor were large casement windows like those of a cottage or the upper rooms formerly occupied as loom shops...the chapel was graced by a handsomely decorated altar, surmounted by three pictures, thought to be of considerable merit. The central and largest picture showed the homage paid by the shepherds at Bethlehem to the infant Saviour. Another depicted the Trinity, with the Father mourning over the dead body of His crucified Son whilst the Holy Spirit, in the shape of a dove, hovered above them...The third picture represented the Holy Family. [17]

The chapel, named after St Chad, was opened 3 June 1776. John Orrell wrote to William Walton at York, 5 July 1776, detailing the financial situation of the Manchester Mission:

| The Income of Manchester Incumbency July 5th 1776 | | | |
|---|---|---|---|
| | *L* | *s* | *d* |
| Trafford Family (precarious) | 8. | 8. | 0. |
| Lord Fauconberg, for Sutton | 5. | 5. | 0. |
| 2 Houses in Church Street | 11. | 4. | 0. |
| Old Chapel House (supposed) | 16. | 0. | 0. |
| Cellars and stable of present Chapel | 11. | 15. | 0. |
| Benches in New Chapel (when all set) | 84. | 0. | 0. |
| | | | |
| | 136. | 12. | 0. |

*13. The Income of the Manchester Incumbency July 5th 1776*

According to this statement the income from 'Roman Entry' was £16 for the Old Chapel House and £11 4s 0 for two houses in Church Street. In the sale of 'Roman Entry' in November 1808 there were four cottages on Church Street, 1, 3, 5, and 7,and the building which housed the chapel, house and stable were listed as 42, 44, 46, and 48 High Street, although the usage may have been long altered to meet the needs of renters. The plot was still the same size and was sold on an agreement to pay the trustees of the Manchester Mission, one of which included Broomhead, a chief rent of £54 per annum gross.

## Notes

1. G. Anstruther, *The Seminary Priests: A Dictionary of the Secular Clergy of England and Wales 1558–1850* (London, Mayhew McCrimmon, 1969), vol. 3, p. 245.

2. Dicconson's list of 1741 reads as follows: 'Salford Hundred, Henry Kendall at Manchester & Sutton in Cheshire', and then it has 'Do: Paris' which suggests that he had come from Paris to serve the Manchester and Sutton area (UC/M3/124 [1741]. List by Bishop Edward Dicconson with additions for the later 1740s (copy made in 1864 from Bishop Goss's copy) Anstruther, vol. 4, p. 159.

3. J. Gillow, *A Literary and Biographical History or Bibliographical Dictionary of the English Catholics from the Breach with Rome in 1534 to the Present Time* (London, Burns & Oates, 1885–1902), vol. 3, p. 263.

4. Saintsbury's, *Plan of Manchester and Salford about 1650* (Manchester, Chetham's Library).

5. *Manchester Cathedral Title Deeds* (Manchester, Chetham's Library), Mancath. (CE 1/Pars/1/1).

6. J. M. Reilly, *The History of Manchester* (Manchester, Judd & Glass, 1865), p. 259.

7. F. O. Blundell, *Old Catholic Lancashire* (London, Burns Oates & Washbourne Ltd., 1938), vol. ii, p. 34.

8. Orrell, *Letter to Walton 5 July 1776* (UCA: 11/472).

[9]   Appendix 2/1 *Manchester Trustees 29 November 1784* (SDA. 479).

[10]  Appendix 2/2 *Original Indenture 30 November 1808* (DP4A2). Extract of Indenture by Rev J Rowntree 18 April 1940 (DP4A3).

[11]  A dwelling-house with its outbuildings and curtilage (a small court yard, or piece of ground attached to a dwelling-house and forming one enclosure with it) and the adjacent land assigned to its use.

[12]  Broomhead, *Letter to Marsh 27 February 1796 (UCA: Eyre Correspondence 43).*

[13]  F. S. Fairey, Entwistle & Co. Yorkshire House, 45 Cross Street, Manchester, *Letter to J & N Philips, 35 Church Street, Manchester dated 26 July 1944, and dimensions of the land at Roman Entry* (MCL: M97/10. 22/8).

[14]  Papist Returns: The word 'papist' was a general term of contempt and hostility for Catholics during the seventeenth and eighteen centuries, referring to their adherence to the Pope. The phrase' Papist Return' was used when Parliament demanded information about known or reputed 'Papists' (Catholics) to be returned by the vicar of each parish to his bishop. The listed Catholics, who were convicted of not attending and refusing to attend service in a church of the Church of England, were known as 'recusants' (refusers).

[15]  P. Hughes, *St Chad's Manchester 1847–1947* (SDA: 'The Harvest' 1947), pp. 154–5.

[16]  Anonymous, *A Description of Rook Street Chapel* (Manchester, The Manchester Guardian, 1845).

[17]  D. Lannon, *Rook Street Chapel Manchester* (Manchester, North West Catholic History, 1989), vol. 16, pp. 10–17.

# 5 BROOMHEAD AS ASSISTANT PRIEST 1778–1787

CHARLES HOUGHTON PRIEST-IN-CHARGE and Rowland Broomhead his assistant arrived in Manchester coincidental with the first Catholic Relief Act, which permitted Roman Catholic worship; the acquisition of property either by purchase or by inheritance; repealed the statute forfeiting estates for recusancy; abolished rewards to informers and perpetual imprisonment for priests and schoolmasters however, the reward to the informer against parents who sent their children to be educated abroad remained on the statute book. The Act only repealed some of William III's penal laws and other statutes still remained unchanged.[1]

The clergy, at least from 1778 onwards, were able to go about their business without fear of being taken up by pursuivants. However, the Act gave rise to an anti-Catholic response and riots in some places, especially London. There is no doubt that Houghton and Broomhead would have been aware of and seriously concerned about the possibility of riots spreading to Manchester, which happily did not transpire, but there was much resentment in the Town with the relief.

There was no overnight acceptance of Roman Catholics rather a spirit of distrust but the English Vicars Apostolic were careful to underline the importance of Catholic prayer for the Sovereign. An agreed pastoral, between the Vicars Apostolic of the London, Midland and Northern District, 4 June 1778, was sent to their respective clergy, both secular and regular, requiring:

> that all and every one of you should offer up your most ardent prayers to the Almighty, for our most gracious

Sovereign King George III and his Royal Consort Queen
Charlotte, and all their royal family (when you shall be able
to meet without danger to yourselves or your flocks from
the many grievous penal laws which stand out against the
Catholics of this kingdom) you shall recommend the rest
of the faithful to offer up also their prayers for the same
intentions: this being a duty which by the law of God all
Christian people owe to their respective sovereigns.

The statement 'when you shall be able to meet without danger to
yourselves or your flocks from the many grievous penal laws which
stand out against the Catholics of this kingdom' resonated amongst
families who for generations had worshipped in the 'Old Faith' and
who had been shackled by heinous penal laws. Broomhead, coming
from a recusant[2] family which had held the faith in Stannington
since the Reformation and supported by missioners in their secret
journeys to bring the Mass and the sacraments, now became a
missioner walking in the same footsteps of those who had walked
before him but now without the fear of pursuivants.[3]

Broomhead, from 1778 to 1787 was largely involved as a missioner travelling around south-east Lancashire on the same circuit
as the travelling missioners of earlier years. In general his work in
Manchester was between Tuesday and Thursday. He rotated his
work with the wider mission so that he saw each mission once a
month, travelling on Fridays and returning on Mondays. Obviously
the best time to make contact with his congregations was when
they were not working.

Broomhead had spent the first fourteen years of his life in the
countryside and the next ten years in a secluded and protected
environment in Rome. He returned to Sheffield, which was still a
small town and he often spent time out in the countryside at the
family home in Stannington. In 1778 he was propelled into the

beginnings of an industrial city which would have demanded adjustments in anyone's life.

Familiarizing himself with the Town was one of his priorities for he needed to know the streets, so he could find his flock. The maps of 1772 were evidence of the burgeoning streets of Manchester: Deansgate ran north, with the river Irwell to the west, and off Deansgate, to the east and west, the main thoroughfares of the town. The key ones, reading from the south to the north, were Quay Street; King Street; Market Street Lane and Cannon Street. Around Christ Church and Chetham's College there were a number of important thoroughfares especially Long Mill Gate, Fennel Street, Withy Grove, Shudehill and Millers Lane. At the southern end of Deansgate and the northern end at Millers Lane and easterly at the top end of Market Street Lane, the town ran into fields.

Broomhead lived with the dramatic increase of population and the resulting extension of streets and buildings. By 1794 Market Street Lane continued into Levers Row and on into Piccadilly, Shooters Brow, and Bank Top and on into Ardwick. Millers Street continued into Swan Street and Great Ancoats Street. Quay Street was continued into Peter Street and on into Oxford Street. A whole web of interconnecting streets was developed between these larger thoroughfares. Manchester developed at a dramatic pace and continued to do so throughout Broomhead's time in Manchester.

The improvement of roads had brought improved communication and this in turn brought expansion. The Mersey and Irwell were navigable up to Hunt's Bank near Chetham's College. The Duke of Bridgewater's canal by 1776 ran as far as Runcorn on the Mersey. The most important strands of communication, namely good roads and navigable waterways, were in position.

The population expanded dramatically during the eighteenth century. Estimates of the population in 1717 in Manchester, suggest a figure of about 10,000. The following figures are extracted from W. H. Thomson[4]: (1756) 16,530 from a local enumeration; (1773–74) 22,481 a census paid for by a few gentlemen of the Town; (1788) 42,821 again another local enumeration; (1811) 79,459 the first national census; (1821) 108,016 the second national census. These increases were phenomenal and presented massive problems for the leadership of all institutions at work in the Town, including the churches.

The huge increase of population was the result of a number of different factors coming together. The improved transport system brought both more reliable supplies of food and an influx of immigrants from Ireland, Scotland and from the English countryside, looking for work in the booming town. The establishment of the Manchester Royal Infirmary in 1752 and later the Lying-in Hospital in 1790 led to a significant improvement of health. A visitor[5] to Manchester in 1775 wrote:

> The bustle of active commerce was conspicuous throughout the town, and every house among the poorer class might be called a factory, from the number of hands and of spinning wheels in perpetual motion... To all the ingenious processes of preparing the cotton, from the first carding of it to the completion of the fabric.

The inventions of John Kay with his flying shuttle (1733), Richard Arkwright with his spinning frame (1767), James Hargreaves with his spinning jenny (1768) and Samuel Crompton with his spinning mule (1765–1769) revolutionized the cotton industry. Once these inventions could be harnessed to water or later steam power, the need for a cottage industry decreased rapidly and the construction of huge mills began apace. The first cotton mill to be erected in Manchester was at Millers Lane which was recorded in a pamphlet written in 1783: 'Mr Arkwright's machines are setting to work by a steam engine, for carding and spinning of cotton.'[6] Between 1783 and 1802 there were fifty-two new spinning mills and by 1830 there were ninety-nine.[7]

In 1778 there were ten churches in Manchester and Salford. There were eight churches of the established religion. They were: The Collegiate Church (now Manchester Cathedral) founded in 1419; Trinity Chapel, Salford founded in 1635; St Anne's Church, St Anne's Square, in 1709; St Thomas's Chapel, Ardwick, founded in 1741; St Mary's Church, situated in the Parsonage Gardens area, near the river Irwell, founded in 1753; St Paul's Church in Turner Street founded 1756; St John's Church, at the bottom of St John Street, founded in 1768 and St Thomas's Chapel, Pendleton, consecrated in 1776. Besides the established churches there was the Old Dissenter's Chapel in Cross Street and the Roman Catholic Chapel of Rook Street.

A series of letters refer to the numbers of communicants, confirmations and the size of communities from 1778 to 1787. Bishop William Walton was in Manchester 6 December 1778 and the records detail that:

> There were 261 confirmations and 500 communicants. Here his Lordship was again laid up in the gout for about a month at the house of Rev R. Broomhead & Houghton Incumbents.[8]

In 1780, the number of Catholics at Manchester was recorded as 400 and the priests were Messrs Houghton and Broomhead. John Chadwick, Grand Vicar of Lancashire, in a letter dated 3 February 1783 to Bishop William Gibson informed him that the Manchester mission had four hundred Catholics.[9] Matthew Gibson, 6 December 1784, confirmed 261 and there were 500 communicants at Manchester.[10]

The baptismal figures from Rook Street give some idea of the rising numbers in the chapel during the period of Houghton and Broomhead's incumbency. In the first three years 1778 to 1780 there were 124 baptisms, an average of three baptisms per month. From 1781 to 1783 there were 137 an average of about four baptisms per month. From 1783 to 1786 there were 237 baptisms, an average of seven baptisms per month. For most of the period 1778 to 1787 Broomhead was rarely in Manchester at weekend for he was travelling in the wider Manchester Mission.

## Notes

[1]    B. Ward, *The Dawn of the Catholic Revival in England 1781–1803* (London, Longmans Green, & Co., 1909), pp. 2–3.

[2]    D. Attwater, *The Catholic Encyclopaedic Dictionary* (London, Cassell and Company, Ltd, 1949), p. 420. Recusant: One who was convicted of not attending and refusing to attend service in a church of the Church of England. The word nearly always indicates Catholics who were specifically indicated in several Acts of Parliament against recusancy. The Act of 1714 provided that anyone refusing the oath of allegiance and supremacy when lawfully tendered became subject to the penalties of 'popish recusant convict': these were fixed by the Act of 1593 at a monthly fine of £20 with various civic disabilities; failure to abjure the realm on non-payment was a capital felony. These laws were not enforced with uniform strictness at all times but were far from being neglected.

[3]    Pursuivants: Royal or state messengers with power to execute warrants or warrant officer to summon or arrest.

[4]    W. H. Thomson, *History of Manchester to 1852* (Manchester, John Sherratt & Son Ltd., 1967).

[5]    Thomson, *History of Manchester to 1852,* p. 216.

[6]    *Ibid,* p. 228.

[7]    W. H. Chaloner, *The Birth of Modern Manchester: Manchester and its Region* (A survey prepared for the British Association Meeting held in Manchester 29 August to 5 September 1962), ch. 9.

[8]    Bishop W. Walton, *Records of confirmations and communicants 6 December 1778* (UCA: II/196c).

[9]    Chadwick, *Letter to W. Gibson 3 February 1783* (UCA: 11/129).

[10]   Visitation and Confirmation etc. of the Vicars Apostolic of the Northern District, 6 December 1784 (LRO transcript: RCV 2/6; MS. Ushaw College).

# 6 BROOMHEAD IN THE WIDER MANCHESTER MISSION 1778–1820

M ICHAEL GAFFEY wrote of Rowland Broomhead's work in the wider mission:

For Manchester was not the only place
To feel the effects of such amazing grace,
The towns and villages, for miles around,
Were by his presence and his works renown'd:
Over hills and dales, steep rocks and mountains high,
This bird of Paradise was wont to fly;
He thought no place too distant to do good,
And scatter blessings over whilst he could;
No time he thought too soon, no hour too late,
To labor, but with zeal affectionate,
He brought the wand'ring sheep, that went astray,
Back to the fold of Christ, and led the way.
For this, in summer, heedless of the heat,
He trod his usual rounds with blister'd feet,
The sweat in torrents streaming from his face
Thro' toil, and travelling from place to place:
And in the winter, fearless of the cold,
Both zealous, watchful, diligent, and bold,
Thro' snows that deep upon the surface lay,
This faithful shepherd always found a way;
For pains and miseries, he understood,
Are pleasures when they terminate in good.

The missionary circuit was the Hundred of Salford; Sutton with Macclesfield in Cheshire and Glossop in Derbyshire. This missionary area had been sustained by the priests who served from 1661. There were seven priests: Thomas Weedon, 1661 to 1719, John Shepherd, 1706 to 1734? George Kendall, 1734 to 1741, Henry Kendall, 1741 to 1752, Edward Helme, 1753 to 1773, John Orrell 1773 to 1778, and Rowland Broomhead (and his assistant priests) 1778 to 1820.

Broomhead's work as a missionary priest was governed by the areas which had the greater Catholic numbers and it is in these places that we can to see the early development of Catholic communities, which developed around the support of the Catholic gentry at Barlow Hall, Lostock Hall, Sutton Hall, Trafford Hall and later Glossop Hall. When Broomhead arrived in the mission the Barlow family estate had been sold to the Egerton family and the Anderton family estate at Lostock had passed into the hands of the Blundell family.

The size of the Catholic population in each town can be extracted from the Papist Returns of 1767, but this evidence cannot give us the whole picture because the clergy of the Established Church did not always enter reliable returns and within the Catholic population there were those who conformed outwardly to the Established Church, who came to be known as 'Church-papists',[1] and were consequently not listed in the Papist Returns.

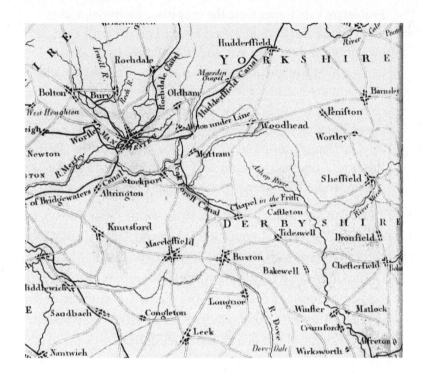

*14. Map of Manchester showing the extent of the Manchester Mission adopted from John Aiken,* A Description of the Country from Thirty to Forty Miles Round Manchester *(1795)*

Broomhead had set times for visiting these far flung hamlets:

> But whilst assiduous in attendance in every priestly duty in the town (of Manchester) he was by no means neglectful of those members of his flock who lived many miles away from their Catholic centre. He had fixed times for visiting them throughout the year, to instruct them and to administer to them the Sacraments. He was with them in sickness, and in case of death went fifteen and twenty miles to give them the rite of Christian burial, and as in those days

Protestant cemeteries were the only place for burial, and as
many of the Anglican ministers insisted on the body being
brought into their churches and the full Protestant service
being gone through, he first performed the Catholic burial
service at the house of the deceased, and as a substitute for
consecrated ground he blessed some earth and placed it in
the coffin; then when the dead were laid in the grave, recited
an 'Our Father' and a 'Hail Mary' together with the 'De
Profundis' for the departed soul a beautiful custom that
continued for a long time[2]

In 1778 the wider Manchester mission comprised: Sutton with
Macclesfield; Trafford; Glossop; Rochdale and Bolton. Only eleven
years before Broomhead arrived in Manchester, the 'Papist Returns
of 1767' had identified those who were Catholics within the wider
Manchester mission. This list of the named members of each
mission is as important as the names of the priests who served them,
for both the laity and the clergy were dependant on one another.
Many of those listed in 1767 would have been still alive when
Broomhead began to visit these missions. Their names were as
important to Broomhead as they are to those whose faith is traced
back through generations of their Catholicism. It is appropriate
that the family names of each community, where possible, should
be listed alongside that of their missioners, for these so-called
'papists' laid the foundations of their Catholic communities.

## *SUTTON & MACCLESFIELD*

Despite the penal laws the Sutton family supported local Catholic
worship and provided both a chapel and a priest for the local
people.[3] Through the failure of the male line the family name
descended from Sutton to Davenport to Belasyse.

Sir Humphrey Davenport continued to allow Catholic worship at Sutton. Sir Rowland Belasyse in 1698 settled £5. 5. 0 upon the mission at Sutton Hall, and it was to be paid 'to such priest or priests as should assist the Catholics of Sutton'.[4] Thomas Belasyse, 4th Viscount Fauconberg, became a Protestant circa 1716 and because of his apostasy the Catholic community in 1716 had to find alternative accommodation for their worship.[5]

During the period, 1716 to 1720, the Catholics of Sutton and Macclesfield used a hay-loft at Ridge Hill Farm, just outside Macclesfield; and sometimes at Rainow. In 1720, two sisters, the Misses Orme, provided the congregation with a large room in their home at Sutton Lane Ends, just outside Macclesfield town. This chapel served the local Catholic community for the next seventy-two years. It was at this chapel that Broomhead met with the Catholic community.

Some eighty years after the original benefaction of Sir Richard Belasyse, the endowment was still being paid and continued to be paid from the manorial mill on Mill Green till 1821.[6]

There was evidence of a significant Catholic community in Macclesfield and Sutton for there were twenty-nine 'papists' listed. The introduction to the 'Papist Return' comments on the information gathered:

> All the reputed Papists within the Chapelry of Macclesfield, computed to comprehend in Circumference full Twenty Miles & in wch [sic] after the best enquiry I can make, I find only thirty seven reputed Papists and those chiefly in Macclesfield & Township of Sutton where Mass is performed by Mr Hulme (Helme) the priest once a month. Of these I find only two of any Landed Interest & that very small, the rest being either lowe Mechancks or Journeymen, artificers of no settled Residence.

The Return is divided into two lists. The list for Sutton supports the view that this was the original enclave of Catholics, for the information about their length of residency was much longer than the Macclesfield return and there were no Catholic landowners listed. The family surnames were: Brokenhough, Doson, Callicon, Davy, Tompson, Warren, Crammock, Bottom, Stoddart, Perry, Young, Lea, Orme, Goodfellow, Warrington, Windop, Shore, Davenport, Melampy, Cassidy and Bassall. Some of the names suggest that there were Irish present in the area and this is supported by a note attached to the Prestbury Return 24 August 1767:

> There are a few Irish Papists in Macclesfield; and in Sutton there is a Mass-house very near ye Hall which belongs to Lord Falconberg.

After the death of Helme in 1776, the priests who lived at Manchester were missionaries to Macclesfield including John Orrell, Rowland Broomhead and Edward Kenyon. In a letter to William Walton, 5 July 1778, John Orrell listed the income for the Manchester mission and in it recorded 'Lord Fauconberg for Sutton £5. 5. 0.'[7]

Economic change in the third quarter of the eighteenth century, driven by technological innovations in the textile industry, saw the advent of the age of the factory. Macclesfield had specialised in the production of silk by handloom but the advent of textile mills, powered by water, led to the mechanisation of production which brought people to the town for work. This led to pressure for a new church to meet the needs of a growing Catholic population.

Chart: Papist Return for Macclesfield & Sutton

| Townships | Persons Name | Ages | Occupations | Years of Residence |
|---|---|---|---|---|
| MACCLESFIELD | James Brockenhough | 35 | Carpenter | 35 |
| | Patrick Doson | 70 | Cobbler | 20 |
| | John Callicon | 40 | Journeyman Barber | 3 |
| | John Davy Senior | 70 | Shoemaker | 70 |
| | John Davy Junior | 35 | Shoemaker | 35 |
| | His Wife | 35 | | 35 |
| | Samuel Tompson | 60 | Carpenter | 10 |
| | His Wife | 60 | | 10 |
| | Martha Warren | 52 | Button Maker | 7 |
| | Mary Warren | 50 | Widow | 7 |
| | Mary Warren her daughter | 29 | Button Maker | 7 |
| | John Crammock | 40 | Shagweaver | 12 |
| | Thomas Bottom | 30 | Servant to Copper Company | 1.5 |
| | Margaret Stoddart | 60 | Widow | 60 |
| | Edward Perry | 55 | Journeyman Chandler | 10 |
| | His Wife and 5 Children | | | |
| SUTTON | Mr Hulme | | Priest resides chiefly in Manchester | |
| | Mr Wm. Young | 60 | Steward to Lord Falconberg | 30 |
| | Mr John Lea | 70 | Yeoman Estate | 70 |
| | James Orme | 45 | Yeoman Estate | 45 |
| | James Goodfellow | 70 | Husbandman | 70 |
| | Widow Warrington | 80 | Button Maker | 80 |
| | Ellen Warren | 80 | Button Maker | 80 |
| | Elizabeth Tompsons | 70 | Button Maker | 70 |
| | Widow Windop | 80 | Button Maker | 80 |
| | Her Daughter | 38 | Button Maker | 38 |
| | Her Daughter | 36 | Button Maker | 36 |
| | Elizabeth Shore | 65 | Button Maker | 65 |
| | Elizabeth Davenport | 70 | Button Maker | 70 |
| | Daniel Melampy | 40 | Lopis Callim Dresser | 1.5 |
| | Patrick Cassidy | 40 | Lopis Callim Dresser | 2.5 |
| | William Bassall | 60 | Lopis Callim Dresser | 1.5 |
| | James Bassall | 58 | Servant to Copper Company | 0.5 |
| | His Wife | | Servant to Copper Company | 0.5 |

15. *Chart: Papist Returns for Macclesfield & Sutton*

In 1793 the congregation moved from Sutton Lane Ends to a
room in Backwallgate under the leadership of Edward Kenyon who,
in the following year, was assigned to be in charge of the new church
at Mulberry Street in Manchester. The French émigré priest, Louis
Benjamin Robin, was appointed to the mission at Macclesfield and
was responsible for beginning the first baptismal register in 1795.

In a letter from Rev Thomas Longden of Macclesfield to William
Gibson, 23 February 1811, there was news about the building of a
new chapel at Macclesfield:

> I write this to inform your Lordship that we are going on
> with our Chapel very well and with the assistance of God
> we purpose compleating it towards July or August if we
> meet with any reasonable share of liberality from a generous
> Public this spring. We have already expended nearly £600
> and our resource is done which constrains us to beg your
> Lordship's assistance by giving us a Letter of Recommen-
> dation or Patronizing our undertaking to the most Popular
> Congregations in Lancashire by which means we have not
> the least doubt of meeting with all our wishes in enabling
> us to compleat our design: our principal aim at this time is
> to beg for money that we can raise an house annexed to the
> Chapel and school, for the Reception of a Gentleman as
> soon as we can give any reasonable share of support to one.
> We have already had an invitation to visit Liverpool but
> must obtain your Lordship's letter first, before we can go
> out any more a begging at the same time we must beg your
> Lordship's Benefaction and Blessing with it. Your Lordship
> must be informed that the Trustees will give up to his
> Lordship the Chapel and all its dependencies whenever he
> may think proper to take it under his protection and then
> make not the least doubt of it please God to spare him to
> visit Macclesfield what has been done will meet his Lord-
> ship's approbation for which we shall have to return
> Almighty God our thanks for His assistance in all the little

crosses we have met with and in enabling us to prosecute the object before us to the end, in hopes that his Blessing will crown all our endeavours with success and merit a part of his Blessings in Eternity is the sincere wish of your Lordship…Nb. Our little Congregation has added ten pounds a year more to Rev Mr Blundell's yearly income exclusive of all the other incident expenses attending the Chapel so that for the future he will receive from Macclesfield £20. 5. 0.a year.[8]

Broomhead wrote to William Gibson, 7 July 1811, part of which letter referred to the new chapel at Macclesfield:

I am going to open the new Chapel at Macclesfield in a few Weeks & therefore must beg leave of your Lordship permission to bless it before it is used according to the form laid down in our new Ritual. To save your Lordship the trouble of granting me this leave in writing I shall presume the leave is granted except you write to the contrary. I got £10 for it from Mr Tempest of Broughton. I expect something from Mr Maire from Hartington to whom I have written on the subject, & meant to have written to Sir John Lawson, whose death is very much lamented in this County by every one that knew him.[9]

The new chapel, dedicated to St Michael, was opened in Chester Road by Broomhead, 25 August 1811, and from, 1811 to 1821, James Blundell served Macclesfield from Stockport, until the appointment of John Hall as resident priest.

There is evidence that the Fauconberg family continued to support the Catholics of Macclesfield for there are two entries for benefactions from Lord Viscount Fauconberg for £10, 30 November 1810, and another £10, 13 December 1810, both donations to the Rev Dr Rigby of the Secular Clergy Fund.[10]

## GLOSSOP

The Glossop estates of the Howard family were a relatively insignificant part of the whole and it didn't even merit a manor house. The area was a scattered collection of farms and hamlets. The Howards did not build a manor house there until the eighteenth century and then probably as a response to industrial changes in Glossopdale. It was built circa 1729 by Ralph Standish Howard and was known as Royle Hall, but later renamed Glossop Hall. After his death in 1737, the family agents who managed the estate lived at the Hall. These were Vincent Eyre and his son Nathaniel, who were related to the Eyre's of Hassop, a family who were noted for their Catholic influence in Derbyshire.

Thomas Shimell born in Shropshire, 22 September 1716, entered Douai, 24 October 1729, and was ordained 1 April 1741. He remained at the College for two years in the role of prefect-general and left for the English mission, 3 September 1743. These dates are supported by the archives. There is a gap of ten years which is not covered by any evidence before he became chaplain to the Eyre's at Warkworth Castle, Northamptonshire in August 1753. Sometime later he became chaplain to Nathaniel Eyre, agent of the Howard family at Glossop Manor. In November 1773 he was made executor to the will of Rev Edward Helme. Later he was with Nathaniel Eyre at Crumpsall where he died, 23 August 1779. According to John Kirk he was 'many years at Glossop' and in the 'Return of the Papists 1767'[11] the entry for Glossop lists 'a male, aged 50, reputed priest, 23 years resident'. This description agrees with a large part of the above evidence. He was born in 1716/17 therefore in 1767 he would have been 50 years old. If we accept that Shimell is the subject of the Papist Return it follows that he would have spent only a year as chaplain at Warkworth Castle. This suggests that Thomas Shimell was in Glossop from circa 1744.

Unfortunately, the names of those who were Papists in Glossop were not recorded in the Papist Returns of 1767, nor were the ages of children. The reputed priest, aged fifty and the steward, of the Howard family aged fifty-three, had both been in residence in Glossop since 1744 based on the 1767 Return. The servant to the hall and his wife a servant were both thirty; he was a native, but she had arrived in Glossop nine years previously. A female publican, aged sixty-four had been born in the Town circa 1703 and she had a daughter. The next longest resident was a woman cotton spinner, aged forty-two, who had lived there since her birth. A male weaver aged thirty-six was a native of the Town as was a male butcher, aged thirty-four. There were four female cotton spinners. The first, aged twenty-six, was a native and had two children. The second was thirty-six and had been in the town for fifteen years and had a son. The third aged thirty had been resident for seven years. The fourth was thirty and she had a son but residency was not enumerated. A male labourer was listed aged forty, with a daughter aged eighteen but again residency was not enumerated. There were in total nine-teen Catholics, which comprised thirteen adults and six children.

Broomhead took Thomas Shimell's place as chaplain, visiting Glossop Hall monthly and saying Mass in a temporary chapel in the Hall. He travelled over from Manchester on Saturday when he would have heard confessions in preparation for the Sunday Mass and returned on the Monday. The following story was recorded by Mgr Croskell:

> The chief agent of the Duke of Norfolk resided at Glossop Hall, near the town of Glossop, in Derbyshire, and he had a domestic chapel in the Hall. Thither Father Broomhead went once a month to hear confessions, celebrate Holy Mass and give Holy Communion; on the occasion of one of these monthly visits, he was riding his pony between Manchester and Ashton-under-Lyne, when he fell in with another gentle-

man on horseback. He was young, and had the appearance of a clergyman. He asked the reverend father if he could direct him to the town of Ashton. Father Broomhead said he was going there, and should be happy to accompany him.

They fell into conversation, and soon became quite friendly; but they were both quite silent as to their respective business, or to what place they were going. This reserve was occasioned in Father Broomhead from the persecuting times which were still more or less prevailing, and on the other hand the young clergyman was loath to make known his business to an entire stranger. But they went so far as to let it be known that they were both on their way to Glossop, and in the end they found they were going to the same house, Glossop Hall—Father Broomhead to discharge his monthly duty at the Hall, and the young clergyman to be inducted into the living of Glossop, which was in the gift of the Duke of Norfolk.

The point of the story consists in the manner in which the young clergyman found that he was in the company of a Roman Catholic priest. Priests at that time avoided dressing in clerical garments, and the young parson found out that his companion was a priest by a circumstance which he long afterwards remembered, and often told it as a good joke. They had got to Hollingworth, a village on the way to Glossop, a little after mid-day, where two hand-loom workers were standing at the door of the cottage after their dinner, taking a little fresh air before resuming work. As the two travellers were passing, the parson heard one of the man say to the other, 'See thee, Bob, yon's the Popish priest, but I wonder who's t'other devil wi' him?' He had no doubt heard at school, or from the pulpit, that a Popish priest was near akin to the black demon, and of course anyone travelling with him in a friendly manner could not be much better, hence the expression. However, the two arrived at the Hall together, and afterwards became good friends; but the parson all his life repeated the story of his first acquaintance with a Roman Catholic priest.[12]

A new family of Howard agents began their long and devoted service in Glossop when Matthew Ellison was brought from Sheffield to manage the Howard estates. He moved into Glossop Hall in 1797. Bernard Edward Howard, who succeeded to the Glossop estate, had lived there for a long time as a youth. Educated at Douai, he was heir to the Duke of Norfolk, and he supported the Catholic cause at national level. It was Bernard who later funded the building of All Saints church.

Glossop, a wool processing centre for generations, changed quite rapidly towards the end of the eighteen century to specialising in the production and printing of calico and coarse cotton bringing increased population to the area. The increase of the numbers of Catholics and the need for a resident priest and more chapel space was addressed by William Gibson.

In March 1800, Matthew Ellison wrote to William Gibson, asking that an émigré priest might be recommended to Glossop in succession to Fr Tolly. The wording of the letter suggests that he had been resident chaplain to the Ellison's but this has not been confirmed. The Ellison's request for a priest was granted with the arrival of Joseph Barbe, one of a large number of clergy who had fled from France at the Revolution. Under his direction they formed the mission of All Saints, based at the chapel at Royle Hall in 1803.

## TRAFFORD HALL

Sir Cecil Trafford succeeded to the estates of Trafford and Booth in 1620. He was already a knight, having been invested at Houghton Tower in Lancashire, 16 August 1617. Initially, Cecil was a persecutor like his father, levying '12d per head for non-attendance at church on each Sunday'.[13] However, when his friend Francis Downes of Wardley Hall converted to Catholicism in 1632, Cecil tried to get him to change his mind. Cecil was unsuccessful and came under the influence of the Benedictine monk, Richard Huddleston, who received him into the church in 1636. As a result, Sir Cecil Trafford was stigmatised as the 'Arch Papist', arrested by the order of Sir John Seaton and imprisoned in Manchester. His estates were sequestered but subsequently restored to him by Charles II.[14] He died in 1672. From then on the Trafford family maintained an unbroken link with Catholicism.[15] They were said to have:

> Kept a low profile with regard to their Catholicism, this in no way seemed to inhibit their own private devotion and they continued to provide most generously for the religious observance of their Catholic tenants and employees, affording mass and other devotional facilities upon the estates.[16]

The family had a series of chaplains assigned to Trafford Hall. The independent chapel at Barton was not built till after Broomhead's death. James Wagstaffe, 21 July 1791, registered the chapel of Trafford as required by the Act of that same year.[17] He also served as chaplain to John Trafford at Croston Hall from 1792 till 1805 and in 1792 James Haydock arrived from Douai and was assigned to Trafford House to be chaplain to John Trafford.

The mission included Barton, Eccles, Pendleton, Pendlebury, Patricroft, Stretford, Sale-Moor and Altrincham is reputed to have contained about three hundred Catholics. It is difficult to find proof for Gillow's figure[18] of three hundred for Eccles and Stretford which were the only 'Papist Returns', which combined totalled only thirty-nine, which included Humphrey Trafford of Trafford Esq., but they did not include the Trafford family and their servants who spent much time in York. According to Connolly:

It would appear that substantial numbers of those employed on the estates in the late eighteenth century and early nineteenth century belonged to known Catholic families who had worked the estates for a considerable time. A number of servants also appear to fall into this category'.[19]

*16. Trafford Hall*

In the Papist Returns for Eccles, the enumerator separated the males from the females making it difficult to link families together:

The first entry at Eccles is John Cooke, aged forty, described as a gentleman. Then there are two families, Marsh and Tomson, who were the largest proportion of the entries. The Marsh family had Bryan, aged 72, a weaver; Richard, aged 38, a hatter; Margaret a wife, aged 35 and Elizabeth a wife, aged 42, four in all and no children. The Tomson family had James, a husbandman and Catherine his wife both aged 60; Thomas aged 25 and Samuel aged 22 were both husbandmen; Joseph Tomson aged 18, a labourer and there were two infants William aged 3 and Betty aged 1, a total of seven. Mary Wallwork, aged 35, was widowed and had an infant Elizabeth aged 2. Jane Pollet, aged 33, was also a widow with a possible daughter Margaret, a weaver, age 17. In the list there was only one person who was not a native of the area. She was Elizabeth Evans, aged 27, resident ten years and mother of Samuel aged two. The Eccles Return had a total of eighteen recusants.

Mr Stopford, the curate of Stretford, listed the following Papists in his chapelry but did not say how long each had been resident but the nature of their work, mainly farming, would suggest a long held local occupation:

The Anderton family were farmers and there were three involved, namely John and his wife who were both aged about 60 and their son William aged about 30.

The Gibbon family comprised John, a labourer, and his wife Ann Gibbon, both aged between 60 and 70. There was also Ann, a midwife, aged 30.

Another branch of the Gibbon family was also in farming. There was James and his wife Jane both about 40 and 6 children the youngest under 1 year, the oldest about 15 or 16.

The wives of William Johnston and Jonathan Pilling both labourers and Thomas Syddall the innkeeper were aged 25; 30 and 35 respectively.

John Morrice, aged 60, was a shopkeeper and his wife Ann was aged between 50 and 60.

The only weaver mentioned was Thomas Fazackerley who was about 50.

Mr Stopford, the curate, mentioned that Humphrey Trafford of Trafford Esq. was residing in York for the most part. The Stretford Return had a total of 20.

The chapel at Trafford was attached to the house and was sufficient to hold the small numbers that were likely to assemble at any one time. In 1807, James Haydock exchanged places with James Smith at Lea Chapel near Preston. After a short time James Smith retired from the chaplaincy at Trafford House and was replaced by Thomas Sadler who registered the Hall chapel at the Quarter Sessions, 14 October 1807, according to the law.[20]

According to the general meeting, August 1808, for the General Fund of the Secular Clergy, Thomas Sadler was entered as priest at Trafford House and there is a further entry for him, October 1815.[21] Three of this generation of the Trafford family made donations to the Secular Clergy Fund: Mrs Trafford £20, 30 September 1813; Mr Edmund Trafford £10, 23 December 1813 and John Trafford Esq. of Trafford £20, 18 November 1814 and Masses were said on their behalf.[22] John Trafford died 29 October 1815. There is an entry in the Lancashire Secular Clergy Fund for a donation of £20 for Masses to be said for Henry Trafford dated 10 July 1822.[23]

It was not until 1827 that the mission had its own independent chapel which served the area in conjunction with the domestic chapel of the Trafford family. The Trafford family funded their chapel and priests but Broomhead, as dean of Lancashire was responsible to the bishop with regard to placements at Trafford and the family also made contributions to the charitable needs in the town of Manchester and to the building and upkeep of Catholic chapels.

## ROCHDALE

Thomas Wray, Vicar of Rochdale recorded 25 August 1767, a list of the Papists in the Parish of Rochdale in the County Palatine of Lancaster, except for the Chapelry of Saddleworth. There was a nil return for Littleborough. Children were not recorded in his list.

Out of the fourteen people listed, thirteen had lived in Rochdale from birth and three had been born there in the late seventeenth century. This suggests that there had been a small but significant group of Catholics in Rochdale which would have been brought to the attention of the missionary priests and we may surmise that the chapel recorded as being licensed by Rowland Broomhead in 1791 was licensed because there was already a significant Catholic community in existence. In the visitation and confirmation lists of Bishop Matthew Gibson, 8 December 1782:

> Matthew Gibson went to Preston with a view to meeting the trustees from Liverpool. Afterwards set out from Heaton and on his return called at Manchester and Rochdale.[24]

| Chart: Papist Return for Rochdale 1767 | | | | | |
|---|---|---|---|---|---|
| Townships | Persons Name | | Ages | Occupations | Years of Residence |
| ROCHDALE | James Turner | | 80 | Weaver | 80 |
| | Cornelius Holt | | 74 | Cloth Worker | 74 |
| | Daniel Holt | | 40 | Weaver | 40 |
| | William Roberts | | 36 | Shoemaker | 36 |
| | Elizabeth, His Wife | | 45 | | 45 |
| | John Wolfenden | | 40 | Shoemaker | 40 |
| | Lucy, His Wife | | 34 | | 34 |
| | James Chadwick | | 70 | Weaver | 70 |
| | Robert Holt | | 37 | Cloth Worker | 37 |
| | Anne, the wife of James Holt | | 35 | Farmer's Wife | 35 |
| | Mary, the wife of James Sharrocks | | 33 | Farmer's Wife | 33 |
| | Timothy Grindred | | 40 | Weaver | 40 |
| | Mary His Wife | | 60 | | 60 |

*17. Chart: Papist Returns for Rochdale 1767*

This indicates that Matthew Gibson visited Rochdale in 1782 and confirmed some of the community and received a report on the progress of this mission from Broomhead who served Rochdale from Rook Street. Early correspondence referring to Rochdale shows that the mission had been the beneficiary of £1,000. There is no indication in the records as to where this money came from. The earliest mention of this sum refers to interest paid on capital and is contained in a letter, 12 January 1784, from John Chadwick, at Chorley to the Vicar Apostolic, Matthew Gibson, at Darlington:

> Mr Dunn told me on his return from your parts, that you saw no impropriety in applying ye money that comes in annually for Rochdale, towards paying the interest of wh. he owes for his purchase in Blackburn provided you give me your sanction for so doing, I shall have no objection: But without that I certainly shall not do it.[25]

Some of the interest on Rochdale's money was being used to support the Blackburn Mission. In further correspondence from Chadwick at Weld Bank Chorley to Matthew Gibson 31 January 1787, the interest of the Rochdale money is again being used for Blackburn:

> I must begin with the Blackburn concern... The payment for the premises by the contract is to be completed in 3 years viz. next May. The sum payable £500 with int [interest] at 5 p [per] c [cent] besides this an annual ground rent of betwixt 50 and £3 I believe. All that has been paid towards it is £50 which was paid as you agreed at Warrington it should be, from the Blackrod and Rochdale money, adding to that 12s. 6d out of 13, Petre's money to make up the £50. There remains therefore upwards of £500 still to be paid. Now for the ways and means, which, I fear will prove very inadequate. A Mrs. Hodgson left £400 to Blackburn on the demise of either of her sons. One of them is now confined

for madness amongst the xx's at Liege. The other, not overwise, lives at Duncan. At present, indeed, I'm told, he is at London on a 3 weeks tour. If any money could be raised, a security might be given by you and Mr Dunn for repaying it, which this cash falls in three months ago ....[26]

In the accounts for the Northern District, May 1791, the £1,000 belonging to the Rochdale Mission, was entered with the £30 interest which was divided between the priest from Manchester who cared for Rochdale £10 and the Vicar General, John Chadwick £20 which he used where ever he felt there was most need:

Copy taken from the account of monies in Mr John Chadwick's hands, which account he communicated to R.R. Wm. Gibson at York May 1791. For Rochdale-£1000 (capital) Interest per annum £30. Nb. Ten pounds of this interest has been paid to the Priest at Manchester for attending Rochdale. The remainder of the interest is put out by Mr John Chadwick. [27]

In accordance with the Act of 1791, Broomhead registered a chapel at Rochdale, which confirmed that there was already in existence a community of Catholics and this is supported by the evidence from the Papist Returns of 1767. The registration document read as follows:

In pursuance of an Act of Parliament made and passed in the Thirty-first Year of the Reign of his Majesty King George the Third, and in the Year of our Lord One thousand Seven-hundred and Ninety-one, entitled, "An Act to relieve upon Conditions and under Restrictions certain Persons therein described from certain Penalties and Disabilities, to which Papists or Persons professing the Popish Religion are by law subject," I, Rowland Broomhead of Manchester in the County of Lancashire, officiating Priest and Minister at a certain Chapel situate in Rochdale in the said County, do hereby certify to the Justices of the Peace assembled at the General Court of Quarter Session of the

Peace, holden by adjournment at the new Bailey Court House in Salford in and for the said County of Lancaster, on Thursday the twenty-first Day of July in the year afore-said: that the Place of my Congregation or Assembly for Religious Worship and Meeting is held at the said Chapel at Rochdale aforesaid, and I do hereby request that the said Place of Congregation or Assembly for Religious Worship and Meeting may be recorded at the said General or Quarter Sessions, and also that my Name may be recorded as officiating Priest and Minister at the Chapel aforesaid. And I do demand the Clerk of the Peace for the said County of Lancaster to record the same in the Manner provided, directed and required in and by the said Statute. Dated the twenty-fifth Day of July 1791.

To the Justices assembled at the General Quarter Session of the Peace, holden at the New Bailey Court aforesaid in and for the said County.

Signed: Rowland Broomhead. [28]

The Manchester priests were responsible for the Mission at Rochdale until 1794, when Joseph Shepherd took charge at Bolton and also became the missioner for Rochdale and Bury. There is a list of communicants for Rochdale for 1796 attached to the baptismal records of Bolton, which reads as follows:

Daniel Holt, Th. Buckley, Mary Hardman the miller, Elizabeth Holt the shoemaker & daughter.[29]

In the 'New Annals of Rochdale', printed in 1931, there was an entry for 1820:

The Roman Catholics met for Mass in a room over the "Hark up to Glory" Hotel, now the Harkaway Hotel, St Mary's Gate.[30]

In the Commercial & Trade Directory for Rochdale, dated 1825, there was a reference to where the Roman Catholics worshipped:

> In addition to which places of worship, the Roman Catholics assemble for divine service, in a room over a dwelling house at the top of Blackwater Street.[31]

Both these references were referring to the same hotel/dwelling house which was situated on St Mary's Gate right opposite Blackwater Street. This is the earliest known place of Catholic worship in Rochdale, since the Reformation. The first the chapel of 'St John the Baptist' was built in 1829 on Anne Street. Alongside the Chapel was a school, chapel house, a house for the master and a graveyard.

## *BOLTON*

The Returns of the Papists for 1767 for the ancient parishes and townships of Bolton total one hundred and fifteen listed recusants which includes all ages. The family names suggest they were mostly of English derivation. They were:

> Shepherd; Pilkington, Pendlebury, Walkden, Hilton, Bolton, Eastwood, Bushell, Brimelaw, Ramele, Hosking, Lee, Ownsworth, Rylance, Bratherton, Langshaw, Marsh, Sedgwick, Daggart, Etock, Siddalt, Low and Headley. In some cases names were not listed. Of those who recorded their occupation, the majority were either weavers or spinners. Out of 34 adults who recorded how long they had resided there, 16 had been there under 10 years; 3 under 20 years; 4 under 30 years; 6 under 40 years; 2 under 50 years; 2 under 70 years; and 1 under 80 years.

The Catholic population had begun to rise in the Bolton area somewhere between 1757 and 1767. Prior to that time the numbers of adult Catholics was sparse.

The first entry in the Papist Returns of 1767 was Robert Shepherd, a saddler by trade, whose wife Anne Shepherd (née Ratcliffe) was of the Established Church. They were the parents of Joseph who was brought up as a Catholic. At the age of twelve he presented himself at the English College of St Alban in Valladolid in Spain for training to become a priest, where he was accepted by his uncle, his Father's brother, also called Joseph. After his ordination 17 December 1791, he was appointed to the staff of Tudhoe School in Durham as a teacher. After three years his wish to work in Bolton was granted and he arrived there in 1794.

There was already a small mission at Bolton based on a small chapel in Old Acres, behind the Balmoral Hotel. The Manchester priests, including Broomhead, were responsible for the Catholics in the Bolton area and the Rochdale area until 1794, when Joseph Shepherd took charge of both of these Missions.

Broomhead was called to attend someone who was sick in Bolton on the very day of his arrival in Manchester in 1778. In the first register of the Catholic Chapel of Saints Peter & Paul, Bolton, the first entry is in 1794. Prior to that date baptisms for Bolton people would have been recorded in the Manchester records at Rook Street, which date from 1772.[32]

An extract from 'A Portrait of Father Broomhead' written by Provost Croskell, who came to Manchester in 1835, includes the following incident which he had been involved in during his early missionary days. He wrote:

> Such was the primitive mode of instructing followed by Father Broomhead, and it was imitated by the Rev. Jos. Shepherd, of Bolton, as I gather from a little incident which occurred on the occasion of a visit which I paid to SS. Peter and Paul's during my early missionary days. I was shown by a decent-looking woman, somewhat advanced in years, a book which she said was given to her by the Rev Father

Broomhead, who was accustomed from time to time to visit his friend and neighbour, Father Shepherd. 'On one of these occasions,' said the woman, Father Shepherd called me to him and said to his friend, "Father Broomhead, this young woman has done a world of good by devoting herself to the work of instructing young and old for the Sacraments'. Father Broomhead seemed very much pleased, and said he would make me a present of a book which would help me in my most excellent work of preparing my classes for the more perfect practice of their religion. 'Depend upon it, if you go on as you have been doing, you will shine like the stars in Heaven for all eternity'. The good woman showed me the book given her by Father Broomhead a simple book of instruction and she seemed to prize it more than if it had been the most rare and valuable work ever written by man.[33]

The year after Shepherd arrived in Bolton, he established his mission at a house in Wood Street. As priest and minister of Bolton he presented himself at the New Bayley Court House at Manchester to record the Chapel at Wood Street, Bolton 21 January 1795. This was required under the Act of Parliament of 1791, entitled 'An Act to relieve upon Conditions and under Restrictions certain Persons therein described from certain Penalties and Disabilities to which Papists or Persons professing the Popish Religion are by Law subject'.[34] In 1800 a new church was established at Pilkington Street called Saints Peter and Paul.

In the 'Return of the Papists for 1767' for the parish of Bury in Lancashire, recorded by J. Stanley, Rector of Bury, August 1767, there were no Papists listed in the hamlets of Bury, Elton, Walmersley, Heap and Holcombe chapelry. There was only one entry in the Bury parish, and this was Alice, the wife of James Kay, a spinner, a reputed Papist, living in the Edenfield chapelry.

*18. Saints Peter & Paul Bolton*

The census of 1801 which recorded the population of Bury as 7,072 had by 1831 risen dramatically to 15,086 and this increase can be traced to industrial change, which drew in both indigenous British workers and Irish migrants, the latter escaping from the upheavals in their native land. There is no evidence of a place of worship in Bury till 1825 but we cannot discount the possibility of missionary priests stopping off to respond to the religious needs of the Catholics there. It is not beyond the bounds of possibility that the Manchester priests, in travelling to Rochdale, from pre-1791, the date that the chapel was registered, and Bolton till 1794, did not include a visit to Bury. The room that Fr Michael Trappes, the Rochdale priest, opened at Clerke Street, Bury in 1825, suggests that a nascent Catholic community already existed in the Town.

## STOCKPORT

In the eighteenth century, Stockport was known for its silk weaving, but later in the third quarter of the century, due to the import of cheap foreign silk, the town went through a period of decline, but its workforce, conversant in textiles, responded to the huge development in the cotton industry in the latter part of the century. The size of the population depended to a large extent on the work available. In the early part of the eighteenth century, it was about 2,000, but by the latter period it had grown to approximately 5,000.

The 1767 Papist Returns for Stockport register eight adults but no children; hardly evidence for a need for a chapel but by the end of the century the rise of the population had changed enough for Broomhead to begin to establish a mission there. In 1798, Broomhead and his assistant priest, Richard Thompson, were responsible for collecting funds to establish a mission.

They set up a chapel, 1 May 1798, in a small room, in Hempshaw Lane, Stockport and between them 'continued to ride out from Manchester each Sunday for the next 16 months to offer the Holy Sacrifice of the Mass'[35] and recorded thirteen baptisms during this time. Mass was first said, 22 July 1798, in a room in Windmill Street by Richard Thompson.

In a letter from James Blundell from Stockport, 22 April 1800, to the Rev Mr Rigby, at Lancaster, one of the priests responsible for the Lancashire Infirm Secular Clergy Fund, regarding his membership of the fund, he referred to the fact that he had only just arrived in England in the previous summer and his place of abode was at No. 50 Union Street, Stockport, Cheshire.[36]

| Chart: Papist Return for Stockport | | | | |
|---|---|---|---|---|
| Townships | Persons Name | Ages | Occupations | Years of Residence |
| STOCKPORT | Nicholas Chadwick | 82 | Taylor | 40 |
| | Anne Chadwick | 59 | Throwster | 30 |
| | Robert Chadwick | 21 | Felt Maker | 21 |
| | Charles Chadwick | 17 | Taylor | 17 |
| | Stephen Purcell | 28 | Shag-Weaver | 1 |
| | Stephen Harris | 50 | Shag-Weaver | 10 months |
| | William Rushton | 58 | Linen Weaver | 13 weeks |
| NORBURY TOWNSHIP | Lawrence Woodcock | 40 | Collier | 1 year 3 months |

*19. Chart: Papist Returns for Stockport*

Blundell established his chapel in a rented apartment in Windmill Street, at the corner of Edward Street, in Stockport, summer 1799. In 1801 he purchased land in Edgeley, a short distance from Windmill Street, to build a chapel, presbytery and school. In 1802, Rev Richard Thompson laid the foundation stone for the three buildings and on 1 May 1803, the feast of Saints Philip and James, the chapel was opened and dedicated in the names of the two saints. Sermons were preached by Broomhead and Thompson, who had both been instigators of the new mission.

Three letters give us some insight to the developing mission at Stockport. The first refers to a gift of £100, which was left in the will of Ann Heatley, to provide income for the Hull Catholic Chapel, but Bishop William Gibson, did not think that this gift would be advantageous for Hull, and his Grand Vicar, Anthony Lund, suggested Stockport, which was a new mission, and in desperate need of funds. The letter, dated 8 December 1804, from Anthony Lund of Fernyhalgh to the Right Rev William Gibson, Old Elvet Street, Durham contains the following extract:

*20. Saints Philip & James Stockport*

Moreover Mr William Heatley Esq. has left in my hands £100 more, this money was left by his late sister Ann Heatley with intention of mending the income of Hull Catholick Chapel but as your Lordship has informed us, that it can be no advantage to that place, but rather a detriment. Mr Heatley is willing for the above sum to be given to any other place your Lordship shall appoint, which stand in need of an increase of salary. I recommended to him Stockport as that place is a new place & has not as yet a sufficient salary affixt to it. Mr Heatley desires that for 30 years to commence from this time a greater number of Masses should be annually said for his sister Ann who died the first of June 1803 and after 30 years are past only one Mass to be annually said on or about her anniversary. In my opinion 10 Masses per annum or at most one Mass per month should be sufficient for thirty years to come … at present this money

is in Preston Bank and will there remain till I have your
orders about it... [37]

The second letter, 26 April 1805, was from Thompson, who was
then the Grand Vicar in Lancashire, based at Weld Bank, Chorley,
to William Gibson at Durham. The extract refers to the poverty of
the Stockport mission, the importance of the mission and the priest
in charge Blundell:

> If your Lordship could spare a few Pounds for Mr Blundell,
> Stockport, I am well satisfied the trifle could be no where
> better applied, both on account of the poverty of the place,
> the importance of that Mission & the (—-) of Mr Blundell
> himself... [38]

The third letter, 12 February 1807, from Broomhead, Rook Street,
Manchester to William Gibson, Old Elvet, Durham, emphasised
the problems facing the mission at Stockport:

> Mr Blundell's Congregation at Stockport is increasing fast;
> after his last Public Instructions, he added 50 to its number,
> partly Converts & partly Catholics who did not before
> attend their duty: but the whole at present are but poor, not
> one opulent person amongst them, who can afford to assist
> him any more than paying their Bench rent, & now, owing
> to the stagnation of trade, a great part of his Bench holders
> are unable to pay. If your Lordship has any monies to
> dispose of to indigent places, it could not be better applied
> than there. I know he has been much distressed of late, tho'
> he says little of it himself. He is far from being extravagant:
> he lives sparingly & with great economy; for after paying
> ground rent & taxes he told me himself, that he had not
> more than £30 per annum to keep himself & his Maid
> Servant on. Had he not had an old careful & steady house-
> keeper, who formerly lived with me, & who I am sure will
> put everything to the further most I do not know how he

must have lived. And yet I am certain, that in a little time the place will support him very well: but being an infant Institution it will want nursing for a time.[39]

Besides his work in Stockport, Fr Blundell, was a missioner to Macclesfield from 1811 to 1821.

## TAMESIDE

The River Tame flows south through Saddleworth, Mossley, Stalybridge, Ashton-under-Lyne, Dukinfield and Hyde. The 'Returns of the Papists 1767' for Stalybridge lists two Papists or reputed Papists and were recorded by John Cradock, 12 August 1767:

> Bartholomew Irwin of Highfield in ye Parish of Saddleworth
>
> Mathew (sic) Williams of Grasscroft in the Parish of Saddleworth
>
> Irwin is 52 years of Age, and has resided in this Country, 20 years.
>
> Williams is 40 Years of Age and has resided in this Country upwards of 4 years, Irwin & Williams are woolen(sic)-Clothiers.

Stalybridge was within the parish of Ashton-under-Lyne so the records place them together in the Returns. The names of the Papists or reputed Papists, within the Parish of Ashton-under-Line (sic) in the County of Lancaster and Diocese of Chester were listed in the 'Returns of the Papists' 6 August 1767. There were two entries which were submitted by J. Spicer, Curate of Ashton:

> Robert Gommins of Ridgehill aged about sixty by Trade a Woollen-Clothier has resided in this Country about twenty years.

> Christian Whitefoot of Staileybridge (sic) Widow aged about thirty years, by Trade a wool Spinner Resided in this Country about five years.

Dukinfield and Hyde were not mentioned in the Papist Returns.

Within the boundaries of what today is known as 'Tameside', there was a total of only six people in the Papist Returns of 1767, and none of them listed had lived in the area since their birth. Tameside covers a large area and it would not have made sense to establish a mission there until there were viable numbers, which arose as a result of the influx of Irish migrants and others responding to the opportunities in the textile industries in Lancashire and Cheshire in the latter quarter of the eighteenth century.

The Catholic population in the Dukinfield area expanded as a result of Irish migration and by 1798 or 1799 the Catholics, through the work of Broomhead and his fellow clergy, had taken over an abandoned Methodist chapel in Harrop's Yard, off Cricket Lane, which was served by the Manchester clergy from Rook Street Chapel.[40] Duckinfield St Mary's was built in 1823 and this became the mother church of St Mary's Oldham (1828); St Peter's Stalybridge (1839); St Paul's Hyde (1845); St Mary's Ashton-under-Lyne (1856) and St Anne's Ashton-under-Lyne (1857).[41]

## OLDHAM

In the first three quarters of the eighteenth century the Oldham district was a scattered area of homesteads, which through the grazing of sheep, supported a cottage industry producing woollen garments. The first cotton spinning mill to be built in the Oldham area was Lees Mill in 1778.

The Oldham 'Return of the Papists 1767' covered the area of the Township of Oldham, and Chadderton, Shaw, Crompton and Lees.

The latter two areas recorded nil returns. In Oldham there was the Lees family (5), the Whitehead family (2), the Mey family (3) and Alice Taylor. In Chadderton there was the Buckley family (10) and in Shaw, Philip Buckley. In all there were nineteen of working age and three children. Of the nineteen working, there were three people involved in the fur industry; eight weavers; seven cotton spinners and one clothier, all of whom conducted their businesses in cottages, because the mills had not yet been built.

Chart: Papist Return for Oldham

| Townships | Persons Name | Ages | Occupations | Years of Residence |
|---|---|---|---|---|
| OLDHAM | Samuel Lees | 47 | Weaver | 47 |
| | James Lees his Son | 21 | Weaver | 21 |
| | Elizabeth Lees his Daughter | 18 | Cotton Spinner | 18 |
| | Mary Lees his Daughter | 15 | Cotton Spinner | 15 |
| | Susanna Lees his Daughter | 5 | | 5 |
| | Edmund Whitehead | 41 | Weaver | 41 |
| | Mary Whitehead his Sister | 44 | Cotton Spinner | 44 |
| | James Mey | 48 | Fur Cutter | 15 |
| | Catherine Mey his Daughter | 14 | Fur Cutter | 14 |
| | Nancy Mey his Daughter | 12 | Fur Cutter | 12 |
| | Alice Taylor | 30 | Cotton Spinner | 10 |
| CHADDERTON | Robert Buckley | 41 | Weaver | 35 |
| | Martha Buckley his Wife | 46 | Cotton Spinner | 35 |
| | Edmund Buckley their Son | 22 | Weaver | 22 |
| | John Buckley their Son | 21 | Weaver | 21 |
| | Abigail Buckley their Daughter | 18 | Cotton Spinner | 18 |
| | David Buckley their Son | 15 | Weaver | 15 |
| | James Buckley their Son | 12 | Weaver | 12 |
| | Sarah Buckley their Daughter | 8 | Cotton Spinner | 8 |
| | Paul Buckley their Son | 5 | | 5 |
| | Elizabeth Buckley their Daughter | 5 | | 5 |
| SHAW | Philip Buckley (Batchelor) | 83 | Clothier | 83 |

*21. Chart: Papist Returns for Oldham*

In the last quarter of the eighteenth and the first quarter of the nineteenth century there was a large number of cotton and weaving mills erected in and around Oldham and as a result there was a large increase in the population, due to migration from areas around the country and from the increase of Irish migrants, especially following the events in Ireland in 1798.

The mission of Oldham was overseen by the priests, firstly from Rook Street Chapel and later from St Augustine's Granby Row in Manchester. One of the priests who assisted Broomhead in Manchester, John Worswick, visited Oldham during the period 1789 to 1791.[42] Mass was said in a room over a public house, known as the 'General Cornwallis' which later was called the 'Harp and Shamrock'(which suggests a large number of Irish people in the area) and afterwards changed to the 'Lamb and Lark'. The first Catholic Church in the area covering what today we call Tameside was St Mary's Duckinfield built in 1823, which was the mother church of Oldham.

## Notes

[1]   Church-papist: In the seventeenth century, a Roman Catholic who conformed outwardly to the Church of England. (Shorter Oxford English Dictionary).

[2]   P. Prendergast, *Old Catholic Manchester, a Sketch*(Manchester, John Ryland's Library, c. 1905), R166830) p. 6.

[3]   M. J. Ullman, *St Alban's Macclesfield* (Macclesfield,1982), p. 5.

[4]   C. S. Davies, A *History of Macclesfield* (Macclesfield, 1961), p. 149.

[5]   *Ibid.*, p. 350.

[6]   *Ibid.*, p. 149.

[7]   Walton, *Letter to Orrell 5 July 1778* (UCA: II/473).

[8]   T. Longden, *Letter to W. Gibson 23 February 1811* (LDA: WG. 679).

[9]   Broomhead, *Letter to William Gibson 18 March 1811*(LDA: 690).

[10]  *Donations to the Secular Clergy Fund* (LRO: RCCF5/2).

[11]   E. S. Worrall, *Return of the Papists 1767* (London, Catholic Record Society, 1980), vol. 2, p. 92.

[12]   R. Croskell, *Traditions Connected with the Revival of the Catholic Faith in Manchester* (SDA: 'The Harvest' January, 1896), pp. 11–16.

[13]   J. Slater, *History of Eccles and Barton* (Trafford, 1897), p. 21.

[14]   R. Hollingworth, *Mancuniensis or, an history of the towne of Manchester* (Manchester, 1839), pp. 115–116.

[15]   J. P. Earwaker, *Cheshire Past and Present* (London, 1877) p. 93.

[16]   *London and Dublin Orthodox Journal* (Dublin, 3 November 1838), p. 288.

[17]  J. Wagstaff, *Registration of Trafford Hall 21 July 1791*(LRO: QDV/7/34).

[18]   J. Gillow, *The Haydock Papers: a glimpse into English Catholic life under the shade of persecution and in the dawn of freedom* (London, Burns & Oates, 1888) p. 205.

[19]   G. P. Connolly, *Catholicism in Manchester and Salford 1770–1850* (Manchester University, Unpublished thesis for PhD, 1980), TH10287.

[20]   T. Sadler, *Registration of Trafford 14 October 1807* (LRO: QSP/2555/19).

[21]   *Sadler at Trafford October 1815* (LRO: RCCF5/2, 1783–1844).

[22]   *Trafford Family donations 1813–1815* (LRO: RCCF/5/2).

[23]   *Trafford Family donations 10 July 1822*(RO RCCF/2).

[24]   M. Gibson, *Visitation and Confirmation lists 8 December 1782*(LRO: transcript RCV 2/6).

[25]   Chadwick, *Letter to M. Gibson January 1784* (LDA: MG. 11).

[26]   Chadwick, *Letter to M. Gibson 31 January 1787* (LDA: MG. 11).

[27]   Chadwick, *Letter to M. Gibson May 1791*(LDA: MG. 57, p. 111).

[28]   Broomhead, *Registration of the Chapel at Rochdale, General Quarter Session of the Peace* (Manchester, 25 July 179), LRO: QDV/7/33.

[29]   *Bolton's Baptismal Records with attached list of Communicants at Rochdale 1796* (LRO: RCBO 1/5).

[30]   T. T. Heywood, *New Annals of Rochdale* (Rochdale, 'Rochdale Times', 1931), p.188.

[31]   *Rochdale Commercial & Trade Directory* (Rochdale, Pigot's Directory, 1825) Rochdale Library, A21. 1825.

[32]   *First Register of the Catholic Chapel of SS. Peter & Paul Bolton 1794* (LRO: RCBO MF 9/53–57).

[33]   C. A. Bolton, *Salford Diocese and its Catholic Past* (Manchester, Jas. F. & C. Carter Ltd., 1950), Appendix vi, Includes extract of the above meeting of Broomhead and the woman in Bolton, printed in *The Catholic Monthly* of

SS. Peter and Paul's, Bolton, September 1895.

34  *The Catholic Relief Act* of 1791 (LRO: QOV, 7/2).

35  G. Wright & H. Dove Our *Lady and the Apostles, Stockport, 1799–1999. Two Hundred Years of Witness* (Stockport, 1999).

36  J. Blundell, *Letter to Rev Mr Rigby at Lancaster concerning his membership of the Lancashire Infirm Secular Clergy Fund 22 April 1800* (referred to in Wright & Dove, Our Lady and the Apostles, Stockport), p. 2.

37  A. Lund, *Letter to W. Gibson, 8 December 1804* (LDA: WG 501).

38  R. Thompson, *Letter to W. Gibson 26 April 1805*(UCA: 513).

39  Broomhead, *Letter to W. Gibson 12 February 1807*(LDA: WG. 553A).

40  B. Marshall, *A History of the Parish of St Paul's Catholic Church, Hyde, 1848 to 1998* (Hyde, 1998), p. 6.

41  M. E. Gandy, *Catholic Missions and Registers 1700–1880* (London, Michael Gandy, 1993), vol. 5, North West England.

42  T. Curley, *The Catholic History of Oldham* (St Williams Press, Market Weighton, East Yorkshire, 1911), p. 16.

# 7 BROOMHEAD & THE MANCHESTER MISSION 1787–1820

WITH THE ABSENCE of Houghton in 1787 Broomhead became priest-in-charge of Manchester, Salford and the Greater Manchester Mission. He and his missionary priests continued to minister at: Sutton and Macclesfield till 1795; Bolton and Rochdale till 1795/96; Stockport till 1800; Glossop till 1803; Duckinfield till 1823 and Oldham till 1828. With his new position, and the gradual growth of independence in the outer mission, Broomhead had more time to engage with the local people in the Town and assess the needs of the people of the Manchester Mission.

The arrival of so many people in the Manchester area looking for work, many of whom were negligent of their religious practice, inspired Broomhead to introduce a system, known as 'Public Instructions', which had been tried before: 'What others have attempted, but in vain'. 'Public Instructions' reflected the 'retreat' method of Ignatius, but Broomhead did not call it a retreat, which might have suggested exclusion or separation but rather offered his instructions to all who wished to attend.

Archival material is missing from 1787 to 1805 but there is no doubt that he introduced 'Public Instructions' soon after he took charge of the Manchester Mission for there was a perceptible increase of baptisms after 1787.

Broomhead's key aim was 'to teach the ignorant and point the road to Heaven'. The meetings were open to anyone of any religion or none and they were free. Thousands took up the invitation and all kinds of people from different backgrounds attended the Catholic chapel and Broomhead faced some people, who came to laugh, mock and jeer at him and to treat him with scorn and despite these, others listened. Michael Gaffey, a contemporary of Broomhead narrated his success:

> The scheme succeeded—thousands came to hear
> The mysteries of God by him made clear;
> Among the rest some came, familiarly,
> To satisfy their curiosity;
> Some came to laugh, and others came to scorn;
> Some came for entertainment, some to learn;
> Some came to mock and jeer, but ere they went
> Were frequently by him made penitent;
> Instead of making game, 'twas their delight
> To frequent the instructions every night
> That they were given, and with one accord
> Join hearts and voices to adore the Lord,
> Become good Catholics, reform their lives,
> Convert their husbands some and some their wives-
> In short, a universal change took place...

Letters between the clergy, chronicle the story of Broomhead's introduction and development of 'Public Instructions', the repercussions and the favourable outcomes, the labour required to hear confessions and to examine those wanting to become Catholics.

The earliest evidence is a letter sent to Thomas Eyre, at Crook Hall, Durham, 6 November 1806. Broomhead addressed the results of Thomas Lupton's 'Public Instructions', which had resulted in examinations of converts, listening to first confessions (many of whom were Irish), many long absentees from their religious duties, hearing General Confessions and two other priests had joined with them in order to help them to give confessions which ran very late into the night. Besides all the postulants the everyday visitations to the sick had to be made:

> I should have answered your letter sooner but after Mr Lupton's Public Instructions which ended a fortnight since we have not had a moment to spare: one week has been employed in examining converts, first Confessions many from Ireland of this class from 30 to 40 years old & long absentees from their duties another week with the assistance of 2 other priests has been employed from morning to night in hearing their General Confessions & our sick who have given us some respite for these 2 months past, are now calling on us daily 3 or 4 time.[1]

Broomhead shared the statistics of the growing Catholic population with his congregation:

> Two or three times each year it was the good father's custom to announce to his congregation the increase in the number of baptisms, Easter Communicants, and converts to the Church, for year by year he saw the little flock around him steadily growing in numbers, increasing to his delight, his responsibilities and labours.[2]

In a letter to Bishop William Gibson, 12 February 1807, Broomhead asked him to grant faculties to émigré priests, to church women, as the large numbers of these women were interrupting his work in the confessional, especially on a Sunday morning when the clergy were responding to confessional needs. The number of Catholics in the congregation was given as ten thousand and there were so many requiring confession that the priests often worked in the confessional into the late hours of the night:

> And at the same time I must by leave of your Lordship to grant faculties to Church[3] Women both for him on Mr Kenyon's account, as well as to Rev Mr Hardy on our account, as it is attended with great inconvenience & loss

of time for us to quit the Confessional 2 or 3 times on a
Sunday morning to church Women. In such a Congregation
as this, consisting of above ten Thousand Catholics, it is
frequently more than we can do, to hear the Confessions of
those who apply for it; we are frequently engaged on the
Saturday night from 6 or 7 o'clock till 11 or 12 at night, &
sometimes later, & from early in the morning till the end of
High Mass which is half past 11 (except while we are saying
Mass)… We have never less of a common Sunday out of
Indulgence time than from 20 to 40 communicants & of
these some, either very long, General Confessions.[4]

Broomhead compared the Manchester Mission with that of Liverpool in 1807. Manchester had two chapels whereas Liverpool had
four, and twice the number of priests, yet Liverpool had half the
numbers of confessions than Manchester. Broomhead laid the
success of confession at the door of 'Public Instructions'. He
informed the Bishop that he would soon embark on building another
church in Manchester, for the two chapels, St Chad's Rook Street and St
Mary's Mulberry Street, were overflowing:

Liverpool may have as many nominal Catholics; but by
means of Public Instructions which we have thrice in the
year we hear Double the number of Confessions; tho they
are 6 priests & 4 Chapels We are much in want of a very
large Chapel & I mean to set about it, as soon as a favourable
opportunity offers: trade is now so bad, that I fear little or
no Subscriptions could be raised. Our 2 Chapels at present
will not hold our Congregation by many thousands.

In the same letter, Broomhead records success with 'Public Instructions'
closer to home. These had been taken up at Fr Blundell's chapel at
Stockport and the mission had increased in size after the last 'Public
Instructions' which suggest that there had been previous instructions.
The poverty of the Stockport mission was giving cause for concern.

> Mr Blundell's Congregation at Stockport is increasing fast; after his last Public Instructions, he added 50 to its number, partly Converts & partly Catholics who did not before attend their duty: but the whole at present are but poor, not one opulent person amongst them, who can afford to assist him any more than paying their Bench rent, & now, owing to the stagnation of trade, a great part of his Bench holders are unable to pay.

In another letter from Broomhead, 26 February 1807, to Thomas Eyre, part of it described the intensity of work in the mission of Frs Lupton, Thompson, Blundell, Shepherd and himself in dealing with the results of the 'Public Instructions'.[5] Richard Thompson, then Grand Vicar came from Weld Bank in Chorley to help the priests at Manchester. It is quite clear from this letter that Broomhead was leading the team of priests and he was the one who was going to give the 'Public Instruction'. The doctrine of the Catholic Church would be tested on the applicants for conversion and it would take as much as four to five days to complete and that the applicant would be there for all of that time from the Monday morning. This letter would have had some influence on Thomas Eyre, for he was in charge at Crook Hall, where the students were training for the priesthood. Eyre shared the 'Public Instructions' of Broomhead and his priests, as a model for imitation for his staff and students:

> If I cannot find time this week, I shall not be able to do it for a fortnight after, as I shall be totally engaged, along with the Rev Messrs Lupton, Thompson, Blundell & Shepherd, in taking the Converts, Ist Communicants (many from Ireland from 20 to 40 year s old) & other long absentees (old Soldiers, Sailors etc) into the Church. My Public Instructions will finish on Sunday night next: & we begin to examine those who apply to us to be admitted on Monday morning. The examination will take us 4 or 5 days to know if they are sufficiently convinced of every doctrine of the Catholic

Church from what they have heard on Controversy at the
Public Instructions. We have persons of all Religions who
attend them, & in general many Converts who came at first
out of curiosity. This year I have had an unusual crowd the
(—-) entire have had only Mr Thompson to assist us on that
week; but the following week we shall all five be employed
the whole week from morn till night in the Confessional.
After the last Public Instruction we had 194 General confessions to hear of which 34 were Converts besides 7 others of
that description who were not sufficiently then instructed.
We had also a great many after Mr Lupton's Public Instructions at the end of summer: not less than 20 Converts besides
other general confessions of Ist Communicants & long
absentees. I wish Public Instruction were everywhere
adopted: they are of more real service to religion than all
other duties. Mr Thompson has adopted them at Weld Bank,
Mr Shepherd at Bolton & Mr Blundell at Stockport with
equal great success. A few years since neither Bolton nor
Stockport had a Chapel and only a few straggling Irish
Catholics in them: they have each now above 300 in congregation; besides children & you have heard that Mr Thompson has been obliged to enlarge his Chapel.[6]

In an extract from a letter written by Broomhead from Manchester,
18 March 1811, to William Gibson at Durham, Rowland cut short
his letter because he had no further time as he was so occupied with
all the confessions and converts he was attending:

I have not time to say more; for we are taking 20 Converts
into the Church this day; & we have 150 more general
Confessions to hear this Week with the additional assistance
of Rev Messrs Thompson, Penswick & Blundell: this is the
harvest Week of my last Public Instructions, which began
at Christmas and ended a Week since. We spent all last
Week in examining those who attended the Instructions.[7]

Besides the normal routine of the Mission, the hours that had to be spent on confession alone were phenomenal, and it was apparent that without the extra help from priests outside of Manchester, Broomhead would have been hard put to cope. It was said that:

> It was no uncommon thing ( ... ) for him to be kept in his confessional till one and two o'clock in the morning, when, overcome with fatigue, he would come out of the vestry, and, entering his house, would steep his feet in hot water, which had the effect of causing a copious flow of tears, after which he returned to the duty of the confessional quite refreshed to continue his sympathy and kindly advice to his spiritual children.[8]

The Manchester mission seemed to be taking its toll on the clergy. In a letter from Richard Thompson to William Gibson, Vicar Apostolic, 15 January 1818, he makes the following reflections on the situation at Manchester. Thompson was giving the Bishop an update of the problems of the Manchester mission. Fr Lupton has been ill but had recovered enough to go back to Manchester after his recuperation at Chorley. Richard Thompson knew the extent of the work in Manchester and had personally worked there and knew just how exhausting the work was. It was such a laborious mission that it could 'Murder its priests'. The way forward, as he saw it, was to get more priests into the mission:

> I am happy to inform your Lordship that Mr Lupton got over his attack very well. It was a touch of Typhus; but it was taken in time, & removed by prudent attention. He was confined for a short time; but he is now again hard at work, though weak & looking worse than before the attack. Mr Briggs[9] remained with them: but Mr Broomhead says he is not made for much- he does not like work ( ... ) I suggested to Mr Ashhurst by way of trying his dispositions, that your Lordship would perhaps direct him to Manchester. His

answer was he wished to have no disposal of himself & if it were your Lordship's pleasure, he should not object. I was gratified, seeing him so stout since his fever. He is more like Mr Penswick in bulk than like what he was when he left Ushaw. I fear, however, it may not be all health: & I think he would please Mr Broomhead & answer well. And I do sincerely, flatter myself that with another with Mr Lupton or Mr A. (Ashhurst) with Mr Lupton or another with Mr Broomhead, Manchester would be, though a laborious Mission, yet a Mission that would not Murder its Priests; which it is now doing. But all this rests with your Lordship; whose judgment no one can distrust.[10]

The content of these 'Public Instructions' can be found in Michael Gaffey's poem above, and in the writings of Provost Robert Croskell. The latter had come to Manchester in 1835 and died there in 1902. His writings were based on the information which he had garnered from his fellow clergy who had known Broomhead and the recollections of those in the community who still remembered him. Broomhead:

> made it a practice to give two courses of familiar instructions every year in the Chapel, on each Sunday and Monday evening for several weeks, and during the time he employed catechists to train classes of boys and girls in the knowledge required before they went to Confession or to Holy Communion.[11]

A description of Broomhead's success with his Public Instructions was written in 1905 and it would appear to reflect a story that had been passed down by the clergy during the nineteenth century:

> Plain and simple were his methods in all his dealings with his people. Twice a year he gave a course of public instructions on Christian doctrine, embracing the chief points of the Catholic faith and practice, which with all their plainness attracted crowds; many outsiders being drawn by curiosity

to know what the Catholic religion was, that it should be so
banned and penalised on account of its dangers and numerous were the conversions effected by these means.

As a proof of his growing influence in the town and to show his
quiet yet masterful way of dealing with those with whom he came
into contact, we quote the following interesting conversation of a
local preacher to the Faith. Having become acquainted with Father
Broomhead shortly after his coming to Manchester, and being
kindly disposed towards him by reason of his unobtrusive zeal and
his kind and genial character, he thought it a great pity that so good
a man as Mr Broomhead should be engaged in the errors of popery,
so after some thought he took it upon himself to talk to Mr
Broomhead, with a view to his conversion.

For this purpose he called upon him one evening, and after some
conversation gradually commenced a discussion on religious
matters, showing the follies of Popery and the absurdities of the
Catholic Faith. The good father answered never a word to all that
he advanced, but, noting down all the points of the discourse, he
thanked him kindly for his visit and his good intentions, and invited
him to come again on another evening.

The preacher, confident that he was making headway, and that
before long he would have Mr Broomhead persuaded to his own
way of thinking, came again at the appointed time and continued
his arguments, the father again pursuing the same course and fixing
up a third meeting, when he took up his turn to speak. He dwelt
upon every point he had noted down in such clear and convincing
terms that the would-be Apostle went away deeply impressed, and
very much disturbed at the answers he had received.

After a little while he came again to the good father's parlour,
but with a very different purpose in view, for, after being fully
instructed in the doctrines and practices of the Catholic Church,

he was received among the faithful, and became one of the most fervent members of Father Broomhead's congregation.[12]

The 'Public Instructions' of Broomhead and his fellow priests pre-1794 were such an achievement that many people came back to the Church and others were received into the Church but the chapel at Rook Street was too small to hold them. Throughout the correspondence there was recognition that a new chapel would be needed. The increase in baptismal figures supported that view. The period, 1772 to 1777, under John Orrell, baptisms were circa two per month; under the period of Charles Houghton, 1778 to 1786, the figures were circa three baptisms per month. Under Broomhead, from 1787 till 1794 (the year before the opening of St. Mary's Mulberry Street) the average number of baptisms was circa fourteen per month.[13]

The population figures for Manchester during the period, 1778 to 1820, are difficult to pinpoint but there is no doubt that there was a huge rise in the numbers of people in this period. According to one source there were 43,000 in 1773; 76,788 in 1801; 91,136 in 1811 and 129,035 in 1821.[14]

The population and baptismal statistics mirror one another in that they both suggest a fast upward trend. The increase of the Catholic community brought with it increasing demands which Broomhead and his clergy in Manchester had to tackle. These were: the cost of finding space to accommodate the increasing numbers; reaching out to the growing population whether they were Catholic or Non-Catholic, believer or non-believer; and the difficulty of responding to a Catholic congregation who were, to a large extent, illiterate.

Increasing numbers of migrants within the British Isles, especially from Ireland, responded to the enormous job opportunities in Manchester, in the period of Broomhead's incumbency at Rook Street, 1778 to 1820. A Manchester historian, Joseph Aston,[15] expressed in poetic form, the decision of the Roman Catholics to build a new chapel in the town:

The same year the Catholics deem'd it quite meet
To build up a chapel in Mulberry Street.
For the trade of the town, and hands wanted for weaving,
And bread to be found here, poor Irishmen craving,
Brought an influx of Catholic weavers to town,
And fill'd Rook Street Chapel to near breaking down ...

Michael Gaffey, in his poem on Broomhead, mentions the reason for building a new chapel:

This Reverend Pastor, seeing his success
Had crowded his small chapel to excess
Resolv'd to build one on a larger scale

William Gibson in a letter to Mr Eyre at Crook Hall, 3 January 1794, raised the question of the size of the size of chapels:

Almost all new chapels are already found to be too small.[16]

The immediate problem for Broomhead was how to provide for the overflow from Rook Street Chapel until the new chapel was built, for the needs of these people could not be neglected. The first step was the establishment of a chapel-of-ease to hold the overflow from Rook Street whilst subscriptions were gathered; negotiations begun for the purchase of the land; the appointment of an architect and the commencement of the new building.

Monsignor Canon Charles Rothwell, the editor of 'The Harvest', wrote an article in that journal, to celebrate the first centenary of St Mary's, dated 15 August 1895:

The centenary will be kept on Sunday, August 18th, when the Bishop of Salford will preach. In preparation for the celebration, Father O'Dwyer proposes to renovate the interior, and for this he appeals for outside aid. St Mary's, he says, has claims upon the Catholics of Manchester at large, for here the great-grandfathers of the Catholic community were baptised, here the sacraments were adminis-

tered, here the Faith was handed down to us at a time when
the last penal laws were but of yesterday'.

Monsignor Rothwell raised the possibility of an older chapel,
named under the title of the Blessed Virgin Mary, which opened
30 November 1794 and closed about 1812:

> From the biographical sketch of Father Kenyon and Gil-
> low's Dictionary, and the Baptismal Register kept at St
> Mary's, we gather that another St Mary's, wherever situated
> was opened for Divine service on November 30th, 1794, and
> blessed in honour of the Blessed Virgin Mary, and this older
> chapel continued in existence after the opening of Mulberry
> Street Chapel till about 1812.[17]

It is feasible that during 1794 there was a temporary chapel somewhere, probably close to the site of the intended building plot in
Mulberry Street, which took the overflow from St Chad's Rook
Street and was called the Chapel of the Blessed Virgin Mary. It may
have been a Sunday school room which was used for the children in
the afternoon and might have been available for service in the
morning or it might have been a room in a building nearby possibly
'Church Street'. In 'Manchester's Hidden Gem' Broomhead was
listed 'in charge of Mulberry Street from 1792 until 1794, which may
indicate that Mass was said in the area before the church was built'.[18]

The title of the Blessed Virgin Mary would likely have been
reduced in conversations to that of St Mary's. The Baptismal
Register for St Mary's Mulberry Street listed only two baptisms in
1794 dated 7 December,[19] a week after 30 November 1794 opening
of the older chapel of the Blessed Virgin Mary (unknown location)
or St Mary's Mulberry Street. These baptisms may well have taken
place in a chapel-of-ease, which would have carried the name of the
future chapel.

In the minutes of the Manchester Sunday Schools, 7 December
1795, Mr Hall, secretary, was asked by the General Committee to

write 'to the two Romish Ministers to preach a Sermon at their respective Chapels for the benefit of the Sunday schools'. The first chapel was that of Broomhead at Rook Street and the second that of the Rev Edward Kenyon at Mulberry Lane. The sermon at Mulberry Lane by Kenyon was not given until after 1796. Kenyon was based in Macclesfield before his appointment in Manchester for he moved his congregation from Sutton Lane Ends to a room in Backwallgate in Macclesfield in 1792. Backwallgate had 'Two rooms, to serve as a chapel and priest's house'[20] and Kenyon was the first resident priest there but was then assigned to be in charge of the new church at Mulberry Street in Manchester, sometime late in 1794.

The French émigré priest, Fr Louis Benjamin Robin was only appointed to the mission at Macclesfield in 1795 to take Kenyon's place. Fr Robin was responsible for beginning the first baptismal register in that year.

*22. The First Chapel of St Mary Mulberry Street*

The following legal document was a licence issued by the Justices assembled at the General Quarter Sessions of the Peace, holden by adjournment at the New Bayley Court House:

> In Pursuance of an Act of Parliament made and passed in the Thirty-first Year of the Reign of his Majesty King George the Third, and in the Year of our Lord One Thousand Seven Hundred and Ninety-one, entitled, 'An Act to relieve upon Conditions and under Restrictions certain Persons therein described from certain Penalties and Disabilities to which Papists of Persons professing the Popish Religion are by Law subject' I Edward Kenyon of Manchester in the County of Lancaster, officiating Priest and Minister at a certain Chapel situate in Mulberry-Street in the said County, do hereby certify to the Justices of the Peace assembled at the General Court of Quarter Session of the Peace, holden by adjournment at the New Bayley Court House in Salford in and for the said County of Lancaster, on Wednesday the twenty-fifth day of January in the Year aforesaid: that the Place of my Congregation or Assembly for Religious Worship and Meeting is held at the said Chapel at Mulberry-Street aforesaid; and I do hereby request that the said Place of Congregation or Assembly for Religious Worship and Meeting may be recorded at the said General or Quarter Sessions, , and also that my Name may be recorded as officiating Priest and Minister at the aforesaid Chapel by the Name and Description of the Reverend Edward Kenyon officiating Priest and Minister at the Chapel aforesaid. I do demand the Clerk of the Peace for the said County of Lancaster to record the same in the Manner provided, directed and required in and by the said Statute.

> Dated the twenty-fifth Day of January 1795. (Signature) Edward Kenyon

In the following documents for the Mission of St Mary's Mulberry Street, there were none that referred to the purchase of the land, which was owned by John Leaf, who conveyed the land to the trustees: John Trafford, James Orrell and James Taylor, with a chief rent of £49. 10. 0., 25 December 1794. This would suggest that John Leaf made a gift of the land on Christmas Day 1794, which was freehold, but retained a chief rent.

On Christmas Day, 1794, the land for the new chapel was conveyed by John Leaf to three trustees as follows:

> John Leaf to John Trafford, James Orrell & James Taylor: Conveyance of plot of land containing 664 square yards. Freehold. Chief rent £49. 10. 0. Declaration of a trust as in the next deed. Declaration of a trust made between Trafford, Orrell & Taylor of the one part and Wm. Gibson of the other part to maintain the priest appointed to the Church on the said plot with power to mortgage (no power to sell).[21]

Attached to these trust forms was a statement dated 8 September 1848:

> These deeds were not enrolled and as possible trouble was anticipated in consequence of this omission a new conveyance was executed by the representation of John Leaf.

In the 'Rules and Regulations of 1823' the following entry was made:

> The ground on part of which the Chapel & House are built, pays an annual Rent of £49. 10. 0 to John Leaf Esq., on the 24th June and 25th December i.e. half yearly ... [22]

Michael Gaffey referred to the support that Broomhead received to build the chapel at Mulberry Street:

> Nor did he in that undertaking fail;
> For the respect and honor he acquired
> Immediately procured him the desired
> Assistance, and beyond description proved
> How much he was esteemed and belov'd
> By all who knew him—every one that could

Contributed to aid a man so good;
Not only Catholics, but likewise they
Who from the Mother Church had gone astray?
None lagg'd behind, whate'er their faith might be,
But gave their aid alike promiscuously...
 So they who were not bound by duty's laws,
And they who had no int'rest in the cause
Join'd hand in hand with Catholics to raise
The temple, and deserve an equal praise.
Thus Broomhead was enabled to complete
The chapel standing in Mulberry-street.

Towards its completion eight hundred guineas (£840) was borrowed from the executors of Mr Casey at five per cent interest, which had been bequeathed for the relief of the poor of Manchester, at the sole recommendation of the Catholic clergy. The phrase: 'Towards its completion eight hundred guineas were borrowed' would suggest that the mortgage was not set up till after the death of John Casey Junior, October 1795. John Casey, an Irish linen merchant, died 13 September 1792 and left on his death:

> the remainder & residue of his Personal property to Trustees that they should place out this money on Mortgage, or Government security that the Interest of it might be forever hereafter applied to the relief of the Poor Catholics of this Town; not by the Priests except they be Trustees, but by their direction & appointment as expressed in his will.[23]

John Casey's son, John, had a right to the interest on £300 that was held by the Trustees, but should the son die, then the £300 went into the Casey Fund. His son perished in a shipwreck on the banks of Newfoundland, October 1795, and the £300 devolved to the Casey Fund. Broomhead, as a trustee of the fund, turned to the fund, to find the money to build the new chapel at Mulberry Street:

I called out of Mr Leaf's hands by degrees as it was wanted
by Mr Needham the treasurer for the Building of the New
Catholic Chapel in Mulberry Street Manchester & I got a
Mortgage on the said Chapel for £840. The interest of this
at the rate of 5per. cent is to be pd. to me for the benefits of
the Poor Catholicks of Manchester.

Until October 1795, the date of death of John Casey Junior, the
£300 was not available to the Trustees for it provided 5per cent
income for John junior. Therefore the mortgage of £840 must have
been set up some time after the death of John junior.

Towards the completion of the Building £840 was borrowed of
the Executors of the late Mr Casey at 5 per cent, which interest was
forever to be applied to the Relief of the Poor of Manchester at the
sole recommendation of the Catholic Clergy, as by will devised (£42).
This sum (£840) was sunk into the Building. The Executors of Mr
Casey were: Ben Sanford, George Gibson and Mr Leaming Esq.

The oldest description of St Mary's Chapel in Mulberry Street
was printed in 'The Manchester Guide' of 1804:

> The NEW CATHOLIC CHAPEL is a very handsome, large
> building of brick and stone, situated in Mulberry Street. If
> the pews of this chapel had been of oak (instead of deal) or
> were neatly painted, it would scarcely yield in neatness to
> any place of worship in the town. The pulpit is very light,
> airy, and elegant fabric. The altar is very handsome, and has,
> perhaps, the very best painting which ever came from the
> pencil of WILLIAMS. The subject is the descent from the
> cross. Upon the altar, stand the four Evangelists, in alabaster,
> brought from CAMBRAY[24] during the late war. On the
> front of the altar, is painted the Holy Lamb, by TOWNLEY,
> in his best manner. The altar recess loses much of its effect,
> by a black gummy kind of adhesion which disfigures it. It is
> supposed to arise from the breath of a very crowded congre-
> gation, which rushes towards that part of the chapel, when,

in the course of their ritual, six large lighted candles, and a lamp, rarefy the air. A ventilator, immediately over the recess, would probably remedy this inconvenience. The light air would be at liberty to escape, and the damp particles of breath, instead of flying all to one point, would be more uniformly dissipated, as in other places of public worship.

The glass dome produces a very fine effect, and is perhaps worthy of imitation, in designs for other chapels. The architect however made some mistakes in the roof which was intended to have supported itself, but recourse was obliged to be had to iron pillars. A neat organ adds to the appearance of the chapel, as well as contributes to the swell of devotional praise, which is chanted by some very good voices. This chapel was built in 1794, by subscription, in which the names of many persons of different religious persuasions, very much to the credit of their liberality of sentiment, were found for handsome sums. The present priest is the Rev Edward Kenyon.[25]

The beauty and magnificence of this chapel was a haven in the middle of poverty:

In those days the vicinity of Mulberry Street was vile in every way, and the idea of its being the site of a place of worship was to the last degree a glaring and nauseous incongruity ( ... )the chapel was surrounded by small, poverty-looking cottages, with untidy kitchen gardens, whilst the roads and lanes round about the near neighbourhood were not then, as now, neatly paved, with sidewalks marked off, and flagged for pedestrians, for oftentimes, we learn, the members of the congregation must have waded ankle-deep in mud in coming to the chapel, whilst here and there along the lanes heaps of refuse might be seen, all combining to mark the place as a most unlikely site for a place of worship.[26]

Broomhead was soon aware that both the churches of St Chad's Rook Street and St Mary's Mulberry Street were insufficient to hold the number of Catholics in the town, and by 1807 he was telling his bishop that he was going to build another church.

Many of the people in Manchester in Broomhead's time were illiterate and the paintings and statuaries would have been a way for them to contemplate and reflect on the life of Christ. They would also have used the age-old method of praying the beads, reflecting on the mysteries of the rosary.

Images were the normal part of the furniture of a church. Due honour and reverence were given to them not because it was believed that there was a divinity or power in them, but the honour shown to them referred to the prototypes that they represented. In Rook Street Chapel there were images to help the people to pray and meditate on the important events of Christ's life. A description was given in 1804:

> The altar is handsomely decorated: and over it, are three paintings, which have considerable merit. The largest, in the centre, is the homage paid by the shepherds, at Bethlehem, to the infant Saviour. Another is a representation of the Trinity, in which the Father is represented mourning over the dead body of his crucified Son while the Holy Spirit, in the form of a dove, seems to hover over him. The third painting is the Holy Family; in which the Virgin and Child have some merit but there is an air of vulgarity in the countenance of Joseph which destroys the effect as a whole.[27]

The Latin Mass was difficult for them to understand but they imbibed the sense of the divine in the chapel and in time responded with some Latin phrases. This extract from Michael Gaffey's poem with his emphasis on the fatherly figure of Broomhead, talking to his congregation in words that could be easily understood, and addressed with a smile, won over so many of his congregation:

Thus, in a little chapel of his own,
The truths of Christianity were sown
For more than forty years, in words that could
By every auditor be understood.
Methinks I see him at the altar side
Teaching the faith for which his Master died,
With wisdom's tongue, a countenance serene,
And pleasing smile that could not fail to win
The hearts of all his hearers, and impress
Upon their minds a sense of their distress
In being slaves to Satan (who, perchance,
Had ta'en advantage of their ignorance
To plunge them into hell, and leave them there,
Victims of folly, torments, and despair,)
Exhorting them, by fatherly advice,
To follow virtue and abandon vice-

There were some attempts in the seventeenth century to introduce a vernacular version of the Mass. In 1614 John Heigham produced *A Devout Exposition of the Holie Masse,* which was certainly being printed as late as the nineteenth century providing a complete translation of the Ordinary of the Mass.[28] James Dymock, in the 1630s wrote *The Great Sacrifice of the New Law, Expounded by the Figures of the Old (Testament).*

Despite the fact that Pope Alexander VII, in 1661, forbade any further vernacular translations under the threat of excommunication, priests continued to write them. John Goter's contribution to liturgical writings had such a great influence on the liturgy of the Catholic Church in England that much of his work was printed even into the nineteenth century. Goter's ideas about congregational participation are set out in his 'Instructions and Devotions for hearing Mass 1699'. His liturgical translations were incorporated into Fr William Craythorne's *The Holy Mass in Latin and*

*English 1718* commissioned by Bishop Gifford, remained in use till the end of the eighteenth century.

The clergy could not use the vernacular, but Rome never ruled on whether the congregation could use vernacular material, so Goter and Craythorne made translations of the Missal, responding to the needs of the people.

Richard Challoner's response to the needs of Catholics was the *Garden of the Soul*. When Rowland Broomhead attended school at Sedgley Park in 1764, the students were required to bring a copy of it.[29] It became one of the most influential prayer books and the term 'Garden of the Soul Catholic' was given to 'one who displays the solid and unostentatious piety of penal days in England'.[30] From 1740, when it was first written, through to the nineteenth century, it was subject to revision and Thomas Haydock, printer and publisher, who established his business in Manchester circa 1799, annotated and published a new edition in that same year.

The contents outlined the liturgical practices prevalent at the time of Broomhead. In summary they were: doctrine, sacraments, the Mass, prayer, hymns, matins, meditation, devotions, family devotions, feasts and fasts and preparations for death. Challoner wrote a commentary of the Mass which emphasised the key Latin word beginning a specific prayer and then a prayer or reflection or both was given in English on what the priest was doing or saying at that point of the Mass. This commentary allowed the congregation to be able to follow the stages of the Mass.

Broomhead and his priests officiated at High Mass, known as the 'Missa solemnis' which required 'the presence of a choir and of a certain number of servers or acolytes and the use of incense'.[31] In a letter, 12 February 1807, from Broomhead to William Gibson, he referred to 'a High Mass at half past eleven on Sunday at Rook Street Chapel'.[32] Low Mass was the norm. Besides the priest it normally required a male server. The prayers were all spoken by the celebrant either inaudibly or in a clear tone but always in Latin. The collect, epistle, gospel and post-communion were said aloud but the canon of the Mass said in secret. It also consisted of a number of parts, some of which varied according to the day or the feast and were known as the 'Proper of the Mass'; the unchangeable parts of the Mass as the 'Ordinary of the Mass'.[33] All this was said and done by the celebrant at the middle of the altar with his back to the people, except the gospel and the last gospel, said at the gospel-side (the north or left-hand side facing the altar) and the introit, collects, epistle, gradual, preparation of the chalice, lavabo, ablutions, communion-verse and post-communion at the epistle-side (the south or right-hand side facing the altar).[34]

The Sunday Mass was offered for the people of the whole congregation whereas Masses, if they were said on the other six days were often said for the particular intentions of individual members of the congregation. It was canonical for a priest to accept a stipend and the amount was set by the bishop. This system traced back to times when the congregation would have provided the necessary items required for the saying of the Mass such as candles, bread and wine. These, in time, were replaced by a money payment which donation would be for the upkeep of the priest, the supply of materials for the liturgy and for alms for the needy.

The subject of 'Mass Offerings' was broached in part of a letter from John Chadwick, to Matthew Gibson, 31 January 1787 a sentence of which emphasised Chadwick's understanding of what a 'Mass Offering' was for:

> It is generally thought here ... we can hardly suppose that people leave their money merely with a mercenary view of Prayers only, but upon a more liberal and charitable motive, for support of Religion in certain districts and for procuring all religious help for their poor neighbours.[35]

Catholic devotion was not expressed openly in Manchester. Roman Catholicism in England had been outlawed and marginalized for hundreds of years. Broomhead and his fellow clergy were working within a country which mainly adhered to the Church of England, and they could not openly express their Catholicity, as did the Catholic countries on the Continent. The Relief Acts gave rise to riots and anti-Catholicism, so the Catholic community was careful not to antagonise with outward displays of devotion.

From a prayer book of 1801[36] the motives and practices were presented for devotion to the sacrament of the altar, which promotes love for the Saviour. The devotions which were applicable to an English church were retained, but not those peculiar to usage in Continental Europe 'since the liberty of religious worship cannot be supposed to be the same here as in Catholic countries'. The openness to processions and other public worship was not judicious at this time in England, however, 'although we cannot practice(sic) this devotion in the extent to which it is carried in Catholic countries, we may at least regret our inability, and supply by private devotions, our want of public opportunity'. Examples of such devotions might be:

> to go a little earlier to chapel every Sunday, and to dedicate ten minutes, or a quarter of an our hour, to make some kind of amends, for the many abuses, sacrileges and profanations, committed against the infinite majesty of God, in the divine Eucharist or we may turn ourselves every morning when we arise towards some chapel, where the Blessed Sacrament is kept and say: Praised for ever be the adorable sacrament of the altar.[37]

An advertisement printed on the back page of the above prayer book of 1801, listed the range of prayer books available to Broomhead and his congregation, thirteen in all. The books had been certified and licensed by The Right Rev Doctor William Gibson,

Vicar Apostolic of the Northern District and T. Haydock of
Manchester was given the right to publish and sell the books, two
of which were certainly used by Broomhead. They were

> A new edition of the Garden of the Soul with considerable
> additions and improvements annotated and published by
> Thomas Haydock. (First written in 1740 by Bishop Chal-
> loner titled 'Garden of the Soul or a Manual of Spiritual
> Exercises and Instructions for Christians who (Living in the
> World) Aspire to Devotion), and Daily Companions, with
> a complete Preparation for the Sacraments, Litany to St
> Joseph etc.[38]

Haydock lived in Market Street (Stead) Lane in Manchester where
he conducted his business as a Catholic publisher. Broomhead,
living only a short walk away in Rook Street, had close contact with
Haydock in his capacity of confessor and purchaser of books and
pamphlets for his congregation and his Sunday school.

The extent of the religious books printed and published by
Haydock suggests that there were a significant number of local
people who were purchasing prayer books. To be involved in the
spinning, weaving and dyeing industry in Manchester might not have
required literacy, but Manchester was more than just a producer of
cotton for by the second half of the eighteenth century it had become
'a provincial centre of the first rank, already attracting interest for its
urban growth, commercial life and transport innovations'.[39] Mr Eyre,
from the Catholic Eyre family of Derbyshire, steward to the Duke of
Norfolk and his wife and son Vincent were living in Manchester from
1766 for they were listed as 'professors of the Romish faith in the
Township of Manchester' according to the Returns of the Papists
1767.[40] The people involved in the commercial dealings of Manchester had to be able to read and write and there were certainly Roman
Catholics involved in business who were literate.

*23. Southerly View of Market Street*

Broomhead's congregation at Manchester was subject to the legal requirements of the Marriage Act of 1753 and the requirements of the Council of Trent which presented applicants for marriage with something of a dilemma. The State required, under Lord Hardwicke's Marriage Act, officially entitled 'An Act for the Better Preventing of Clandestine Marriage':

that all marriages, except those of Jews or Quakers, had to be performed in a Church of England and that banns had to be read on three consecutive weeks in the parish church or chapel and the contracting parties were required to be there to listen to the reading of their banns.

The Council of Trent, 11 November 1563:

required the contracting parties to be present in the Roman Catholic chapel or church to hear their banns read out by the priest in charge, on three consecutive Holy Days, and the Council also laid down that the Roman Catholic Church had to keep baptismal and marriage registers.

The marriage registers of the Manchester Mission for most of the period under consideration, 1778 to 1820, have not survived or more likely were not kept. Only the marriage register for Bolton combined with Rochdale, which started in 1795, are in existence so maybe the answer is that the 'priests were aware that their marriages had no legal force and that registration was not actually necessary'[41] or possibly they might have feared being seen to be undermining the role of the Church of England by registering a marriage, which was the business of the local vicar.

Catholic Bishops, through their priests, advised couples to have two ceremonies, a religious one before a Catholic priest, and one according to the Church of England rites, which was, in the eyes of the bishops, a civil marriage. This arrangement necessitated two sets of marriage fees and poorer Catholics often opted for a single service in the parish church.

A marriage was important for the poor as much as the rich. The poor might have had nothing to leave when they died but they needed the certificate from the Church of England for poor relief and parish status, and, in the case of the rich, to ensure legitimacy and inheritance.

Certain times of the year were closed to the solemnities of a marriage but an ordinary marriage without a nuptial Mass was allowed. Broomhead would not have been allowed to celebrate a nuptial mass during two periods of the year. These were Advent to St Hilary's day, 13 January and Septuagesima to Low Sunday. [42]

Sickness, death and burial in the Community were unexceptional and Broomhead spent much time visiting from one house to the next. Gaffey described his work with the sick, the poor and the dying:

How oft I've seen the subject of my song
Trudging with short but hasty steps along
The streets of Manchester, before the sun
Could shed his beams above the horizon;
From house to house he went, from door to door,
To see the sick, and to relieve the poor–
Throughout the day this tender Father would
Be, like his Master, always doing good;
And ev'n at night he from his bed would rise
To give the sacrament, and close the eyes
Of such as on their pallets chanc'd to lie
Struggling with death, and teach them how to die.[43]

Written just after Rowland Broomhead's death, by a man who knew the very essence of Broomhead's character the picture portrayed, mirrored that of Christ moving among His people and emphasised the tenderness of Broomhead and saw him 'like His Master, always doing good'. Broomhead's actions are seen like little vignettes: the description of seeing him before sun up, hurrying from house to house; his solace to the sick; his relief for those who were poor; his preparation for those who were dying and the final anointing with the sacrament of Extreme Unction.

In the time of Broomhead, Extreme Unction would have been defined as 'a sacrament in which the sick in danger of death are anointed by a priest for the health of soul and body, the anointing being accompanied by a set form of words'.[44] The words of St James described the liturgical actions and the effects of this sacrament:

> Is any man sick among you? Let him call to himself the presbyter of the Church, and let him pray over him, anointing him with oil in the name of the Lord. And the prayer of faith shall save the sick man, and the Lord will raise him up, and if he has committed sins, it shall be forgiven him.

Broomhead's care of the sick began as soon as he arrived in the Manchester Mission, 19 March 1778:

> At that time the duties of a Priest stationed in Manchester, were less confined to the immediate town, than they now are, by the greater number of labourers in the vine-yard; and the morning after his arrival he was obliged to go to Bolton to visit the bedside of a dying member of the Catholic Church, and administer the last consolations ... [45]

The application for oils from the Bishop for the sacraments of Baptism and Extreme Unction does not appear in any of the Broomhead letters. Every so often the Vicar Apostolic visited Manchester to confirm and would of course have brought his own oils but individual missioners needed the oil of catechumens and the oils of Chrism for Baptism and the oil of the sick for Extreme Unction. It seems likely that the difficulty of bringing or sending the oils would have been overcome by the Vicar Apostolic giving permission to the Grand Vicar or another denoted priest to bless the oils themselves:

> The matter of the sacrament, according to the Council of Trent (sess. Xiv. Cap. 1) is 'oil blessed by the bishop'. Most theologians hold that this blessing is essential, though it suffices for validity if the blessing has been given by a priest who has received jurisdiction to do so.[46]

Death and burial records were not kept by the priests for the burial had to take place at a Church of England parish graveyard and the service there was conducted by the local vicar and Broomhead would have taken no part in the actual burial. However, at the home of the deceased, Rowland would have led the service and 'as a substitute for consecrated ground he blessed some earth and placed it in the coffin'. When the dead were laid in the grave, the relatives and friends, before departing, knelt around the grave, recited an 'Our Father' and a 'Hail Mary' together with the 'De Profundis' for the departed soul.[47]

Oliver Carter, a fellow of the Manchester Collegiate Church, and some associate preachers complained in 1590:

> that prayers for the dead were still recited, and that the corpse, before being brought to the churchyard, was set down at every cross, the people kneeling in prayer.[48]

Most Catholic funerals were in the Anglican churchyards till 1853, for after that year there was a move to open Borough cemeteries. In the last fifteen years of Broomhead's life, St Mary's Mulberry Street had a graveyard as did St Augustine's by 1820.

When Broomhead arrived in 1778 the prison in Manchester, which he visited in his first twelve years, was situated on Hunt's Bank where 'the present Palatine buildings now stand, now Victoria Street, a prison known as the 'New Fleet' and later known as the House of Correction'. It was built in 1580 and rebuilt in 1774.[49]

The 'New Fleet 'was replaced as a result of the Town obtaining an Act of Parliament in 1782 enabling them to build the New Bayley prison, which was opened 22 May 1787 by T. B. Bayley, the chairman of the Quarter Sessions. There was a chapel in the new prison and there is no reason to think that Broomhead would do anything else but visit the prisoners there.

*24. Hunt's Bank Prison*

*25. New Bayley Prison*

# Notes

1   Broomhead, *Letter to Eyre 6 November 1806* (UCA: Eyre correspondence 47).

2   P. Prendergast, *Old Catholic Manchester* (Manchester,1905), JRL: 166830, special collection, p. 6.

3   Churching of women was an act of thanksgiving after childbirth. The mother came to church to receive the blessings contained in the Roman Ritual.

4   Broomhead, *Letter to W. Gibson 12 February 1807* (LDA: WG. 553A).

5   Fr Thomas Lupton, priest in charge at St Mary's Mulberry Street; Fr Richard Thompson formerly assistant at Rook Street became Grand Vicar in 1802; Fr James Blundell priest in charge at Stockport and Fr Joseph Sheppard priest in charge of Bolton, Rochdale & Bury.

6   Broomhead, *Letter to Eyre 26 February 1807* (Eyre correspondence, 49).

7   Broomhead, *Letter to W. Gibson 18 March 1811* (LDA: WG. 690).

8   Prendergast, *Old Catholic Manchester*, p. 6

9   John Briggs, Vicar Apostolic of the Northern District 1836–1840.

10  Thompson, *Letter to W. Gibson 15 January 1818* (LDA: WG. 1044).

11  C. A. Bolton, *Salford Diocese and its Catholic Past*, pp. 254–255.

12  Prendergast, *Old Catholic Manchester*, pp. 5–6.

13  Appendix Three: Chart of Manchester Population Statistics 1714–1821; Chart of Manchester Roman Catholic Baptisms 1772–1819; Annual Baptism Returns for Rook St & Mulberry St Chapels 1772 to 1819.

14  A. Kidd, *Manchester a History* (Lancaster, Carnegie Publishing Ltd, 2008), ch. 1.

15  J. Aston, *A Picture of Manchester 1816* (MCL).

16  W. Gibson, *Letter to Eyre 3 January 1794* (LDA: WG 155).

17  C. R. Rothwell, *Centenary of a Manchester Church St Mary's Mulberry Street* (SDA: 'The Harvest' 15 August 1895), p. 188.

18  D. Clinch, *Hidden Gem: A Celebration in Words and Pictures of St Mary's Mulberry Street, The first two hundred years 1794–1994* (Manchester, J & E. W. Jackson Ltd., 1994), p. 19.

19  *Register of Baptisms for St Mary's Mulberry Street 7 December 1794 to 1 January 1812* (LRO: RCMM 1/MF9/21).

20  Ullman, *St Alban's Macclesfield* (Macclesfield, 1982).

21  *Deed Index for St Mary's Mulberry Street*, SDA, p. 5.

22  Appendix Two, part 1: Documents Concerning 'Church Street' (Roman
    Entry) & Rook Street Chapel, Manchester Trustees 29 December 1784;
    Old Trust as to Rook Street Chapel. Declaration of Trust & Rules and
    Regulations written by Rev Rowland Broomhead and accepted and signed
    by Bishop William Gibson 7 May 1790). Part 2: *Rules & Regulations, agreed
    upon by the Bishop and Secular Clergy Priests, in the Hundreds of Salford &
    Macclesfield, for the future care and management of their Funds and Temporal
    Affairs 1823* (SDA).

23  *An Account of the Late John Casey's Fund left for the Poor Catholicks of
    Manchester* (SDA).

24  Cambray in northern France on the Escaut River during the late war. The
    City suffered from the Revolution and most of the religious buildings were
    demolished in the period 1794/1795 and the old cathedral, known as the
    'wonder of the low countries' was sold to a merchant who exploited the
    stone.

25  J. Aston, *The Manchester Guide: A Brief Historical Account of the Towns of
    Manchester and Salford, the Public Buildings and the Charitable & Literary
    Institutions* (Manchester, printed and sold by Joseph Ashton 84 Deansgate,
    Manchester, 1804), p. 121.

26  Prendergast, *Old Catholic Manchester*, p. 15.

27  Aston, *The Manchester Guide*, pp. 123–124.

28  The unchangeable or practically unchangeable part of the Mass into which
    the proper of the Mass is fitted, (those parts of the Mass which are variable
    according to the day or feast).

29  *Sedgley Park School, Account Book 1762–1766* (BAA)

30  D. Attwater, *The Catholic Encyclopaedic Dictionary* (London, Cassell and
    Company Ltd, 1949), p. 206

31  Attwater, *The Catholic Encyclopaedic Dictionary*, p. 230

32  Broomhead, *Letter to W. Gibson 12 February 1807* (LDA: WG. 553A).

33  The preparation, *introit*, Kyrie eleison, the Gloria in excelsis (on feasts, and
    Sundays outside Advent, Septuagesima and Lent), *collect(s), epistles,
    gradual, gospel*(followed sometimes by a sermon which however was not
    considered part of the Mass), the Nicene Creed (only on Sundays and chief
    feasts), *offertory-verse*, offering of the bread and wine, lavabo, prayer to the
    Holy Trinity, *secret, preface*, sanctus, the canon wherein takes place the
    consecration, the Our Father, the breaking of the Host, Agnus Dei, three
    prayers preparatory to communion, communion of the celebrant and then
    of the people, ablutions, *common-verse, post-communion prayer(s)*, the

dismissal, blessing, the last gospel.

34    Attwater, *The Catholic Encyclopaedic Dictionary,* p. 406

35    Chadwick, *Letter to M. Gibson 31 January 1787* (UCA: PA/C20).

36    H. M. Boudon, *The Love of Jesus in the Adorable Sacrament of the Altar* (Manchester, a new translation from the French, printed by R. & W. Dean and Co. Market-Street Lane for T. Haydock, 1801).

37    Preface to *'The Love of Jesus in the Adorable Sacrament of the Altar'.*

38    Appendix Four: List of the other eleven prayer books.

39    Kidd, *Manchester a History,* p. 9.

40    Worrall, *Return of the Papists 1767.*

41    M. Gandy, *Catholic Missions and Registers 1700–1880* (London, Michael Gandy, 1993), vol. 5 North West England, p. IV.

42    W. E. Tate, *The Parish Chest, A Study of the Records of Parochial Administration in England* (London, Cambridge University Press, 1969), p. 62.

43    Gaffey, *A Panegyric of the late Rev Rowland Broomhead.*

44    W. E. Addis & T. Arnold, *A Catholic Dictionary containing some account of the doctrine, discipline, rites, ceremonies, councils, and religious orders of the Catholic Church* (London, revised with additions by T. B. Scannell , 9th edition, 1925) pp. 342–344.

45    Anonymous author, *Manchester Exchange Herald Brief Memoirs of the Rev Rowland Broomhead of Manchester with an Account of his Funeral; and a Funeral Elegy* (Manchester, Exchange Herald, 1820) MCL.

46    See Addis & Arnold, *A Catholic Dictionary containing some account of the doctrine, discipline, rites, ceremonies, councils, and religious orders of the Catholic Church,* p. 343: 'The Greek priests bless the oil of the sick by commission from the bishop and this custom of theirs was approved by Clement VIII, in a constitution dated 1598.'

47    Prendergast, *Old Catholic Manchester,* p. 6.

48    O. Carter et alia, *Description of the State, Civil and Ecclesiastical, of the County of Lancaster 1590* (Manchester, printed by Chetham's Society, 1875), CLM.

49    W. E. A. Axon, *The Annals of Manchester, A chronological record from the earliest times to the end of 1885* (Manchester, John Heywood, Deansgate and Ridgefield Manchester, 1886).

# 8 ECCLESIASTICAL CONNECTIONS

## 1. Broomhead in the Correspondence of the Clergy

THE CORRESPONDENCE BETWEEN various ecclesiastics presents us with a backdrop of chronological events and activities that had a bearing on the life of Rowland Broomhead. The ordinary day to day matters sit alongside the great events of State and Church.

While Broomhead was still at the English College in Rome, the first sign of a 'favourable disposition' to Catholics in Ireland was the 'Act for the reclaiming of unprofitable bogs' of 1771. Further concessions were given in the Irish Relief Act of 1774 in which Irish Catholics took a prescribed oath testifying loyalty to George III. The conflict of the English government with the American Colonies can be seen as the spur to conciliation with the Irish and the hope that this would lead to less Irish sympathy for the American Colonies and willingness to enlist in the conflict itself. This Act did not rescind any of the penal laws but from then on they were not enforced and the Irish Catholic people were recognised as subjects of the Crown. These events in Ireland gave the English Catholics hope that change would come to them.

Within a short time, after the Acts of 1771 and 1774, there followed the Irish Acts of 1778 and 1793, the latter giving them the franchise. Logically the granting of concessions to Catholics in Ireland had now to be carried in England and an Act was quickly passed into law. The oath in the English Act of Relief of 1778 embodied the Irish oath of 1774 and Catholics had to swear allegiance to George III and renounce any obedience or allegiance to the exiled Stuarts, within six months of the passing of the Act.

One of the key themes in this correspondence was the provision of priests. Church students from the Northern District were educated at one of the English Colleges either Douai, Rome, Valladolid or Lisbon, during the penal times. All of these seminaries were a long distance away from the north of England and students would have remained on the continent throughout their training, until they were ordained and appointed to a mission. Some students were as young as ten, which would mean they would be abroad for at least fifteen years as they were ordained normally at the age of twenty-five. It was no light decision to decide that a boy was a suitable candidate and if they got their decision wrong it would have been an expensive mistake.

Until the second half of the eighteenth century in the north of England, missions were not centred on towns but rather in outlying areas often in small hamlets. The numbers of priests needed was not the same as the number that could be sustained and it was always a difficult decision for the Vicar Apostolic and his advisors and they could end up with more priests than they could afford to employ. Charles Houghton who joined Broomhead at Manchester in 1778 had been without a placement since 1775. Bishop Walton of the Northern District wrote to his Grand Vicar, John Chadwick, at Weld Bank near Chorley, raising some of the problems for the supply and demand of priests:

> But when there are more hands than can be provided for, it would be great imprudence to increase the number. And this seems to be our situation at present. Messrs Houghton, Parkinson, Marsland are out of work, another is daily expected from Hilton, so that there is no want, but, on the contrary, an evident abundancy, and, of course, no room for Mr Spenser.[1]

Their education to priesthood would have cost considerable sums of money, no matter whether it came from family funding or charity, and it would have been imprudent to educate further students. He does not say, that until such time that they can be placed in employment someone has to pay for their upkeep, and whether the family of the student was able to support him, nor would support come from the funds of the Northern District?

> After the death of Bishop Petre, Walton succeeded as Vicar Apostolic of the Northern District, 24 December 1775, and lived at York. Matthew Gibson was vicar general in the latter part of Walton's life.

The revoking of the penal laws would not have come about unless there were reasons of political necessity or expediency. The offensive and defensive alliance between France and the American Colonies, 6 February 1778, influenced the decision of Roman Catholic peers and commoners of Great Britain to address the King, in the hope that George III would grant Roman Catholics relief from penal laws. The English Catholics were aware of the need for unity in the face of war and the need of the Government for Catholics to join them in the fight. George III was very much against any relief for the Roman Catholics but his government's need in 1778 led to the removal of 'the prohibitive oaths technically required of those who served in the king's forces'. The Relief Act of 1778 allowed 'military recruits simply to take an oath of fidelity to the Crown'.[2] For Broomhead, arriving in Manchester in the same year of the Act, it was an important liberation from some of the penal laws and he and Houghton took the oath.

Two letters, 17 January 1780, contain invalid information about the clergy in the Salford Hundred. The first contained a note by Thomas Eyre 'Clergy in Salford Hundred 1' in correspondence between Matthew Gibson and John Chadwick Grand Vicar of Lancashire. The second[3] letter, dated the same day, from the newly elected Vicar Apostolic

Matthew Gibson to Chadwick records 'the number of Clergy Priests in this Vicariate viz. in the counties of Cumberland, Westmoreland, Lancashire and Cheshire are at present 35'. Salford Hundred 1 out of 28 in Lancashire'. Broomhead and Houghton had been in the Manchester Mission from 1778 and Houghton did not leave until 1787. However a third letter[4] , dated circa 1780, from Matthew Gibson to Chadwick has 'The number of Catholics at Manchester recorded as 400 and the priests were Messrs Houghton and Broomhead'.

Following the Act of 1778 a general meeting of Catholic laymen met in 1782 and appointed a Committee for 'five years, to promote and attend to the affairs of the Roman Catholic body in England'. A fault-line can be seen to run through the establishment of this Committee and that was the exclusion of any of the bishops and clergy and it was this decision that led to a great deal of dissention between the various parties trying to further the cause of Catholic Emancipation.

Matthew Gibson sent information to Rome, 8 January 1787, regarding the Mission of Lancashire. The computation read as follows:

> For Lancashire there were 23,000 communicants; 62 incumbents; 32 clergy; 15 Jesuits; 12 Benedictines; 1 Dominican & 2 Franciscans.[5]

Only a few weeks later John Chadwick wrote to Matthew Gibson, 31 January 1787, concerning the problems that had arisen with the severe winter; the rise in the cost of staple foods and the need for the clergy to be provided with an increased allowance.[6] The February meeting of the Lancashire Secular Clergy Fund was imminent. As Grand Vicar, John Chadwick was in touch with all the clergy in Lancashire, including Broomhead. Chadwick informed Matthew Gibson of these matters of importance:

> I waited for the sentiments of several of our Brethren before
> I answered you about Lent. All that I have consulted, and

the same may be said of most people in these parts, are of opinion that there never was a greater necessity of ample allowances, than this year: Potatoes are one farthing dearer than they have been some years past and it is commonly reported that great quantities are spoiled by the frost, so tis thought they will be uncommonly scarce and dear. Two other most essential articles viz. butter and milk, will I doubt be ill to be got, owing to the scarcity of fodder. The former article has all last summer and autumn been dearer by 2 and 3d per lb. than ever known in this part and there is the highest probability of its being still dearer till the cattle are turned to grass. On the whole I suppose there never was more need of good allowances than this year.[7]

By 1787 Broomhead had become priest-in-charge at the Manchester mission following the absenteeism of Charles Houghton who had: left to travel with Mr Battersby through Italy, which gave great offence to his bishop, from whom he had not obtained leave to quit his post In consequence of this he was suspended but on his return he was appointed chaplain at Carlton, the seat of the Stapletons in Yorkshire, and died at York, Sept. 7, 1797, aged 47.[8]

Further matters arose concerning Catholic Emancipation. In May 1787, a new Committee of ten members was formed, the aim of which was 'to watch over and promote the public interest of the English Roman Catholics'. It presented a memorial to Mr Pitt, the Prime Minister, 9 May 1788, which 'described the state of Catholics under existing laws, abjured certain opinions falsely attributed to them, and asked for relief'.[9] The response from Pitt was supportive but before any bills could be brought before Parliament he asked that 'he should be furnished with authentic evidence of the opinion of the Catholic clergy and Catholic universities, with respect to the existence or extent of the Pope's dispensing power'.[10] The resulting document published by the Committee was known as the 'Protestation'. One of the key aims of this declaration was to:

free Ourselves from such Imputations, because divers
Protestants, who profess themselves to be Real Friends to
Liberty of Conscience, have, nevertheless, avowed themselves hostile to us, on account of certain Opinions which
we are supposed to hold.

The final paragraph of the 'Protestation' was an appeal to

the Justice and Candour of Our Fellow-Citizens, Whether
We, the ENGLISH CATHOLICS, who thus solemnly
disclaim, and from our Hearts abhor, the above-mentioned
abominable and unchristian-like Principles, ought to be put
upon a Level with any other men who may hold and profess
those Principles?

Broomhead, who was then Rural Dean of the Salford Hundred,
signed the document in 1789[11] as did all the Vicars Apostolic,
except Matthew Gibson of the Northern District, who was Rowland's superior. (After 1787 Broomhead, as chairman of the Lancashire clergy, was an important leader and documents that came
out of that county were stamped with his hallmark).

The Lancashire clergy, in 1789, addressed the Committee of the
English Catholics, lamenting the division between the various
Catholic parties. It gave primacy to the bishops regarding matters
ecclesiastical; regretted the possible fatal consequences of disunity
and recommended that any oath had to have been sanctioned and
approved by the bishops:

To the Lords and Gentlemen of the Committee of the
English Catholics dated 1789.[12]

My Lords and Gentlemen

We the undersigned beg leave to address you in the present
critical juncture of affairs. We cannot but lament the variety
of opinions which have of late and still do subsist amongst
the English Catholics, and we most earnestly wish to suggest

such means as may be likely to bring about the unanimity so much wanted. We actually consider some parts of the oath lately or now in agitation, as being particularly within the ecclesiastical department and we foresee that unless these things are so altered as to be sanctioned by our Bishops and also so framed as to be ensured from the censure of the acknowledged Head of our ecclesiastical government, the said oath must ultimately be refused by the Catholics of this nation who will undoubtedly think themselves justified in opposing its being passed into law and as such deemed a test of their allegiance. We cannot persuade ourselves that any member of the Committee or the body at large can be so little aware of the fatal consequences of disunion amongst us as not to be willing to sacrifice everything to prevent it, and under this impression We come forward to recommend, 'that no oath be presented to Government or brought before Parliament which has not received the approbation and sanction of our Bishops'; and we recommend this previous step as essentially necessary to secure unanimity in a business of such immense consequence as is that of settling the form of an oath, which will in all succeeding times be considered as a Criterion of the allegiance of English Catholics.

We are my Lord and Gentlemen,

Your most obedient & humble Servants.

Broomhead signed the address and very soon after he and his fellow Lancashire priests, numbering fifty-five in all, wrote 1 January 1790 to their Vicar Apostolic, Matthew Gibson, earnestly requesting him to use his influence to get a new oath, but at the same time suggesting that they would be happy enough with the Irish Oath, which had been used in 1774 and 1778. Deep concern that a schism amongst the Catholics would be the worst of consequences, permeated the latter part of the address:

Induced by no other motive than that the Catholic religion may be preserved in all its purity. And the minds of the faithful kept free from all doubts in matters of Faith, we, whose names are hereunto subscribed, earnestly request your Lordship to use all your influence that a new form of Oath, if required by the Legislature, as comprehensive as possibly in what relates to civil government, be presented to Parliament, that our allegiance as subjects may be firmly established, and our religious rights preserved inviolate. Would not the Oath taken by the Catholics of Ireland in the year 1774, and approved, as we believe, by the See of Rome, answer this salutary purpose, being deemed sufficient by the Parliament of that Kingdom?

We are fully convinced that a schism amongst the Catholics of England would give you the greatest concern, scandalise the Christian world, and produce the worst of consequences, not only to the souls of those who break the bonds of unity, but to the property and persons of those amongst us who, from motives of conscience, should refuse to take the Oath now before Parliament; and that a Schism will be the consequence if the Oath be tendered in its present form is beyond all doubt.

The 'Address to the Catholics of England' has come to our hands, but it does not satisfy the minds either of the Ecclesiastics or laity of this County of Lancaster; few indeed of either will take the Oath in its present form: a large and respectable body of people may consequently be exposed to the rigour of those laws which yet stand unrepealed against us.

We therefore, in the name of the Almighty, humbly entreat your Lordship in conjunction with the other Bishops, to strike out some other line by which peace and union may be preserved amongst us; prejudices of education, ignorance or malevolence be removed from our Protestant fellow-subjects; and our fidelity to our King and country fully ascertained.

We have the honour to be, my Lord, with the greatest respect,

Your Lordship's humble servants.[13]

The pastoral letter of Matthew Gibson, 15 January 1790, written to his dearly beloved brethren and children in Christ, during the negotiations taking place for a new Relief Act for Roman Catholics, expressed deep understanding of the persecution of two hundred years of the 'remnant of Catholicity in this nation':

> Our blessed Redeemer told his disciples that they should be reviled and persecuted by men, speaking all evil against them, untruly, for his sake. In the earliest ages of Christianity, the brightest models of virtue and learning were calumniated as enemies to the state, fomenters of rebellion, and avowed adversaries to every principle of honesty, honour, and conscience. These, with many other charges of the blackest die, stand recorded in the writings of St Justin, Origen, and other incontestable monuments.
>
> For these two centuries past, have not the same arms of defamation, with uncommon asperity and violence, been levelled against the small remnant of catholicity in this nation? The dark pencil of misrepresentation, painting them in the hideous colours of disaffection, disloyalty, and revolt– invectives, virulent and envenomed-bloody scenes, the sport of malevolent fancy, exaggerated with every circumstance of horror, and displayed in the most terrifying language, have been all successively employed to exhibit a distressed people, writhed under calamities, as an object of distrust, danger, and popular detestation. That they have not been utterly exterminated and rooted up; that they live to lament their miseries, is a kind of miracle, for which,

under a partial Heaven; they are indebted to the enlightened humanity of their supreme governors; to the mild and gracious reign of a sovereign, in whom benevolence and lenity shine, with peculiar lustre, amidst the brightest of his virtues.[14]

Broomhead, as required, read the pastoral letter of Matthew Gibson to his congregation at Rook Street Chapel. Gibson died 17 May 1790 and William Gibson, his brother, was appointed Titular Bishop of Acanthus and Vicar Apostolic of the Northern District and was consecrated 5 December 1790, at Dorset.

In a letter sent to John Chadwick from Rook Street chapel, Manchester, on 6 March 1791, Broomhead expressed his concern on liturgical and other problems:

> As I have not yet received orders for Lent, should be glad you would send them as soon as possible. It has been a great disappointment to the Congregation that they were not given out today; but have promised to publish them on Wednesday or Friday next, that they may know how to make their marks etc on Saturday. Manchester always is the last to receive information of this kind from Mr Boardly's neglect, who has formerly pretended to make himself a rural Dean over Salford Hundred as well as his own, & consequently undertook to inform Mr Orrell of these things when he lived here. In future, therefore, as Manchester is the only Clergy Congregation in Salford Hundred should be glad you would give what information on this or any other head is necessary. As we have not yet received the £10 due at Christmas for serving Rochdale should be glad you would send it, as my finances at present is at a very low ebb; I began on the last guinea yesterday of course my purse is empty & so it must remain till the 25th instant except you replenish it. Must therefore demand your immediate assistance that we may not keep too strict a Lent both from meat & fish.[15]

The second Roman Catholic Relief was passed 7 June 1791. A letter from William Gibson, to all the faithful, clergy, and laity in the Northern District dated at York, 30 June 1791,[16] celebrated the repeal and abolishment of most of the penal laws due to the favours granted by the Legislature to the Catholics of the Kingdom and with the words 'recent extension of the favours' was referring to the first Relief Act of 1778:

> With great joy we seize this opportunity of expressing to you our congratulations, on the present repeal and abolition of great part of the penal laws; and on the recent extension of favours granted by the Legislature to the Catholicks of this Kingdom.

Gibson recalled the problems that the four Vicars Apostolic had in searching for an appropriate oath. The failure to agree a new oath that had led to the use of the Irish Oath of 1774 with the addition of an Act of Settlement on the present Hanoverian family, which sealed and determined the allegiance of the Catholics to George III and his successors, discounting in effect the Stuart line:

> To several clauses of the Oath, which was first inserted in the Bill that was presented for obtaining the aforesaid privileges, we had serious objections, and induced by our zeal for the publick welfare, we ventured respectfully to lay the same before Parliament. We are truly happy in being able to assure you, that Parliament graciously attended to them, and finding them, according to our principles, well founded, kindly condescended to substitute the Oath taken by the Irish Catholicks in 1774, with the addition of the title of the Act of the Settlement of the Crown in the reigning Family. And this too solely to fix and determine our Allegiance to his Majesty's Family, without the most remote intention of infringing on any of our religious tenets or principles in the smallest degree, or of hurting the feelings

of the most timorous, as the explanations given by several of the Lords in the House in their official capacities, and admitted by the rest, as the sense of the whole House, plainly demonstrate.

William Gibson then gave his approval to the use of the Irish Oath:

> Wherefore we now inform you, that you may lawfully, and conscientiously acquiesce, in taking the Oath inserted in the said Act of Parliament.

The final section of his letter called upon the clergy and laity to be faithful in allegiance to the King and obedient to the civil government and to give thanks for the repeal and abolition of the penal laws but they were also warned to be 'discreet and prudent' in their use of these freedoms. He called for prayer for the Country and the King and his family and advised the clergy and laity to avoid offence, so that it would not provoke the possibility of actions which would be worse than they had endured. He stressed the importance of edifying others by good works which would make them pleasing to those around them:

> It may appear unnecessary to exhort you to be faithful and steady in your Allegiance to the King, and constant in your obedience to the civil Government, as we are well convinced of your dutiful sentiments in that regard. We earnestly intreat you to thank God for these signal favours, and to beseech him to direct and inspire you, to make a discreet and prudent use of them. Express your obligations and gratitude to the mildness and condescension of the Legislature, and of our present benevolent Government. Pray for our Country, and our gracious Sovereign, and the Royal Family. Be particularly vigilant, to avoid every offence that may again provoke the anger of God, and draw down heavier judgments upon our heads, than those from which we have been delivered. Strive by every means to render

yourselves pleasing to him, and to edify others by your good works. Love one another, and study peace: remembering withal, that notwithstanding any privileges that can be granted in any Country, or any favourable circumstances that may present themselves of acquiring a greater share of the goods of this world as they are called; that still we are only pilgrims here, and have not a permanent city; but must continue to seek a Country, in which alone we can find secure peace and eternal happiness. The Grace of our Lord Jesus Christ be with you all.

Broomhead, with thirty other priests of the County of Lancaster, signed an address to the Vicars Apostolic, Charles Berington of the Midland District; William Gibson of the Northern District and John Douglass of the London District, at the Annual Assembly of Roman Catholic Clergy of the County of Lancaster, held 30 August 1791 at Preston. It was a document of praise and congratulations to the Vicars Apostolic written in Latin, with an attached rough translation of the document in English:

We the under mentioned missionary priests of the Lancashire province cannot but express and congratulate you on your untiring vigilance and invincible strength of mind by which you have firmly established the power of God to influence the hearts of our noble senate. In properly following the precepts of the saviour you have shown the prudence of the serpent and the simplicity of the dove. You have kept the deposit of faith undefiled. You have kept shut the perilous way of the ( … ) schismatic. You have pointed the common bonds between head and members and the holy hierarchy of the divine institution thereby winning the applause even of those not of our fold. You have merited the praise of some of the noblest of men in our most honoured senate. In short through your work you have freed the English Catholics from many grave penal statutes … [17]

Broomhead was required to take the 'Oath' under the Act of 1791, which then allowed him the 'favours'. No longer could he be prosecuted for failure to attend the Established parish church or for acting out his priesthood but the Act made it compulsory for him to attend the Quarter Sessions to license his place of worship and to have his name and description recorded by the clerk of the peace. Once Broomhead had taken the Oath he was exempt from jury service and he and his congregation were protected under the Act from 'any person disturbing a congregation or misusing a priest' which carried a fine of twenty pounds.

There were, however, restrictions to what he and his congregation could do. Roman Catholics, because of the secrecy required to surmount the penal laws, had conducted religious services behind closed doors, and often with a lookout. The Act of 1791 enacted that they could no longer hold services behind locked doors and failure to follow this proscription would have led to the loss of all benefits under the Act. The same loss of benefits would follow:

> if he officiated in any place with a steeple and bell; if he
> should officiate at any funeral in any church or churchyard,
> also if he should wear the habit of his Order, or exercise any
> rite or ceremony of his religion save within a certified chapel,
> or in a private house, where there should not be more than
> five persons assembled besides those of the household.[18]

The Act of 1791 only gave partial relief, but leaving aside the aggravations between the committee and the ecclesiastics which continued, it was a time for appreciating and responding to the possibilities offered there and then, rather than spending valuable time on 'surviving disabilities'.[19] Broomhead had already responded to the small relief of 1778, and the greater relief of 1791 spurred him on to great things in the wider areas of his mission and in Manchester especially. The following extract from William

Gibson's address to the clergy and laity of the Northern District dated, 7 June 1791, resonated in the life of Rowland Broomhead:

> Be particularly vigilant, to avoid every offence that may again provoke the anger of God, and draw down heavier judgments upon our heads, than those from which we have been delivered. Strive by every means to render yourselves pleasing to Him, and to edify others by your good works.

Correspondence between Robert Banister and his nephew Henry Rutter, both priests, give us both insight into high ecclesiastical politics and 'touch upon a wide range of social and personal matters which fill in many details of daily life on the mission in the final years of the recusant era'.[20] Robert Banister wrote to his nephew Henry Rutter, 8 October 1792. Banister had been called by William Gibson to meet with him as soon as possible at Manchester before travelling on to London. It is a window into the travelling difficulties faced by people in the late eighteenth century and also underlines the charity of Broomhead to his visitor but why were Banister and Gibson travelling post haste for a meeting in London? The date would suggest that it was not a meeting to attempt mediation between the Committee, now called the Cisalpine Club, and the Vicars Apostolic, but rather the planning for the reception of so many emigrant priests, following on the attack on the Tuilleries Palace, 10 August 1792; the imprisonment of the French King, and the search for and imprisonment of priests. By the time Banister reached London, Tuesday 21 August, the news of the decree of transportation, 19 August 1792, had reached London:

> On the 12th of last August I was very ill at my stomach and much worse on the 15th about, two hours in the evening. The day following I received a letter from our Bishop calling on me to meet him at Manchester and go up with him to the Metropolis, admitting no excuse nor delay, for the business was of importance and could not be discussed or

settled by a communication of letters but only in a meeting.
This put me to great distress, fearing to be ill whilst abroad.
I therefore on Thursday evening tried whether riding to Mr
Wilson would agree with my health and consulted him what
I should do. He said I must necessarily go and bid me to eat
and drink heartily and allowed me to eat flesh-meat on days
of abstinence, which I did only twice. On Friday therefore
in the morning, August 17th, I rode to Preston on my mare,
Richard walked on foot. At Preston we took a whiskey to
Bolton, 22 miles, but as no post-chaise could be had there,
he took me forward to Manchester, 12 miles more of bad
road, where I arrived at an inn much tired and over-done. I
only saw the Bishop that night at Mr Broomhead's and
returned immediately to the inn, and to bed, and by lying
long in the morning, was pretty well. On Saturday night I
lodged at Mr Broomhead's in his own bedchamber and he
went to Mr Reynolds. On Sunday at 5 o'clock p.m. we left
Manchester and went only 14 miles to Disley. On Monday
66 miles, but on Tuesday from Leicester 98 miles to London
and 2 more to No. 34 Great Ormond Street, Mr Varley's,
where we found at 7.30 o'clock Bishops Walmesley, and
Douglass, the Revd. Messrs. Robert and Charles Plowden,
Barnard, Pilling and Milner.

In 1793, as a result of the religious persecution that emanated from
the French Revolution, the English convents and seminaries on the
Continent were closed and this brought English clergy and religious
back to their homeland to settle down permanently for they had
lost all their lands and possessions.

The seminary at Crook Hall dated from 15 October 1794. John
Lingard and John Rickaby were the first to arrive of the small
handful of students. A catalogue of problems contrived to make life
at Crook Hall extremely difficult:

Students had to deal with cramped conditions; two or three to a room (even Bishop Gibson had to sleep in the same room as Thomas Eyre); the places in which to study were small and close to others; there was even a shortage of books and there was no road to the house. From the early beginnings of a handful of students, numbers by the end of the first year had risen to twenty-five and as more students arrived life became unbearable. Bishop Gibson interfered with the running of the Hall and delayed looking for alternative accommodation. The root of all the problems lay with the lack of funds. John Lingard was of the opinion that 'during the bishop's life, no house will be either purchased or built for us'.[21]

*26. Crook Hall Durham*

It took the best part of nine years to agree to build a replacement of Crook Hall. The key to all of this was money, but who would be willing to subscribe? The immediate problem for the clergy was finding somewhere to accommodate the returning students from Douai. The need to establish a replacement College for Douai was high on the bishops' agenda. Bishop Douglass of the London

District, supported the use of Old Hall Green in Hertfordshire, but Bishop Gibson of the Northern District argued for an establishment in the north of England, where the costs of property, provisions and fuel were cheaper and proposed Tudhoe, a small village, near Durham. Broomhead and his fellow priests of the western part of the northern district supported Tudhoe:

> At a meeting of the Clergy of Lancashire & Westmoreland, Preston May 25th 1795:
>
> Recorded that it is the opinion & earnest wish of the undersigned priests of the western division of the northern District that the three districts, the northern, middle & southern unite in the establishment of one College, on the plan of that formerly existing at Douai. That they see some reasons; on account principally of the comparative cheapness of fewel (sic) & provisions, for wishing that the said common establishment should be in the North; in such manner however, that the bishop of that District shall not have any more influence in the governance & management of the said College than his equals in authority, the Bishops of the Middle & Southern Districts and if such an establishment can be formed they will contribute to the upmost of their power.
>
> Signed by twenty-one priests including Rowland Broomhead.[22]

Bishop Talbot of the Midland District suggested Old Hall Green or Oscott. The Jesuits, who had been ejected from Liege, supported the Tudhoe scheme, but withdrew their support when they were offered Stonyhurst in Lancashire by Mr Welds, an influential member of the laity.

Tudhoe was now abandoned in favour of more suitable accommodation at Crook Hall, near Durham. Bishop Gibson and Thomas Eyre, both past students of Douai, wanted to replicate the 'life and customs' of their former seminary. In the event it was impossible to get the parties to agree on one seminary for England, and all three Colleges, Old Hall Green, Oscott and Crook Hall continued on their own.

Broomhead had met with William Gibson to discuss what arrangements should be made for missions, where there was more than one priest working. Broomhead had drawn up these Rules and Regulations while he was visiting Stella Hall and they had been accepted and signed for by Matthew Gibson, Incumbents and Trustees dated 7 May 1790, only days before the bishop's death.

Broomhead wrote to Thomas Eyre at Crook Hall, 4 September 1797, concerning the Rules and Regulations which were signed by Matthew Gibson and others:

> The late Bishop had in his possession a Declaration of Trust given by the Trustees of my chapel in Manchester to the Bishop. There is also on the same sheet of stampt (sic) paper Rules and Regulations etc. signed by the Bishop, Incumbents, and Trustees. Some little time after the death of the Bishop you proposed sending the above deed to Manchester, but I did not answer your letter, and of course you did not send it; as I find it will be of use to me now, I beg you will send it by Post as soon as you can, and you will much oblige.[23]

The document was sent to Manchester, for the Rules and Regulations were printed there later.[24] In summary this document laid down the organisational needs both spiritual and temporal to avoid any dispute between the parties involved:

> The chapel at Rook Street had to be served by the secular clergy only. The laity were not permitted to kneel within the aisles or rails during the time of Communion. Trustees had to agree and sign the Declaration of Trust and Rules; had no power to sell part of the premises or properties;

could not make alterations or repairs; could not withhold
money belonging to the incumbent; without consent of the
bishop. They also had to have the deeds, writings and
accounts always ready should the bishop call for them.
Arrangements for the purchase or disposal of seats had to
be approved by the incumbent and monies had to be paid
four times yearly. Obnoxious trustees could be expelled.

The senior priest was in control. Broomhead was the first assistant
to a senior priest in the Manchester Mission and that gave him the
insights that helped him to draw up the document with his Bishop.

As early as 1802 there was concern among the clergy that
Broomhead's health was being affected by the work in Manchester.
Thompson[25] wrote (probably from Manchester as the letter suggests) to Thomas Eyre at Crook Hall, near Durham, 1 December
1802, about the letter he had sent to William Gibson which referred
to his appointment as the new Grand Vicar for Lancashire following
on the death of Chadwick at Weldbank near Chorley; the possible
move of Lupton to Manchester to assist Broomhead and the
concern felt for his health:

> I have written to his Lordship urging him to signify to us,
> who is to be the G. Vicar ... he often urged the Bp. for me
> to succeed him but to no purpose. He therefore mentioned
> Mr Lupton. When I wrote this to the Bishop, he answered
> me that I was to repair immediately to Weldbank and to be
> on the mission there and that perhaps he might send Mr
> Lupton to Manchester ... I have another idea. As it will be
> much easier than Manchester and more comfortable, I have
> made an offer to Mr Broomhead to go there, if the Bp. will
> allow it. My motives are, I can labour, Mr Broomhead
> cannot continue long. He is overwhelmed at the thought of
> my leaving and is resolved if possible to leave too, as he
> would long since have done, he says, if I had not been with
> him. Much noise has been made, when it was known that I

was to go from here. He may serve the mission for a long time; he has merited more than I to retire from the crowds and toil of severe labour.[26]

At a meeting of the Secular Catholic Clergy held, at the Black Bull in Preston, 30 August 1803, the following Resolutions were unanimously agreed on:

> It is the opinion of this Meeting that we ought to support the Bishop of this District in his endeavours to erect a College as soon as may be; for the education of Ecclesiastics.

> That each of us will subscribe ourselves, & will endeavour to raise Subscriptions from our respective Congregations for this purpose, & that the sums so raised shall be paid by instalments quarterly the first payment to be made at Christmas next.

> That the Rev Anthony Lund Vicar General be appointed Treasurer, & that all monies so subscribed shall be transmitted to him.

> That the Gentlemen, who were absent when these Resolutions passed, shall be requested to honour them with their signatures to express their Consent, & that the Chairman shall write to each of them for that purpose. Signed: Rowland Broomhead, Chairman.

It is clear from these documents that Broomhead was playing a significant role among the clergy. In a letter dated 28 October 1803, from Rook Street Chapel, Manchester, to William Gibson staying at Fernyhalgh, Broomhead raised the question of the absentees:

> As Mr Thompson said your Lordship wished to be informed, as soon as possible of the sentiments of such of the Clergy of this County as were absent when certain Resolutions passed at our General meeting at Preston

respecting our assisting your Lordship in the erection of a
New College in the north of England.[27]

As chairman, Broomhead reported back to the Bishop on the
progress that he had made since the meeting at Preston, which was
not good, for some were averse and some were unable to contribute
but only two approved of the Resolution:

> I, immediately on my return from Weld Bank, wrote to each
> individual absentee, except those to whom I had an oppor-
> tunity of mentioning it personally in the neighbourhood of
> Black Brook, (where John Orrell, formerly of the Manches-
> ter mission lived) who were averse to the measure. And
> though I have had plenty of time to have an answer from all,
> am sorry to say I have only yet received an answer from Rev
> Messrs Caton of Townley & Marshall of Carlisle, who both
> approve much of the Resolution passed, but are unable to
> subscribe themselves, as well as their Congregation. Mr
> Marshall will spare one guinea of his next year's dividends
> of the Fund & thinks he can get some small contributions.

Broomhead sent a copy of the Resolution passed at the Preston
meeting, and the names of those who signed, to the absentees:

> Dear Sir.
>
> If the above Resolutions meet with your Consent, please to
> notify the same to me by letter, as soon as convenient. Your
> silence will sufficiently express your dissent.[28]

A further appendix gave the names of the signatories twenty four
in all, including Broomhead, who stressed the total commitment
of the Manchester priests by listing the clergy from Manchester
separately:

> Clergy from the Manchester Mission who signed were:
> James Blundell, Joseph Shepherd, Rowland Broomhead,
> Thomas Lupton & Edward Kenyon.[29]

Thompson, Grand Vicar, wrote from Weld Bank in Chorley to Thomas Eyre, President of Crook Hall in Durham., 3 December 1803:

> I have Mr Lupton here with me for a few days, having been a little indisposed lately in Manchester from the hurry of sick etc. usual at this season. I am very happy to assure you he is likely to do much good in Manchester, being not averse to his labour, pleasing to the Congregation and zealous in his duties as well as agreeable, and hand in glove with Mr Broomhead who is delighted with him.[30]

Whilst there were no dissenters at the Preston meeting of August 1803 there was some dissention at Black Brook where John Orrell was incumbent and at Dodding Green where Robert Banister was the incumbent. Banister, in a letter dated 24 April 1804, wrote to his nephew Henry Rutter:

> I am of opinion that our Lancashire Brethren will not even bear to hear a proposal to sell out and to lend the money for building a College. At the meeting in August at Preston (I was not there and intend to go there no more) Broomehead (sic), Kenyon, James Haydock and a few more called aloud for a subscription (not of fund monies) but from each man's private property...Broomehead wrote to me for my subscription saying it would be levied by six instalments but if I did not accede he would take my silence for my negative. I was and am still silent.[31]

It is somewhat surprising to find Banister writing another letter to his nephew Henry, 27 April 1804, only three days later, reiterating the same facts. Perhaps he wanted re-assurance about his decision?

> I was not at our Clergy-meeting the last August. Mr Broomehead, Kenyon, Haydock and a few more resolved to contribute and to get contributions to enable the Bishop to build. Mr Broomehead wrote me a letter to invite me to

contribute but added that he desired no answer if I refused, so I sent no answer.[32]

The letter of Broomhead to William Gibson, 31 August 1804, can be best described as a fine example of artful strategy. Firstly, in his opening remarks, he links both himself and the Bishop to their success:

> I am just arrived from our General Meeting of the Catholic Clergy at Preston; & congratulate with your Lordship's help on the success.[33]

The sum of one thousand pounds as a possible contribution from the Clergy Fund to support the building at Ushaw seems to have been suggested as a possibility, but from the interaction with the different members of the Clergy, Broomhead had deduced that such would be too much and could affect the Clergy fund. Broomhead, alive to this reaction, felt that a motion in such terms would not be carried:

> Had a thousand Pounds been proposed from our fund I do not think it would have been carried, as many were of opinion, that we could not alienate any of the principal.

Aware of the objections, Broomhead and Edward Kenyon prepared a resolution, prior to the meeting:

> Only 4 or 5 knew the Resolution I proposed at the meeting, which Mr Kenyon & myself had drawn up before we went to Preston. We were aware of objections, & therefore would not make use of the words Give or Lend but Transfer, which caused the first resolution to pass unanimously.

At the meeting, Broomhead, who had been the chairman at the previous Preston meeting, appears to have colluded:

> I got Mr Anthony Lund in the Chair, but finding him a stranger to such a position & entirely unfit to act as Chair-

man, I stood by him, opened the business, kept good order & took the votes myself, which gave me an opportunity of speaking my sentiments, which I could not have done as chairman with propriety; as Chairman's sentiments ought to be impartial, & not to be known, except the votes are equal when he gives the casting vote. Mr Wilson of Appleton was to have proposed the Resolutions but finding him slow & bashful I proposed them myself & he seconded them all, which was done without confusion.

Despite the fact that the 'Resolutions' were to be transmitted to William Gibson by the Vicar General, Broomhead took it upon himself to send a copy, because Lund might neglect to do so:

I gave the Resolution to our Vicar General who promised to transmit them immediately to your Lordship, but for fear he should have neglected they are as follows:

Resolved unanimously that the Treasurer do transmit the sum of £500 out of our General Fund into the hands of the Rev Thos. Smith for the immediate purpose of carrying on the College, now building at Ushaw.

Resolved unanimously that in case the General Fund at any time should be found inadequate to the support of indigent Brethren the legal interest of the sum, now advanced, be paid on the dean and of the Treasurer to supply that deficiency.

Resolved that the Treasurer shall require from the hand of the Rev Thomas Smith of Durham an acknowledgement of the sum so paid on the above express condition.

The resolution gave notice that the building of the College had already started,

Broomhead wrote to his bishop:

I have informed them what we had done in Manchester where we were indeed numerous, but few Catholics of opulence. We had already raised a subscription of £587 & hoped before we closed this Subscription (in which the very existence of the Catholic religion in the North of England was at stake) it would probably amount to near £700. This surprised the whole meeting & they all seemed anxious to do something themselves, if other parts of the Northern District would be the same in their respective Congregations.

Another motion was taken and carried unanimously that a circular letter should be sent out to Catholic noblemen and gentlemen:

a motion was made & carried without a dissenting voice that the Vicar should write to your Lordship at the request of the Lancashire Clergy at their General Meeting to request of your Lordship to send Circular Letters to every Catholic Nobleman & Gentleman in England to solicit their subscription to this general cause of Religion; as well as every Priest to do their utmost endeavour to raise what subscription they possibly could in their respective Congregations. This resolution I doubt not but Mr Lund either has, or will be immediately complied with in this County.

Broomhead told the meeting that:

I was immediately informed of one Gentleman in this County who has asserted, that if the Clergy first set the example (which we now have done) & your Lordship would get others to subscribe, he would give £100 I should not fear that by this means we might acquire 20 or 30 thousand Pounds for the good cause of Religion. If anything was raised more than necessary for the Building, it might be appropriate for establishing funds for the education of Boys, for which every well wisher to Religion must be very anxious. We never can have a greater claim than the present opportunity affords us, of requesting pecuniary assistance from every professor of the Catholic Religion.

Broomhead requested that the circular be sent to Manchester although they had already begun their collection:

> When your Lordship sends these Circular Letters, we should be glad to receive them here, though our Subscription is began-perhaps they may arrive time enough to read up in our Chapels when we make our Charity Sermons & collections in each Chapel (as we mean to do) after we have got everything we can other ways by personal application. As I mentioned above we have already raised by subscription £587. I hereby inclose (sic) for your immediate use what I have received of the above Subscriptions the rest I will remit to your Lordship as I can get it paid to me. One Bill is for £256. 10. 0—the other for £50 in all £306. 10. 0. They are made payable to You or Order & must be indorsed by your Lordship before they are payable, by which means, if the Post should be robbed, or the letter be lost, the Bills would be of no value without your indorsement (sic). Besides I have had another advantage by remitting the Bill at 2 months I gain £2. 10. 0 by selling my cash for a Bill at 2 months which I suppose will be of equal value to you & will add the above sum of £2. 10. 0 to the Subscription. I mean to do the same when I make any other remittance except your Lordship should think otherways. There are few other places where there is the opportunity of selling cash for Bills on such advantageous terms & money cannot be remitted in a more safe way than by Bills not indorsed.

Broomhead had received a subscription which he was sending to Bishop Gibson and asked that an acknowledgement be sent to the donor:

> The Bill of £50 is a subscription from Mr George Gibson his brother & Sisters; the Children of the late Mr Gibson of

York. As they wished it to be known to your Lordship that they had subscribed this sum; it might not be amiss for your Lordship to acknowledge the receipt thereof by letter addressed to Mr Geo Gibson, No. 2 Piccadilly, Manchester: it would please them much.

Rowland reiterated that the subscription would be soon with the Bishop:

I know not when we shall finish our Subscription, but I will remit you the money as I receive it, when it amounts to any sum. If trade had been better we should have raised much more. But your Lordship may rely upon it; we will raise all we can. We wish to set an example to others in a cause so very essential to the very existence of the Catholic Religion in the North.

Broomhead gave some heartrending descriptions of the donations given in Manchester:

Many of the common labourers have subscribed 2 Guineas & will pay it as they can spare it from the necessary maintenance of their families. Even the Poor Children of the Catholic Sunday Schools (who work in the Cotton Factories from 5 o'clock in the Morning to 8 at night) of their own accord without solicitation have presented me with £4. 18. 0 & begged my acceptance of it as their Subscription towards the New College. This they had by mutual consent saved from what their parents allowed them to spend in sweet things & fruit. This has also given them another good resolution of each subscribing a half penny a Week to be spent in Religious Books. I was much pleased with their zeal. I wish their example may be followed by many others of riper years. I hope & trust that every other Congregation will do their proportion, as every other subscriber here expects, & then your Lordship need not fear, but the ways & means of erecting a College will be super abundantly found out in the North without a Hampshire Miller leaving us 10,100£ as in the South.

According to the records of Crook Hall, Brian Marsh from Manchester went there as a student for the priesthood in 1804. Broomhead was expected to encourage young men from his own congregation, within the wider Manchester mission, to study for the priesthood, but he and his fellow clergy needed to be very perspicacious and wise in their decision making. This work would have taken Broomhead into the families of his congregation in order to evaluate the practise of their faith, the abilities of a candidate and the depth of involvement of the parents and children in the life of the church. It was a big decision for all involved and others outside the family, especially the priests who would have been canvassed for their views.

He liaised with the Colleges responsible for training, which required evidence that a student had the necessary requisites for priesthood. What this evidence was can be gleaned from the correspondence of Broomhead and the staff of the various Colleges both home and abroad. Money was also an important consideration in the decision, and funds were not always available, and many families did not have enough money to support their sons. Rowland was also a go-between to family and seminary, especially concerning money and discipline.

In a letter from Broomhead to Thomas Eyre dated, 12 February 1806, it would appear that the new College was still not open to students:

> I hope the new College at Ushaw is going on well. I often enquire about it & think of it & wish it every success. When opened for the reception of Students I hope to see it once more, if I can spare time. It does not want for my good wishes.[34]

Broomhead wrote to Brian Marsh at Crook Hall, 27 February 1806, referring to Brian's baptism, and his brother's inability to write:

> Above I have sent you the certificate of your Baptism extracted from Register Book of my Chapel. I find that I christened you myself. I have only just received your letter this afternoon & shall be wanted immediately in the confessional, as there are people now waiting for me. I, however, just have spared time to run down to your Father, to know if he had anything in particular to say to you, and told him I was writing to you in haste this night. He says as your Brother complains his hands tremble since his last illness so that he cannot write, he means to write to you himself in the course of a Week if not sooner.

The next part of this letter referred to his father's inability to provide for Brian and the solutions that might be considered:

> As I told you, when at Crook, that your Father was not able to provide you any longer with money for clothes & I have arranged matters with him in this way; that your Uncle has made his Will & left you sufficient property at his death to repay the College any money they may advance for you during your Studies, that you should give them a bond or some other legal security to repay them the money, they may advance for you. As your Uncle is old & infirm, I should think the College could not be long, before it was repaid by you any expenses, in a moderate way that you might have incurred. As your Uncle (who you know is very positive in his own way of thinking) will not give any security himself, this must come from you, either by Bond, Promissory Note or in any other manner Mr Eyre & Lingard may think proper. I desired Mr Lupton long since to say this to Mr Lingard, but he tells me, he forgot to do it. I beg therefore you would inform Mr Lingard of this, & inform him at the same time that I doubt not, but that your Uncle will enable

you by his Will to give ample security at his death to repay
any expenses the College may have been at about you. I have
not myself seen his Will, but I have been informed of some
of the Contents from those, who knew it.

He then turned to the latest news on the building of Ushaw:

I am happy to hear the College at Ushaw is advancing again:
nor am I sorry that during the short days of winter it was not
carried on, as Workmen's wages (which in these days are
very high) would have been almost as high in the short days
in winter as they are in Summer time. The Bishop sent me
a ground plan & elevation of the Building, which I much
wished for. I hope you will occupy part of it before the end
of summer.

In the final part of the letter Broomhead and Lupton sent their
greetings:

Give my best respects to Mr Eyre, Lingard, and Bradley &
Gradwell. Mr Lupton desires his complements to the aforesaid Gentlemen. I partly expect Thomas Pinnington will
return again to you, he has lived in Manchester since he left
& has behaved remarkable well in every respect: he has ( ... )
unhappy ever since he took his sudden & rash resolution of
leaving you, which was done without thought of delibera-
tion. I have been concerting measures with Mr Wilson of
Appleton to get him (at his own earnest request) readmitted
in the College: but am not yet certain whether my application will be successful ... '[35]

According to reports from Thomas Eyre, Brian Marsh was giving
them great concern. In a reply to Thomas Eyre dated, 6 November
1806, Broomhead shared his anxieties:

I received yours, which has given me no little concern: nor
do I know how to act myself in the affair. I never thought
the Person alluded to possessing great abilities, but always

thought him a person of good dispositions & religiously inclined, but more zeal than prudence … The Portrait you draw of him astonishes me; as I ever thought him a proper person to stop up a gap, where no great exertions or abilities were required but only a religious & good behaviour & attention to duty … It would be a pity to expel him at his advanced time of life, when his education has already cost so much & when it is almost too late to learn any trade … Is there no chance from proper admonitions & threats of consequences, to work a reform in him? Do you think him incorrigible? Of this, you & other Superiors, who have the greatest opportunities of inspections into his conduct, must be the best & indeed the only judges.

Broomhead addressed the problem of dealing with a recalcitrant student:

If, after repeated admonitions & dispositions & he still persist obstinate in his temper & dispositions which you describe, nothing can be done but to expel him as soon as possible: for if he should be ordained to do no good, but on the contrary a great detriment to Religion it would prove an irreparable evil. We have already too many of this sort, who have brought a disgrace on their Cloth. One scandalous Priest does more harm to Religion than many worthy characters can do good. If these be your sentiments in his regard & you have no hopes of a reform, I think you could find no difficulty in telling him yourself plainly that he is thought an improper person for the Sacred Ministry; or if there be any difficulty in your doing it, I will write to him myself to say he is thought an improper person for our Profession & it is the desire of his Superiors that he should quit Crook Hall immediately.[36]

In a postscript, Broomhead raised the possibility that should Brian Marsh be expelled, that another student might be considered as a replacement:

> P.S. If BM must necessarily leave you I mean to apply for a Son of the late Mr Calvert's (who succeeded your father at Glossop) to succeed him on the same pension. He is a very fine lad about 13 has learnt some Latin, is very fond of study & of most amiable dispositions: he is very quick at learning & though brought up under a mother has never been petted, but always kept under strict discipline.

He wrote again to Thomas Eyre 20 November 1806, as he had not received a reply to his letter of the 6th instant:

> As I have not heard from you respecting the Person mentioned in my last, I partly expect that you mean to give him some further trial before you dismiss him entirely. If so, I should be glad to know, that I may write to him myself & give him a serious advice & severe reprimand for his past conduct, & I will get the same from his Father who is a very religious worthy man. If this has not its desired effect you may give him up entirely... Please in this case to point out to me any particular subject of complaint I may dwell upon, if you can point out to me anything more than you insinuated in your last & you may depend on me saying everything I can say to him on the Business. But if you really think him all incorrigible & not to be reformed by any exhortations, admonitions or threats whatever I certainly would not keep him any longer.[37] ...If he does not continue with you, please to inform me how I may get Frederick Calvert (I mentioned him in my last) in his place. Both in my opinion, as well as Mr Lupton's he is likely to be a valuable member & perhaps a shining character in the Mission. He possesses great abilities for his age, is very studious & of the best good

dispositions I could wish for a child of his age (between 13 & 14).

He continued in his letter to ask Thomas Eyre for advice where he might get support for Calvert:

> If no vacancy happens from the reform of the above men-
> tioned person could you point out to me where I might
> apply, I am a total stranger in the business myself. I suppose
> both the Bishop & yourself have nominations to Funds. I
> am told by Mr Thompson that Messrs John Orrell, Cray-
> thorne & Co., have no vacancies at present & also that Mr
> Dennet (successor to the late Mr Boardley) has given his
> funds up to the Bishop. As this boy is now studying Latin at
> the grammar School here (where they ground them very
> well in the Latin tongue) I wish not to be in any hurry about
> sending him immediately, as he will be coming forward.

Broomhead made an application to William Gibson, for the acceptance of Frederick Calvert as a student at Ushaw, 12 February 1807:

> When it is open for the reception of students I wish to
> recommend a Boy of my Congregation who wishes to take
> to the Church & I do not know where to apply, except to your
> Lordship. His name is Frederick Calvert son of the late
> Charles Calvert, who succeeded the Rev Thos. Eyre's Father
> as agent to Mr Howard's estate at Glossop in Derbyshire.
> After his death, his Widow & Children came to live in this
> Town. She cannot afford to pay a full Pension as she has six
> Children, but I have got her to allow £20 per annum to clear
> him of every expense so that the College will have to find her
> for this in everything even to pocket money. I think she
> cannot afford more. He is a promising boy between 13 & 14
> yrs. of age, has studied Latin these 2 years & very quick &
> fond of study. His Father was a Man of great abilities & so is
> the Mother & the rest of her Children. From an infant he has
> been kept constantly close to his studies & has never been

petted. On the whole, as far as we can judge, he is likely to turn out a shining Character. Mr Kenyon & Mr Lupton are of the same opinion with myself respecting him. He is of a good breed which added to his good dispositions & abilities give me great hopes of him. If Your Lordship can provide him with a place on the above terms at Ushaw I think you will never repent the choice & you will much oblige.[38]

Broomhead wrote another letter to Thomas Eyre, 26 February 1807:

On receipt of your former letter (which only required an answer to Marsh & not to yourself) I immediately wrote to him a severe reprimand as ever came from my pen. I particularly expected after representing to him the particulars of what has come to my knowledge respecting his misconduct my great wish & desire he would not think of embracing the Ecclesiastical State, if it was, as there was reason to apprehend, that he would be a scandal & disgrace to the Cloth. I told him I had seen myself too many unhappy instances of improper Persons embracing that state, who had done more harm than could possibly be conceived to Religion etc. In answer I received a letter from him expressive of the greatest gratitude & sincere thanks for my Paternal care of him & solicitude for his Welfare etc. [39]

Broomhead referred to Marsh's reply to his letter:

In that letter he acknowledges in part his former misconduct, but seems to palliate most of it, but in the last I received from him, at the same time I received yours by Mr Cowley, he acknowledges it in toto & makes many apologies for not having done it before. He seems of late to write much more sense & better language than formerly; even so late as a year since his letters seemed to have been written by one in low figures, or at least not above the Grammar; his ideas were quite childish. This makes me think that his intellects (however late in life) are opening.

In the same letter, Broomhead took the College authorities to task, for not dealing with Marsh earlier:

> I wish dear Sir you had not been so quiet a spectator of his conduct for so long a time; but that you had given him a proper admonition & if this produced not the desired effect, the most severe reprimand where ever you or any of the other Superiors had observed any, even the least impropriety in his behaviour. A stitch in time saves 9. The best of dispositions may at times go astray, & if not directed back into the right path before they have strayed far, the worst consequences may ensue.

Broomhead recorded some of the events which had given rise to concern:

> In Marsh's first letter to me he owns his intimacy with Stonor, but was ignorant of it being against the Rules of the house on account of the Divines being so few in numbers, whereas at formerly there were sufficient number to keep up a society amongst themselves. He says that Stonor now refused to walk out with him & it was at the same time hinted to Marsh, that Stonor might walk out with any other Divine, but he remarks: 'This came from a schoolfellow, not from a Superior; this was sufficient to convince me, that it was not agreeable I should walk out with him; had I received the least word from Mr Eyre it certainly would have put an immediate end to our acquaintance, as it did to our walking out together.

The College authorities appeared to Broomhead to be concerned about Brian Marsh's sincerity:

> I am happy that my letter to Marsh had some effect. But I think you seem to hint in your last letter that you suspect the sincerity of his repentance from what you wish me to

write to him; viz. Not merely to discharge his duties whilst he is watched, but from a principle of duty. He had only hitherto carried a fair outside in order that he might steal through his studies & introduce himself into the sacred Ministry. By false appearances he may impose on his superiors, but as soon as he once should step on the Mission he cannot prevent the world from very soon finding out what he is in reality. These are the hints you wish me to give & I hope only for his good; for if these be your real sentiments about him I should be sorry, very sorry indeed, that you should present him for ordinations.

Broomhead believed any ordinations into orders should be put off for twelve months, so that they could make a judgment of Brian Marsh's character:

At any rate, if you do not judge him to be sincere, but have the least doubt or suspicion of hypocrisy in him in order to obtain ordinations I should think it advisable to defer his Ordinations (except the lower orders) till both yourself & other Superiors are perfectly satisfied as to his real character. I assure you that it is far from my wish & desire (though I have had much pain & trouble about him) to see him ordained, if he is not likely to answer the purpose of the mission. I do not expect him to be fit for every place; but there are places, if his conduct & moral character be good, where he may be of service; but if he should prove deficient in this respect, as well as in learning it would be the greatest misfortune both for himself & Religion that he should ever be ordained. I would sooner see him beg his bread from door to door; nay even attend him I to execution on the gibbet than this should happen.

He held that he had little chance to assess his character. Mr Kenyon was his confessor and it was his original recommendation that he should train for the priesthood. He left the decision in the hands of Mr Eyre:

> I cannot myself be a judge of his character. I sent him to Lisbon when a child; on his return (on account of his health) I saw little of him. Mr Kenyon was his confessor. He urged me very much to get him admitted to Crook Hall assuring me that all he wished for & desired was to take to the Church. In all his letters from Crook Hall he has always expressed the same wish & desire & assures me he thinks he has a true vocation to take to the Church. This is all I know, or can say of him. I leave everything to you & beg you would not be the least influenced by me to present him to ordinations, if you think him improper.

However, Broomhead counselled deferment of ordination:

> At any rate you might, & hope will, defer his ordinations, till you are thoroughly convinced by his future good behaviour & conduct of his sincerity: & I should think, that in another year's probation you might form a pretty accurate idea of his sincerity & what his real character is. I shall write to him on the subjects you mention to me, as soon as I can spare time.

Broomhead wrote again to Thomas Eyre about Calvert, 7 July 1807, reiterating his qualities:

> The Boy I wrote to you about viz. Fredric Calvert whom I wish to recommend as a boy of superior talents & whom I am persuaded, as well as Mr Lupton is in all probability likely to turn out well & probably a shining character is yet here. I have applied wherever I could think of, but all in vain.

He also raised important financial matters about the support of Calvert:

> Mr Lupton says, that you mentioned in your letter to me, that if I could not get him the addition to what his mother will

allow (viz. £20 per annum) I might send him at any rate ... Mr John Orrell is now at my house & says that he (as one of the Trustees for the Barton Property to educate Boys for the Church) Ms. Craythorne & Shuttleworth will consent (of which he has little doubt) who are his joint Trustees, agree to pay what arrears are due for this boy if admitted, when they have sufficient money for the purpose; which they have not at present, but they expect some on that Fund will soon be of the fund & then they can save sufficient money to pay his arrears before they admit any other.[40]

Locating and purchasing the necessary books to stock the library firstly at Crook Hall and later at Ushaw, was very much on the minds of John Lingard and Thomas Eyre. Broomhead, as a trustee of Ushaw, was mindful of the need to stock the library when it opened. On, 7 July 1807, he wrote to Thomas Eyre about an auction at Manchester:

I have sent you a Catalogue of Books lately sold by auction in this Town. I attended the auction as much as time would permit me & I have purchased those in the Catalogue marked with a Cross. Those marked with 3 crosses +++ thus did not appear at the sale, but I have had a hint where they may be had. If you think they would be of any great advantage or service to the College; if I can get the money say reasonable I will purchase them for you as a present for the opening of the new College. Please therefore to inform me if you wish for them particularly. Those I have marked in the catalogue with a single + I have bought as a present for you, some for the use of the Divines & others for the Classics ... I will send them you all or any quantity of them you may wish for: only say whether you will want them all or which of them you would wish for & I will send them by water carriage to Hull to be forwarded to Newcastle by sea, except you would rather have them by Waggon.

There was competition for the books, from London booksellers and an agent for Stonyhurst, and the cost of the books was very high. Mr Edward Kenyon also bought some books and Broomhead thought, that the agent for Stonyhurst, who had bought many books, would probably give some to Ushaw as a present:

> As I have a Catalogue by me you only need (if you select) to put the No. in the Catalogue I should have bought many more of the Books in the Catalogue but many were sold at very high more than the prices in the London catalogues. Booksellers from London & elsewhere attended the sales. Mr Kenyon also attended the sale for a day or two & has purchased some books at the beginning of the catalogue but both he & myself were opposed by an agent from Stonyhurst who has bought up some hundred volumes. I believe he means to make you a present also of some books he has purchased; & I suppose he will give you a list of what he has bought.[41]

In the second part of this letter to Mr Eyre he referred to Marsh's behaviour and was glad he had not been ordained sub-deacon before they were satisfied with his conduct and this is the last letter that we know of that concerns Marsh:

> I hope Mr M. behaved himself now to your satisfaction. I am glad he was not ord: subd: till you was thoroughly satisfied with his conduct and dispositions & etc. (Brian Marsh was ordained 24 May 1809). The boy I wrote to you about viz. Frederick Calvert whom I wish to recommend as a boy of superior talents whom I a.m. persuaded as well as Mr Lupton is in all probability likely to turn out well & probably a shining character is yet here. I have applied whenever I could think of, but all in vain. Mr. Lupton says, that you mentioned in your letter to me, that if I could not get him the addition to what his mother will allow (viz. £20 per annum) I might send him at any rate… I burnt your letter as you desired me &————-not recollect you said so. Tell me. Mr John Orrell

is now at my house & says that he (as one of the Trustees for the Barton Property to educate Boys for the Church) Ms. Crothorne & Shuttleworth will consent (of which he has little doubt) who are his joint Trustees, agree to pay what arrears are due for this boy if admitted, when they have sufficient money for the purpose; which they have not at present, but they expect some on that Fund will soon be of the fund & then they can save sufficient money to pay his arrears before they admit any other.

According to Ushaw College records Brian Marsh and Thomas Pinnington were ordained in 1812 for the Northern District and there was no entry for ordination for Stay or Calvert, at Crook Hall, Ushaw, Douai or Lisbon.

*27. Ushaw College Durham*

The first students arrived in Ushaw College, 29 July 1808, despite the fact that much work needed to be done before the building was finished.

Rowland Broomhead, Henry Rutter, James Worswick, William. Gibson, and Thomas Smith met 20 May 1817, at a meeting of the Trustees of Ushaw:

We the undersigned do hereby acknowledge and declare that the Conveyance made to us in the Rev Thomas Eyre deceased of the estate called Ushaw farm, Lands, Heredita-

ments & Premises formerly belonging to Sir Edward
Smythe Baronet were made to us in Trust, & we do hereby
engage & promise to transfer the same Premises to the
following Person as a new Trustee & Co. Trustee with
ourselves and we do hereby appoint as a Co. Trustee
Namely Rev Richard Thompson of Weldbank near Chorley
in the County of Lancaster. Given at Durham. this twentieth
Day of May in the year of our Lord, one thousand eight
hundred & eighteen. [Signed] William. Gibson, Thomas
Smith. Signed in the presence of us Rowland Broomhead,
Henry Rutter, and James Worswick.[42]

In a letter dated, 20 December 1817, Thompson wrote to William
Gibson:

Mr Briggs is still with one; and would, I do not doubt be
happy to receive a Mission. I think he has a very good
disposition and now equal to a moderate Congregation. I beg
to be dutifully remembered to Bishop Smith. Mr Broomhead,
who is breathing with me, unites with me … P.S. I open this
to mention that I a.m. this moment favoured with a Letter
from Manchester saying that Mr Lupton is confined to his
Room. They apprehend a fever—as he has been attending
some bad Typhus Fevers & fasting—I hope it will be pre-
vented. Mr Briggs is just gone to help tomorrow. Mr Broomhead is returning to Manchester this morning. I dare not tell
him of Mr Lupton's indisposition; as I am sure it will greatly
unhinge him to hear it. I hope he will find him better. The
Account has alarmed me much.[43]

In a further letter of Thompson, 15 January 1818, to his Bishop,
the document gave an update:

I am happy to inform your Lordship that Mr Lupton got
over his attack very well. It was a touch of Typhus; but it
was taken in time, & removed by prudent attention. He was
confined for a short time; but he is now again hard at work,

though weak & looking worse than before the attack. Mr
Briggs remained with them: but Mr Broomhead says he is
not made for much- he does not like work…I suggested to
Mr Ashhurst[44] by way of trying his dispositions, that your
Lordship would perhaps direct him to Manchester. His
answer was he wished to have no disposal of himself & if it
were your Lordship's pleasure, he should not object. I was
gratified, seeing him so stout since his fever. He is more like
Mr Penswick[45] in bulk than like what he was when he left
Ushaw. I fear, however, it may not be all health: & I think
he would please Mr Broomhead & answer well. And I do
sincerely, flatter myself that with another with Mr Lupton
or Mr A. with Mr Lupton or another with Mr Broomhead,
Manchester would be, though a laborious Mission, yet a
Mission that would not Murder its Priests; which it is now
doing. But all this rests with your Lordship; whose judgment
no one can distrust[46]

Thompson wrote to William Gibson, 12 February 1818:

It is only today I heard that Mr Briggs was returned to
Manchester & I am happy in having to state to your Lordship
that he feels willing & even pleased to accept your Lordship's
appointment of him to Chester. Mr Ashhurst also is satisfied.
I sincerely hope that they will both be happy & well situated;
especially if your Lordship should find it well & could be
enabled, to reinforce Mr Lupton , as well as Mr Broomhead.[47]

In an extract from a letter,12 March 1818, sent by John Gradwell
to his brother, Robert Gradwell, Rector of the Venerable English
College in Rome, he confirmed the movement of some of the
Northern District priests: 'Have you heard that Mr Curr[48] is gone
to Mr Lupton and J. Ashhurst to Mr Broomhead & Mr Briggs is
gone to Chester'.[49]

In a letter dated, 30 April 1819, sent from Preston by John
Gradwell to his brother Robert, rector of the English College Rome,

he mentioned that Broomhead and Joseph Curr were both in Sheffield. This was Broomhead's last visit to his home in Sheffield and Mr Curr, was caring for him, in the light of his ill health at this juncture. The foundations of the new church of St Augustine, Granby Row, Manchester were in place and the building about to be commenced. The library appeared to have been substantial in Rook Street. The old church referred to was Rook Street chapel whereas the new chapel was St Augustine's Granby Row:

> Mr Broomhead and Mr Curr were at Sheffield so we had not the pleasure of seeing them. Mr Lupton and Mr Ashhurst were very well, the foundation was made for their new Chapel and I suppose they will soon commence building, they have brick ready and we saw their plans. I admired the old Church which has lately been dressed and cleansed throughout and the Library when I entered it I said here undoubtedly our brother Robert spent many hours.[50]

Broomhead wrote to Rev Mr Winstanley, rector at the English College, Lisbon, 28 September 1819:

> Rev Thomas Sadler & Rev James Blundell your old acquaintance at the College live within 6 miles of Manchester they are both well as usual, though they neither enjoy very good health. Mr Sadler is of a delicate & weakly constitution & Mr Blundell subject to very severe fits of the gout.[51]

In a letter dated 9 December 1819, Thompson reported to William Gibson on the difficulty of raising money for the new College:

> I fear little money can in these times be raised in Lancashire. It is not possible to conjecture the distress everywhere felt in the present depression & distressed state of the Manufactories. They are sorely felt by all, in every situation of life.[52]

In the same letter Thompson refers to criticism amongst the Clergy about the lack of progress in the usage of Ushaw and he was concerned at the criticisms being levelled at the Bishop:

> But it is truly mortifying to hear the general & strong reflections made by our Brethren or others, in consequence of the Lands of the College being so long held from the object, for which they were destined. It is this that gives general disgust, or raises the most painful observations on the conduct of your Lordship. It is the common topic of conversation, when the College is mentioned both as it is a prejudice to Ushaw, and a point of conscience to the Bishop himself. As far as it lies in my power I will endeavour to prevent any evil from these reflections. But they are frequent and severe.

## 2. Lancashire Infirm Secular Clergy Fund

The Rules of the Fund were listed in an undated document at a time when the Fund encompassed the Counties of Lancashire, Cheshire, Westmorland and Cumberland, but the latter two had left the Fund by 1840, so the document belongs in the period 1736 to 1840 and included the period from 1778 to 1820 when Broomhead was resident in Manchester.[53] In the preamble to the Rules, the reason for the establishment of the Fund was given:

> Lest we should have our minds alienated from our pastoral charge by solicitude for worldly things we have thought proper to constitute a Fund by the aid whereof the publick Ministry may not only be supported but each individual Member thereof may be timely supplied in his necessities'.

The Laws also stipulated:

> that no priest shall be admitted to be a subscriber till he has been one year complete upon the Mission and not then without the votes of the major part of our Brethren and if any subscriber behaves badly, it shall be put to the Votes of

our Brethren (and) if the major part judge him unworthy
to be a subscriber he shall be dismissed and shall not be
admitted again till he is truly reformed.

The rules for 1770 registered that,[54] the General Fund and the
Particular Fund were to be overseen by a Master 'whose business
it shall be to take care of the monies and other effects belonging to
all the particular settlements of the secular clergy in the North-West
District'. These Masters of the Funds were 'not permitted to keep
any monies or securities in their own hands; it being the Rural
Dean's business to manage all money affairs but they shall watch
over the Rural Dean diligent and faithful in their Trust'. The Rural
Deans were required to submit copies of the Registers to the Vicar
General who then submitted the same to the Bishop.

In the case of a particular mission receiving monetary support
it was required:

that on a doubled sided white board an account of what
money belongs to that place shall be written in a fair hand
and on the other side the obligations to be performed for it.
These accounts shall be written or at least signed by the
Rural Dean of the Hundred, such place is in, and the board
shall be hung on a pin or nail on the inside of the Tabernacle.

There had to be two meetings: the General Meeting for all the
clergy at which 'the interest arising from the General Fund and
other donations shall be distributed' and officers elected and the
Particular Fund was for the Bishop, Vicars, Rural Deans and 'some
other of our selected Brethren (if thought proper) to settle matters
concerning our Funds or any other matters that may occur'. The
Rural Deans took down in writing the votes of the clergy from their
particular 'Hundred'.

In August 1781, Broomhead and Houghton were listed as
present at the meeting. In documents from the period (1672 to
1782) there was an entry in the catalogue of the members of the

General Fund for 1782 which included Houghton; Broomhead and John Orrell missioners within the Hundred of Salford, within a list of twenty-nine members.[55]

The list of members of the Fund, 25 August 1795, contained the names of forty priests including those within the Salford Hundred: Broomhead, Edward Kenyon, James Haydock and Joseph Shepherd a new recruit.

The rural deacons were expected to 'collect together the donations of the benefactors and deposit them in the hands of the treasurer'; required to give unanimous direction as to the use of the monies by the treasurer who was required to give account to the archdeacon and his superior once a year. The Secretary was required to keep a table or book:

> in which all those who now or shall in future contribute to this Fund shall subscribe their names in their own hand writing to which the amount of their respective donations together with the names of the Benefactors and Priests residing with them shall be subjoined all of which matters or whatsoever else shall be inserted in the said Tables shall be immediately signified to the Archdeacon or his superior.

There was also an Office of Procurator:

> whose business shall be diligently to communicate the orders of the Superiors and all official papers to the Deacons in order that they may communicate them to the Brethren or if he shall receive from the Brethren thro' the hands of the Deacons on account of anything proper to be done or made known, that he transmit the same reciprocally to his Superiors or their officials for the more ready execution of which let him reside in some place adapted for correspondence and Publick business.

The Superior of the Fund was presumed to be the best judge of what is just and right and he had:

the right of inspecting these offices and of taking cognisance
of the cases of the different officers and of weighing what-
soever he finds they have done well or otherwise in the even
scale of justice.

All the Officers of the Fund were required:

> to certify as many as shall attend the annual meeting of the
> Brethren how each has acquitted himself in his Office to
> that time, and in order that it may be known what has been
> disbursed and what remains in the common Purse, let the
> Accounts of everyone be publicly settled, so as by the
> Testimony of those who are present, they may be manifest
> also to the absent.

The annual general meeting was seen as being conducive 'to
promoting union and concord' and they obviously could not meet
without expenditure, which was defrayed from the Fund. The
members were also concerned that 'the house or family where the
meeting is held may be put to no expense on that account'. The aim
of this charity was clearly defined:

> The Alms or Donations ensuing from this Fund shall be
> proportioned according to the necessities of the Brethren
> whose relief is the principal object of this Establishment (as
> for instance when any one first arrives within this Province
> destitute of all accommodation or is in prison or afflicted
> with any daily infirmity) less they be reduced to want.

The Fund also offered its charity to laymen:

> This Charity may be extended not only to the Brethren but
> also to Laymen in like necessity particularly if occasioned
> by their Profession of the Faith but more especially to the
> Benefactors in proportion to their Subscriptions to the End
> that we may not in word only, but in deed be patterns of
> Piety and Commiseration to our Flocks and examples of
> pastoral charity.

A distribution of the surplus of the Fund took place at the annual meeting:

> Let the Remainder of the Profits annually arising from the Fund of this district (all the necessary matters above mentioned being first fulfilled, common expenses deducted and just Alms or Donations duly paid) be divided equally amongst the Brethren.

An example was that of 21 February 1796, when each secular and emigrant priest of Lancashire was given ten shillings and sixpence and on 12 April of the same year the priests in the Fund received one guinea.[56]

At the meeting of the General Fund for August 1808 there was a list of the clergy of the Salford Hundred with their mission location:

> Thomas Lupton, Rook Street, Manchester
> Rowland Broomhead, Rural Dean, Rook Street, Manchester
> Edward Kenyon, Mulberry Street, Manchester
> Joseph Shepherd, Bolton Moor, Bolton
> James Blundell, Edgeley, Stockport, Cheshire
> Thomas Sadler, Trafford House, Manchester
> In October 1815 at the General Fund meeting, the list of the clergy for the Salford Hundred was as follows:
> Rowland Broomhead, Rural Dean, Rook Street, Manchester
> Thomas Lupton, Rook Street, Manchester
> Joseph Shepherd, Bolton-le-Moor
> James Blundell, Edgeley, Stockport, Cheshire
> Thomas Sadler, Trafford House, Manchester
> John Ashhurst, Rook Street, Manchester
> Joseph Curr, Mulberry Street, Manchester

Within the documents of the Fund there was a list of donations which were received by Broomhead in his role as Rural Dean. They were:

> July 27th 1812 Samuel Swann £10.0.0

July 27th 1812 Mary Swann £10.0.0
September 30th 1813 Mrs Trafford £20.0.0
December 23rd 1813 Mr Edmund Trafford £10.0.0
November 18th 1814 John Trafford Esq. of Trafford

In further records of the Secular Clergy Fund there were a number of invoices paid by Broomhead for two priests who were in the Manchester Lunatic Asylum. These records were written on various bits of paper and there are obvious gaps in the material but nevertheless they do give us some insight into the work of the Fund through Broomhead's care of his fellow priests at the Lunatic Asylum in Manchester, in his capacity as Rural Dean.[57] He settled bills for Thomas Milner and James Parkinson. In the cash book for the period 1797 to 1832 there were numerous entries for cash being paid to Broomhead to defray the costs of Parkinson's stay in the Manchester Lunatic Asylum from 1798 to 1820. He died at the Manchester Asylum, 18 November 1821.

Under the terms of the Constitution of the Fund it was required that:

> every Brother shall use his utmost endeavour by all fit and convenient means to promote this Fund and therefore every priest shall at his death at least, if clear of debt, leave something to this Fund and shall with discretion exhort his friends and patrons to contribute to the support of this pious Institution not only at their deaths, but whenever any other charitable distribution take place.

Each priest had to say Mass once a month for the benefactors of the Fund; three Masses for every priest who was a member of the Fund when they died and one Mass for any priest of the Fund on receiving notice of his death. They were also required to say Masses for benefactors on the basis of their donation; one Mass for a donation of £10 and two Masses for £20 and so on. A priest 'who has no Patrimony of his own nor any settled residence ... shall be

given twenty shillings in consideration whereof he shall say Mass
five times for the Benefactors'.

In Broomhead's will there was a bequest to the Fund:

> I give and bequeath unto my friend the Reverend Richard
> Rimmer of Sheffield in the County of York Clerk and Robert
> Gainford of the same place silver plater (my executors
> hereinafter named) the sum of Ten Pounds in trust that they
> do and shall with all convenient speed after my decease pay
> the same unto the Treasurer for the time being of the
> Society instituted in the County of Lancaster for the relief
> or support of poor sick aged or infirm Clergymen of the
> Roman Catholic persuasion resident in the same County to
> be applied for the charitable purposes of such society.[58]

At the bottom of this list there was a donation of £10.0.0 in the
name of Rev Rowland Broomhead, listed as 12 October 1820,
which was the day of his death.[59]

Nowadays the Lancashire Infirm Secular Clergy Fund supports
the secular clergy of the Archdiocese of Liverpool and the Dioceses
of Salford and Shrewsbury who are members of the Fund and who
are too sick or too old to perform their priestly duties. It is supported by members' subscriptions and charitable donations.
Members offer regular Masses for donors.

### 3. Membership of the Old Chapter of England 1807–1820[60]

In 1623, William Bishop was appointed by Gregory XV, as the first
vicar apostolic with the title, Bishop of Chalcedon, with jurisdiction
over England and Wales, though he held his powers 'at the pope's
good pleasure and subject to the higher authority of the papal
nuncio in France acting as ordinary for England'.[61] A vicar apostolic
ruled a territory called a 'vicariate apostolic' as a delegate of the
Holy See. Vicars apostolic 'had no territorial diocese, cathedral
church or chapter of canons'.[62] Despite the restrictions of his office

William Bishop went ahead and established a chapter of twenty canons, who were geographically located across the country. He also divided England and Wales into six districts. In spite of not being a bishop in ordinary he would appear to have:

> behaved as though he possessed such powers and estab-
> lished a Chapter, not only to advise and assist him and to
> exercise jurisdiction 'sede vacante', but even, according to
> its patent of institution, to elect future bishops.[63]

In 1685, John Leyburn was appointed vicar apostolic much to the chagrin of the Chapter and James II, who wanted a bishop in ordinary. Leyburn was a chapterman but received instructions from Rome 'to act independently of the chapter'.[64] From that point on the Chapter's former authority was somewhat curtailed.

The Red Book of the Old Chapter, 5 February 1807, recorded the following:

> The secretary having reported the death of the late Rev
> Dean Thomas Varley and John Lindow the Dean proposed
> Rev Thomas Wilkinson and the Rev Rowland Broomhead
> to succeed to the canonicate vacant by the death of former
> when there appeared for Mr Broomhead 19 and for Mr
> Wilkinson 7 whereupon Mr Broomhead was duly elected.[65]

Broomhead became the 314th member of the Old Chapter. The secretary reported 18 March 1807 that 'he had informed Mr Broomhead of election and that he had accepted and returned thanks'.[66] Only members of the Chapter were allowed to vote for the introduction of a new member. The General Assembly of 1807 recorded the roll of nineteen capitulars[67] and eleven canons including Rowland Broomhead. According to Burton:

> it continued in possession of all its ancient privileges; the
> most eminent priests of each generation, including most of
> the vicars apostolic themselves, were members, and it

remained the one body, election to which set a seal of something like public recognition to a priest's career.[68]

The eighteen archdeacons listed in the roll below do not appear to have been elected on the basis of living in their named archdeaconry. John Orrell succeeded Edward Helme at Manchester moving in 1778 to Blackbrook, Lancashire and was appointed to be archdeacon of Lancashire and Westmoreland whereas Broomhead who worked almost all his priestly life at Manchester was appointed, 30 October 1817, as successor to Reverend Thomas Johnson archdeacon of Oxfordshire, Berkshire and Buckinghamshire. Thomas Eyre, a cousin of Broomhead, was President of Ushaw College, Durham., and yet he was archdeacon of Cornwall, Devon, Dorset and Leicestershire. The title of archdeacon was a title of honour in the chapter.

Broomhead, as one of the thirty members of the Chapter, was aware of its aims and objectives, which can be derived from the work of 'Sergeant'. The Chapter was in receipt of donations from a number of sources which were used for the 'education of students, provision for pastors, relief for superannuated or other necessitated priests and other good uses'. These donations were covenanted through deeds and if the general chapter should cease then it would:

> run great hazard, in small time, of being lost, there being no
> corporate body or bodies to look after them. Nay, which is
> far worse, no more charitable donations can be expected
> from the piety of any persons whatever, let them be never
> so devoutly or piously inclined, since no prudent person can
> be thought willing to make any donation or establishment,
> where there is no authorized ecclesiastical body able to give
> security for future performance of incumbent duties.[69]

In a period of interregnum a diocese had a Chapter to rule until a successor was appointed, but in a vicariate this was not so. The Chapter argued:

that if there was no chapter then there was no one to provide priests for missions; there would be no governance of the clergy; no infliction of censuses; no one to oversee the granting of faculties or the approval of preachers; no one to give leave for a foreign bishop to administer the sacrament of confirmation.[70]

Following the Restoration of the Hierarchy in 1850, the Old Chapter discussed the way forward as there was no longer any Episcopal role to play. They changed the name to the 'Old Chapter Trust' in 1853, but in 1862 changed its name to 'The Old Brotherhood of the English Secular Clergy'. It still retains this latter title and continues its charitable work to this day.[71]

## Notes

[1]    Walton, *Letter to Chadwick November/December 1775* (LRO: RCV2/5/124).

[2]    J. S. Watson, *The Reign of King George III, 1760–1815* (Oxford, Clarendon Press, 1992), vol. XII, p. 235.

[3]    M. Gibson, *Letter to Chadwick 17 July 1780* (UCA: II/126).

[4]    Walton, *Letter to Chadwick January/February 1780* (LRO: RCV2/5/129).

[5]    M. Gibson, *Letter to Rome 8 January 1787* (LRO: transcript, RCV 2/6).

[6]    Through the Lancashire Secular Clergy Fund's General Fund the interest arising was distributed annually to its members. There were two meetings per year, one in February and the other in August. The Fund was ruled by the Bishop, Grand Vicars, Rural Deans and selected brethren.

[7]    Chadwick, *Letter to M. Gibson 31 January 1787* (LDA: MG. 28. 4).

[8]    J. Gillow, *A Literary and Biographical History or Bibliographical Dictionary of the English Catholics from the Breach with Rome in 1534 to the Present Time* (London, Burns & Oates, 5 Vols., 1885–1902), vol. 1, p. 317.

[9]    W. J. Amherst, *The History of Catholic Emancipation and the Progress of the Catholic Church In the British Isles (chiefly In England) From 1771 To 1820* (London, 1885), vol. I, p. 162.

[10]   Amherst, *The History of Catholic Emancipation* vol. I, p. 163.

[11]   Appendix Five: *The Declaration and Protestation Signed by the English*

> *Catholic Dissenters in 1789 with the NAMES of those who signed it,* printed in 1791(UCA: 475C).

12  *Address of the Lancashire Clergy to the Lords and Gentlemen of the Committee of English Catholics c. 1790* (LDA: MG. 46).

13  *Letter signed by fifty-five Lancashire Priests to William Gibson I January 1790* (Ward, *The Dawn of the Catholic Revival in England 1781–1803*), vol. 1, pp. 201–220).

14  M. Gibson, *A Pastoral Letter January 15, 1790* (Newcastle Upon Tyne, printed and sold by Hall and Elliot and also sold by J. P. Coghlan, No. 37, Duke-street, Grosvenor Square, London), LDA: MG, 1790.

15  Broomhead, *Letter to Chadwick 6 March 1791* (UCA: Presidents' Archives/C20).

16  W. Gibson, *to all the faithful, clergy and laity in the Northern District 30 June 1791 (UCA: X. E. 2. 76).*

17  Broomhead (and twenty-nine other priests), *signed an address to the three Vicars Apostolic of the districts of London, the Midlands and the North, 30 August 1791* (UCA: Library: X. E. 2. 7p).

18  Amherst, *The History of Catholic Emancipation,* p. 180.

19  Ward, *The Dawn of the Catholic Revival in England 1781–1803, vol. 1,* p. 315.

20  L. Gooch, *The Catholic Revival in England, the Banister/Rutter Correspondence 1777–1807* (Wigan, North West Catholic History Society, 1995) Letter no. 90.

21  J. Lingard, *Letter to Orrell 26 December 1802* (AAL: Orrell Papers, 18).

22  Ward, *History of Old Hall* (AAW) document no. 83, p. 153.

23  Broomhead, *Letter to Eyre 4 September 1797* (UCA: President's Archives 42).

24  Appendix 2/1: *Old Trust as to Rook Street Chapel: Declaration of Trust & Rules and Regulations written by Broomhead and accepted and signed by William Gibson 7 May 1790* (SDA 479).

25  Richard Thompson assistant to Rowland Broomhead at Rook Street, Manchester

26  Thompson, *Letter to Eyre 1 November 1802* (UCA: Eyre Correspondence, vol. 2, pp. 381–383).

27  Broomhead, Letter *to W. Gibson 28 October 1803* (LDA: WG. 478).

28  The Names of those Gentlemen who were present & signed these Resolutions were as follows: Reverend Anthony Lund, Vicar General; Richard Thompson; James Blundell; Robert Blacon; Joseph Shepherd; Henry

Parkinson; Richard Edmundson; James Wagstaffe; James Dennett; James Lawrenson; Robert Swarbrick; Thomas Penswick; Joseph Higginson; William Irwing; Rowland Broomhead; Thomas Lupton; Thomas Berry; Edward Kenyon; James Haydock; James Finch; James Newsham; John Lund; James Mawdesley & Mr Caton.As I think your Lordship has not a copy of the Resolutions, nor the names of those who signed them, will copy them on the other side for your Lordship's information.

29  Broomhead, *Letter to W. Gibson 28 October 1803* (UCA: WG. 478).

30  Thompson, *Letter to Eyre December* 1803 (UCA: Eyre Correspondence, vol. 2, p. 384).

31  R. Banister, *Letter to Nutter 24 April 1804* (UCA: 143).

32  Banister, *Letter to Nutter* 27 April 1804 (UCA: 142).

33  Broomhead, *Letter to W. Gibson 31 August 1804* (UCA: WG. 497).

34  Broomhead, *Letter to Eyre 12 February 1806 (LDA: 553A).*

35  Broomhead, *Letter to Marsh 27 February 1806* (UCA: Eyre Correspondence 43).

36  Broomhead, *Letter to Eyre 6 November 1806* (UCA: Eyre correspondence, 47).

37  Broomhead, *Letter to Eyre 20 November 1806* (UCA: Eyre correspondence 47b).

38  Broomhead, *Letter to W. Gibson 12 February 1807* (LDA: WG. 553A).

39  Broomhead, *Letter to Eyre 26 February 1807* (UCA: Eyre correspondence, 49).

40  Broomhead, *Letter to Eyre 7 July 1807* (UCA: Eyre Papers 50).

41  Broomhead, *Letter to Eyre 7 July 1807* (UCA: Eyre Papers 50).

42  Broomhead, *Meeting of the Trustees of Ushaw College 20 May1817* (LDA: WG. 999).

43  Thompson, *Letter to W. Gibson, 20 December 1817* (LDA: WG.1040).

44  J. Ashhurst was an assistant at Rook Street Chapel, Manchester.

45  T. Penswick was born 7 March 1772 in Ashton-in-Makerfield and was ordained priest 1 April 1797. He became Coadjutor Vicar Apostolic of Northern District 13 January 1824 then Vicar Apostolic of the Northern District 30 July 1831. He died in office 28 January 1836.

46  Thompson, *Letter to W. Gibson 15 January 1818* (LDA: WG. 1044).

47  Thompson, *Letter to W. Gibson 12 February 1818* (LDA: WG. 1051).

48  Curr was born in Sheffield in 1793 and educated at Crook Hall County Durham. He was ordained to the priesthood and was made assistant at Rook Street Chapel and St Augustine's Granby Row, Manchester. He was

famous for his disputations with the Manchester Protestant Bible Association and also wrote a number of books. He died 29 June 1847 as a result of working in Leeds at the time of a typhoid epidemic. He gave the panegyric at Rowland Broomhead's funeral.

49  J. Gradwell, *Letter to his brother Robert Gradwell 12 March 1818* (VEC: Scr. 56. 6).

50  J. Gradwell, *Letter to R. Gradwell, rector of the English College in Rome 30 April 1819* (VEC: Scr. 56.6).

51  Broomhead, *Letter to Rev Mr Winstanley rector of the English College Lisbon 28 September 1819* (UCA: English College Lisbon).

52  Thompson, *Letter to W. Gibson 9 December 1819* (LDA: WG. 1144).

53  Lancashire Infirm Secular Clergy Fund (LISCF) *The rules of the secular Clergy who are associated to the general Fund in the Counties of Lancaster, Westmorland, Cumberland and Chester 1736 to 1820* (LRO: DDSC/19/38).

54  *Rules of the Secular Clergy Fund with annotations 1770* (LRO: RCCF 3/1).

55  LISCF *Book of rules accounts of legacies and donations and memoranda 1672–1782* (LRO: RCCF 5/1).

56  Roman Catholic Clergy Fund: *Book containing list of fund members, dates of death, benefactions and dividends 25 August 1795–1831* (LRO: RCCF 1/2).

57  LISCF. *Miscellaneous bills, receipts, extracts from accounts and related papers 1800–1919* (LRO: RCCF), q. v. Appendix Six: *Broomhead's Invoices for Milner & Parkinson at the Asylum*.

58  *The Last Will and Testament of the Reverend Rowland Broomhead of Manchester 5 October 1820* (LRO: WCW/ Rev Rowland Broomhead, 1821).

59  LISCF *Book of rules, accounts of legacies and donations and memoranda 1783–1846* (LRO: RCCF 5/2).

60  Appendix Seven: *Background to the Old Chapter of England*

61  M. C. Questier, *Catholicism and Community in Early Modern England: Politics, Aristocratic Patronage and Religion, c. 1550–1640* (Cambridge, Cambridge University Press, 2006) p. 403.

62  Attwater, *The Catholic Encyclopaedic Dictionary* p. 515.

63  J. A. Williams, *Catholic Recusancy in Wiltshire 1660–1791* (CRS: 1968 Monograph Series) vol. 1.

64  Burton, *The Life and Times of Bishop Challoner*, p. 85.

65  Red Book of the Old Chapter 1779–1825 recorded Broomhead's *election to the Chapter, 5 February 1807* (AAW).

66   Red Book of the Old Chapter 1779–1825 recorded *Broomhead in the list of canons, 18 March 1807* (AAW).

67   The Venerable John Lee, Dean and eighteen Archdeacons: Robert Banister of Norfolk and Suffolk;Edward Beaumont of Surrey and Kent; Christopher Taylor of Staffordshire, Cheshire, Derbyshire;Anthony Lund of Shropshire and Herefordshire; Marmaduke Wilson of Sussex; Joseph Knapp London, Westminster, Middlesex; Richard Southworth of Essex, Herts., and Bedfordshire; John Orrell ofLancashire and Westmoreland; John Griffiths, Treasurer, of Hants. Wilts. and Somersetshire; John Perry of Northamptonshire, Cambridgeshire & Hunts; Rt. Rev Dr John Milner of South Wales; Thomas Eyre ofCornwall, Devon, Dorset & Leicestershire; John Gillow of Worcestershire, Gloucestershire;Joseph Hodgson, Secretary, of Durham, Cumberland and Northumberland; John Earle of Lincolnshire, Rutland and Notts.

68   Burton, *The Life and Times of Bishop Challoner,* p. 86.

69   J. Sergeant, *Transactions of the English Secular Clergy* (London, 1706), p. 117.

70   Sergeant, p. 118.

71   Charity Commissioners 2013: The current membership of the Old Brotherhood comprises twenty-two senior priests from the Catholic Dioceses of England and Wales, elected by their fellows in recognition of their individual contribution to the Church in our country. As a corporate body we administer a modest charitable trust primarily intended for the benefit of elderly ladies who had served our diocesan clergy as housekeepers.

# 9 BROOMHEAD'S CIVIC INVOLVEMENT IN MANCHESTER

## 1. Setting the Scene

IN THE WINTER of 1821 Michael Gaffey composed a poem 'about that truly estimable character, the late Revd. Rowland Broomhead' but did not publish it till February 1822. An extract spoke of Broomhead's involvement in the civic activities of the Town:

> What need have I to put the world in mind
> Of all he undertook to serve mankind?
> How many changes, difficult and hard
> For mortal to perform, claim'd his regard;
> And yet, impossible as they appear'd
> With unremitting toil he persevered.
> He eagerly partook of every care
> That bore the name of useful, good, or fair;
> Witness the public charities which he
> Conducted to the last extremity,
> Largely contributed to their support,
> And gave his aid alike to every sort
> Of institution meant to improve the mind,
> Relieve the poor, or benefit mankind,
> By curing sickness and disorders foul,
> Restoring health to body and to soul.

In his early years at Manchester it would have been difficult for Broomhead to have been involved in the civic activities of the Town for the mission still extended to Macclesfield and Glossop and the other outlying towns and none of the missions became independent until 1794. When the mission was able to support more priests, Broomhead had time to be involved:

With the assistance of these good priests, Father Broomhead was in no small way able to turn his mind to social and municipal affairs to the benefit and advancement of his flock.[1]

## 2. The Manchester Infirmary, Dispensary, Lunatic Hospital & Asylum

*28. Manchester Infirmary Lunatic Asylum Dispensary and Baths*

The Manchester Infirmary was established in 1752. When Broomhead arrived in Manchester in 1778, the full title for the Hospital on what was then Levers Row (later Piccadilly) was the Manchester Infirmary, Dispensary, Lunatic Hospital and Asylum and they lay within the land bordered by Levers Row; Portland Place and Portland Street; Parker Street and Bath Street. In front of the Hospital complex there was a canal known as Daubhole.

In the line of duty, soon after his arrival, Broomhead was a regular visitor both at the Infirmary and the Lunatic Hospital and Asylum, a short distance away from the Rook Street Chapel. By

1787 he had become a member of the Board[2] and remained so till his death in 1820. During those thirty-three years he gave unstinting service to the work of the hospital attending an average of two meetings per month, some eight hundred and nine visits, besides his attendance at the Quarterly and Annual Board meetings and special meetings which totalled ninety-seven in all.

His close work with other churchmen was described in Manchester's 'Exchange-Herald' of 1820:

> At the head of the Board sat the late John Leigh Philips, Esq., a high Churchman; on his right hand, sat the late Rev. Dr. Barnes, the highly and justly respected Minister of the Dissenters, assembling for worship in Cross-street; and on his left, Mr. Broomhead, a Catholic Priest;-all zealously and harmoniously employed in one common cause; as if actuated by one heart, and one soul, in labouring for the promotion, and proper direction, of the Charity applied to the relief of every description of poor afflicted with disease, without regard to sect or party. 'We have different Creeds and modes of Faith,' Mr. Broomhead has often said on those occasions, 'but we are all of the Religion which makes us wish to do good'. The chords of their hearts were in perfect unison; and the harmony of benevolence produced by the trio, composed, as it was, of three such distinctly different Christians, must have been approved in Heaven.[3]

At a Manchester Infirmary Quarterly Board, Broomhead signed three documents.[4] The first was an indenture of February 1805, referring to land of Thomas Carill Worsley of Platt Hall in the Parish of Manchester; the second an indenture of re-lease of 23 and 24 September 1808 of land of the Manchester Public Infirmary and Lunatic Asylum belonging to Sir Oswald Mosley of Rolleston House in the county of Stafford, Baronet and the third was a deed of covenant dated 6 April 1809, to produce some deeds.

The work of the Board for those who attended regularly, as Broomhead did, was quite extensive and at times complicated. As a deputy treasurer he had to take in money from benefactors and also oversee the finances which involved paying bills to tradesmen and wages to the staff. In this role he would have supervised the purchase of medical supplies, as well as food and drink. The Board, 25 April 1796, were concerned about a Bill, which was 'pending in Parliament for the purpose of granting to his Majesty certain additional Duties upon foreign wines imported into the Kingdom'.[5]

The committee decided to appeal to Parliament on the basis of the admission of no fewer than 128,000 patients since 1752, and that they depended solely for support of voluntary subscriptions. The efficacy of port wine was also part of their case against the imposition of duties and the members of the committee, of which Broomhead was a member, argued that:

> Port Wine being found a very necessary article of the 'Materia Medica', a quantity amounting to 5 gallons per day is frequently dispensed to the Patients afflicted with fever to which the poorer inhabitants of the Town are much subjected, & that as the Trustees have daily opportunities of witnessing its excellent Effects as a Medicine they feel anxious that no circumstances should happen to prevent its being used in all necessary cases and they are justified by experience in stating that of nearly 10,000 patients now annually relieved by this Charity a very great number owe their lives to that Medicine which in this point of view cannot be considered as a Luxury.

The Board failed to get an exemption 'as it would open a Door to endless Exemptions'.[6]

The Board oversaw the appointment and discharging of staff. When there was an appointment of a physician or surgeon there might be as many as 300 to 600 of the Trustees at a Special Board[7] meeting and every one of them would have had a vote. There were four hundred and forty-three members of the Board at the meeting 2 April 1812, which appointed Mr Robert Thorpe, but the meeting of the Board on 1 August 1811, when Broomhead was in the chair, could not proceed because there was no quorum. They needed seven trustees to hold a Board. The Board also drew up rules and regulations which they were quite prepared to enforce. A minute, 20 February 1791,[8] read:

> that the matron take care that the nurses scour their respective wards with soap and warm water or with ley every Friday before eight o'clock in the morning. Use of sand totally abolished.

A surgical pupil took upon himself the right to take up a petition within the Infirmary against 'certain Bills descending on Parliament'. The Board decided 'That these laudable Institutions being funded on the sole Principle of charity, they know no distinction of Religions or Political Principles'.

The Board,[9] 31 October 1791, was faced with a problem arising from people who were accessing the Infirmary grounds at night time. A minute records the Board's decision:

> As many disorderly People have made a practice of frequenting the grounds of the Infirmary after dark, and behaving with great impropriety and indecency; the Weekly Board think it necessary to give notice, that in future the Gates will be locked every evening at Dark, and not opened again until the morning; but that a Door is opened at the Baths, a few yards from the said Gates thro' which all persons having immediate business at the Infirmary, Lunatic Hospital and Asylum, or Baths will be admitted by the Bathman.

Correspondence was as diverse as the number of people they dealt with. It could be to the family of a patient, to a tradesman or to all the churchmen in the Town. On the 16 January 1792 it was a unanimous decision of the Board:

> that immediate application be made to the Ministers of
> every Denomination in Manchester and its neighbourhood,
> to preach charity sermons for the benefit of this Infirmary.[10]

As a deputy treasurer Rowland Broomhead was in receipt, on a regular basis, of the thanks of the board, alongside all the other officers of the Charity. They moved, 20 June 1816:

> that the Thanks of this Board be given to Treasurer, Deputy
> Treasurers and other Officers for the zeal and attention they
> have uniformly shewn to the interests of these Charities.

At a General Board Meeting,[11] 17 June 1819, in the penultimate year of Rowland's life, James Touchet, the Chair of the Board, signed a resolution that had been carried unanimously:

> That the thanks of this Board be given to the Reverend
> Rowland Broomhead for his attentive and obliging behav-
> iour in the chair.

Broomhead was coming to the end of his life but he remained constant to the work of the Infirmary. In the last twelve months of his life he attended nineteen Weekly Boards; two Quarterly Boards; two Special Boards and one Annual General Meeting. His final meeting was a Weekly Board Meeting, 17 July 1820.

### 3. The Lying-in Hospital

Dr Charles White, surgeon and his son Thomas, a doctor, held positions at the Infirmary until 1790 when they resigned along with Doctors Edward and Richard Hall. They had a difference of opinion about the management of the Infirmary regarding the establish-ment of a charity to help women in pregnancy. A hand-written document stated the following:

> Rules and Orders of the Lying-in Charity for delivering poor
> women at their habitations and for erecting a Lying-In
> Hospital in Manchester, as soon as the sum of £2,000 can
> be raised. Instituted 5 May 1790.

The document appears to have been prepared prior to a meeting
with the concerned gentlemen of the Town, 8 May 1790, at the
Bridgewater Arms in High Street, Manchester, to discuss the
establishment of a 'Lying-in Charity'. Broomhead became a committee member of the new hospital. As a result of the meeting, there
was at least £2,000 in the kitty, and a house was purchased in Old
Bridge Street for use as a hospital. The business of this charity was:

> to provide professional assistance and domestic accommo-
> dation for pregnant women.[12]

In its early days it was known as 'The Manchester Lying-in Hospital
and Charity for the delivery of poor women at their own habitations' but in 1816 it inserted the word 'married' in front of 'women'.

Broomhead as a trustee and member of the committee was
involved in every part of the structure of the Lying-in Hospital
which included: trusteeship and the rights of subscribers; governance, laws and rules; staffing of the hospital; the education and
training of staff; control of medicines; women who could be
admitted and the terms of their relief and the building and the
boundaries of the work of the charity.[13]

Rowland did not take his work lightly, for the evidence of his
attendance at so many board meetings confirm his deep involvement and concern in the work of the hospital. Some of the earliest
records for the Hospital are not extant. The earliest entry for
Broomhead was in the Weekly Board Book of the Lying-In Hospital, for the period October 1804 to August 1819. He was listed as
attending the Weekly Board as a house visitor, 25 October

1805[14]and in 1806, he attended the Weekly Board on 20 May, and took on more work:

> Ordered that Dr Foxley, Rev R. Broomhead and Mr Hutch-
> inson be requested to prepare the Preamble to the Report.[15]

He was present again, 20 June 1806. At the meeting 15 August 1806, a 'new subscription by Mr Gibson and Mr Leaf, trustees and members of Rook Street Chapel, was testified to by Rowland Broomhead'.[16] At the weekly meeting of 26 December 1806 it was:

> Ordered that a copy of the Resolution made at the adjourned
> General Board of the 5th instant be sent to the different clergy.
> This read as follows: 'Resolved that an application be made
> to the different Clergy of Manchester to preach Sermons and
> cause Collections to be made in their respective congrega-
> tions for the benefit of this Charity.[17]

Broomhead was listed, 20 March 1807, as House Visitor for that week. He was listed, 13 May 1808, as having been inoculated for Cow Pox on the previous Tuesday. (People who were regular visitors to the Lying-In Hospital were inoculated.) He was recorded as a House Visitor in the Manchester Mercury, 17 May 1808, and recorded again for the same role 7 July 1809. In January 1810 the minutes recorded the removal of the Hospital to Stanley Street, near the New Bailey.

He was present at the Weekly Board meeting 15 February 1811, and the Trustees, 19 September, of the same year recorded that 'White's Anatomical Museum' belonged to the Lying-In Hospital. (Drs. Charles and Thomas White were two of the original founders of the Hospital). Broomhead chaired the Weekly Board meeting 11 September 1812, where he proposed:

> That the Roof of the Lying-In Hospital and adjoining
> buildings belonging to the same be repaired...that the
> Hospital be painted on the outside.

By 1816 Rowland Broomhead was one of the four deputy treasurers.[18] According to the Annual Reports from 1815 to 1820 he was one of the four deputies and each year he donated his usual one guinea.

## 4. The Manchester Board of Health

In the latter part of the eighteenth century the factories and mills in around Manchester were seen as breeding grounds for the spread of typhus which was said to have been carried into the country in the raw cotton. Wherever people lived or worked in close proximity, especially the poor who were more susceptible to the vagaries of weather, harvests and the resulting high prices, epidemics were common. Doctors at the Manchester Infirmary saw the need to isolate those who were taken with typhus by removing the sick into a 'House of Recovery' but they had a wider agenda which included access to homes, business premises and markets.

There was considerable controversy in Manchester about the possibility of establishing a House of Recovery, but the proponents of the scheme were in the majority and a meeting was held at the Bridgewater Arms Hotel, 7 January 1796:

> to consider of proper means to secure the general health of the town and neighbourhood of Manchester from the contagion of an infectious fever, which has long prevailed amongst the manufacturing poor.[19]

The meeting was very well attended and the Rev Mr Broomhead from Rook Street Chapel was there alongside the Rev Mr Kenyon missioner of St Mary's Roman Catholic Chapel at Mulberry Street. The Committee, known as the Manchester Board of Health, consisted of the Magistrates, the Physicians, Surgeons and Apothecaries of Manchester and Salford and the neighbourhood; the Boroughreeves, Constables, Churchwardens and Overseers of the

Poor of Manchester and Salford; the Committee of the Strangers Friend Society and fifty Gentlemen.

The meeting heard papers by Dr Percival, Dr Eason and Dr Ferriar as well as the Medical Gentlemen of Ashton-under-Lyne. Dr Percival presented the objects of the Board of Health. They were threefold:

> To obviate the generation of diseases;
>
> To prevent the spreading of them by contagion:
>
> To shorten the duration of existing diseases, and to mitigate their evils, by affording the necessary aids and comforts to those who labour under them.[20]

The first objective was to try to introduce measures which would attempt to stop the disease spreading. They needed to inspect the houses of the poor and try to improve their accommodation. It is through the list of the problems to be solved in the houses of the poor that we get a real picture of their living conditions in the last decade of the eighteenth century. Their houses were often built too close together; they were damp; they were ill-smelling and privies were too close to dwellings.

Dr Percival recommended the

> provision for white-washing and cleansing the houses of the poor, twice every year; attention to their ventilation, by windows with open casements.[21]

He also advocated the inspection of cotton mills and factories. The inspection reports should include:

> condition of health, clothing, appearance and behaviour of the employees and an indication of meal breaks at breakfast and dinner; the hours worked etc., the need for public baths; the cleaning of the streets; the removal of dung and other filth; the reduction of the smells from such businesses as the

fell-monger (a skinner); the tanner and the slaughter houses.

He then turned to the problems of markets in the Town 'with a view to the prevention of the sale of putrid flesh, or fish, and of unsound flour, or other vegetable productions'.[22]

His second objective, stopping the spreading of diseases by contagion considered:

> the speedy removal of those who are attacked with symp-toms of fever, from the cotton-mills, or factories, to the habitations of their parents or friends, or to commodious houses, which should be set apart for the reception of the sick in different districts of Manchester; the requisite atten-tions to preclude unnecessary communications with the sick in the houses wherein they are confined, and to the subse-quent cleansing and ventilation of their chambers, bedding and apparel; and the allowance of a sufficient time for perfect recovery, and complete purification of their clothes, before they return to their work, or mix with their compan-ions in labour.[23]

The third objective saw the need to arrange the supply of medical support; medicines; wine if appropriate, and fuel and clothing.

The key question[24] that had to be faced was whether the Committee of the Police was competent or not 'both to originate and effectuate the proposed reforms' or should the Board of Health 'be appointed by the committee of police, to act under their auspices, and to hold from time to time a communication with them', a third possibility might be a Board of Health nominated by 'the magistrates of the quarter sessions, and act under their auspices in connection with the committee of police'. The Justices of the Peace took charge of the reforms.

Dr Ferriar, from the Manchester Infirmary, then suggested that if lodging houses were to be licensed by the magistrates 'it would perhaps be sufficient to be at the expense of white-washing such places, as shall be reported to be infected and dirty'.

Concern was expressed about the number of ill-ventilated cellars and Dr Ferriar told the meeting that it would be necessary for him to explain to gentlemen, who had not visited such places, what these cellars were like and he proceeded to explain:

> that they each consist of two rooms under ground, the front apartment of which is used as a kitchen, and though frequently noxious by its dampness, and closeness, is greatly preferable to the back-room; the latter has only one small window, which, though on a level with the outer ground, is near the roof of the cellar, it is often patched with boards or paper, and in its best state, is so much covered with mud, as to admit very little either of air or light. In this cell, the beds of the whole family, sometimes consisting of seven or eight, are placed. The floor of this room is often unpaved; the beds are fixed on the damp earth. But the floor, even when paved, is always damp. In such places, where a candle is required, even at noon-day, to examine a patient, I have seen the sick without bedsteads, lying on rags; they can seldom afford straw.[25]

Dr Ferriar told the meeting that in those conditions infection ran from cellar to cellar. He supported the need for either renting a house or building a fever ward but preferred the latter. One of most revolutionary suggestions came from Dr Ferriar who suggested the building of small houses at public expense in a barracks-type plan which could be 'let at small rents, or gratuitously, according to the circumstances of the persons applying'.[26]

He was also concerned about the practice of smoking, for some people held that it could prevent infection, but he was quite

> confident that the acrid, irritating composition used by labouring people, is more likely to excite, than to prevent

disease; and I am persuaded that I have seen complaints in the stomach and bowels repeatedly occasioned by its use.[27]

Broomhead could easily have painted such a picture as Dr Percival and Dr Ferriar gave of the wretched conditions of the poor in their homes. He knew this from his own personal experience, visiting the sick and poor.

> The Board of Health, of which Broomhead had immediately become a committee member, passed a series of resolutions, 17 February 1796:

They ordered that an apartment be immediately prepared for the reception of persons sick of infectious disorders which was to be furnished and staffed with nurses. This apartment was to be known as the House of Recovery. The governance of the Institution was to be in the hands of a committee which was to be of 21 subscribers, and the physicians of the Manchester Infirmary. Every benefactor of five guineas became a trustee of the Institution. Three members of the committee constituted a quorum. The committee was to proceed with all convenient speed, in their enquiries into all the existing causes of infection, and to take all such steps as may to them appear necessary, to the accomplishment of the great object of the Institution of the Board of Health.

The final resolution was unanimously passed:

> that in order to defray the charges of the establishment, and support the House of Recovery, application be made to the clergymen of all denominations in Manchester & Salford, requesting that sermons may be preached, and collections made in their respective places of worship, as soon as possible, in aid of this charity and that subscriptions be now entered into, and further solicited, under the direction of the committee.

In 1784, ten years prior to the meeting at Manchester, the condition of apprentices and that means children, had come to the notice of the public, following a severe outbreak of fever at the Radcliffe mill of Sir Robert Peel the elder, which mill held nearly a thousand children many of whom were affected by the fever. The events in Radcliffe had come to the notice of the doctors at the Manchester Infirmary but it took Peel eighteen years to do something about the conditions in his mill.

The decisions of the meeting 7 January 1794, laid the foundation for the first Factory Act of 1802. Sir Robert Peel the elder introduced 'An Act for the Preservation of the Health and Morals of Apprentices and others, employed in cotton and other mills, and cotton and other factories' in 1802 under the guiding influence of Robert Owen, who was firstly a manager of Chorlton Twist Mills 1792 and later bought New Lanark Mill in 1799, who had attended the first meeting of the Board of Health at Manchester, 7 January 1796 and became a Board member alongside Broomhead. The Act was a step in the right direction but it was limited by its inadequate inspectorate.

This Act limited hours of work to twelve, forbade night work, and provided for instruction in reading, writing, and arithmetic. Boys and girls were to sleep in separate rooms and not more than two to a bed. Inspection was to be by a magistrate and a clergyman appointed by the local justices of the peace.[28]

The first House of Recovery was in an existing house at Portland Street and Aytoun Street corner opposite the Infirmary area, the frontage on Portland Street being 81 yards, and 45 yards along Aytoun Street.[29] It was opened in May 1797, but it was found to be too small for its needs, so further land was purchased adjacent to it, which already contained houses. There was a new House of Recovery built at the Chatham Street and Aytoun Street corner which opened in 1803. It had facilities for about a hundred patients.

As the new Institution contained a Board room there was no further need to hold meetings at the Bridgewater Arms Hotel.

Broomhead was a Board member from its inception. He was committee member no. 22. There are no 'Board' records available for the period 1796 to 1814 but from January 1815 to July 1820 the Monthly Board minutes are extant. During this latter period he attended sixteen meetings of the Board and took the chair on at least two occasions 3 September 1817 and 3 June 1818 and was a member of a select committee that surveyed the premises in Portland and Aytoun Streets, 2 April 1817. The success of the work of the Manchester Board of Health was recognised in the preface to the Proceedings of the Board of Health, 6 March 1805, which reflected on the controversy respecting the establishment of a 'House of Recovery':

> They have now the satisfaction to reflect, that in discussing the theory of contagious diseases, the minds of their fellow townsmen were relieved from many fanciful and absurd prepossessions; that the propriety and urgency of the measures proposed became more generally understood; and that a more powerful interest was exerted for carrying them into effect than could have been expected, had their merit been, in the first instance, allowed to pass unquestioned. The success which attended the execution of this scheme, and the important benefits which have resulted from it, having excited in the metropolis, and several of the principle towns throughout Great Britain and Ireland a very general desire to promote similar establishments.[30]

## 5. *The Manchester & Salford Lock Hospital & Asylum*

In September 1818, Joseph Jordan, William Brigham and Michael Stewart, surgeons in Manchester, with the sanction and support of William Simmons, the senior surgeon at the Manchester Infirmary, agreed to establish a Lock Hospital in Manchester.[31] In their view Manchester was amply provided with 'benevolent institutions for the relief of the sick and distressed poor' however there was a gap in provision for:

> the midnight wanderer (who) had hitherto no place of refuge even in a state of lingering disease nor could the poor unguarded youth when brought to the bed of sickness and distress be admitted as a patient in that benevolent institution the Manchester Infirmary.

A meeting was called to bring supporters together and they met at the Star Inn, Deansgate, Monday, 19 October 1818,[32] so that the instigators of this charity could set up a committee to administer the institution and to appeal for public subscriptions to establish the Hospital.

This committee transacted the everyday business of the Hospital. A ten guinea donation gave a person trusteeship for life whereas a guinea subscriber would have annual trustee status.

At the next meeting, Monday 30 November 1818,[33] at the Star Inn, Broomhead was one of those given the task of producing 'an address to the public on behalf of the Institution'. At the same meeting it was agreed that:

> the premises in Parliament Street engaged by Mr Brigham and Mr Jordan meet the general approbation of the trustees and that the medical Gentlemen be requested to open the Hospital for the admission of patients on Monday, 1 March 1819.

Broomhead frequently took the chair at the meetings of the Committee which were then held in the Board Room of the Hospital. He vacated the chair at one such meeting held 16 April 1819, and Dr Mitchell, who took the chair, moved:

That the thanks of the Meeting be given to the Reverend Rowland Broomhead for his able and impartial conduct in the chair.[34]

At a meeting, 23 April 1819,[35] a resolution was passed:

> that Mr Brigham and Reverend Rowland Broomhead be requested to attend the Quarterly Board of the Lying-in Hospital on the 3rd May to receive the proposals of the Trustees for the sale of their furniture and that they be empowered to treat for any part of the same.

The Committee had agreed with John Wadkin 12 July 1819:

> to take the two Houses in Cumberland Street belonging to you on a Lease of six years. The one nearest Deansgate to be entered upon immediately and the other as soon as R. Collier your present tenant leaves. The rent of the former to be thirty pounds and the latter twenty-eight pounds per annum.[36]

These houses appear to have met the Committee's needs for expansion to its accommodation, in order to include the Asylum. Cumberland Street and Parliament Street mentioned above were to be found on the right hand side of Deansgate between Bridge Street and Quay Street coming from the Cathedral end of Deansgate.[37]

The last weekly board that Broomhead attended was 20 May 1820.[38] At the Special General Board[39] of 22 May 1820, his place on the board was taken by his assistant priest at Rook Street, the Rev Mr Lupton.

## 6. The Portico Newsroom & Library

Known locally as the Portico Library it was established in 1806 at the corner of Charlotte Street and Mosley Street, Manchester. Its architect was Thomas Harrison and its builder Thomas Bellhouse. The foundation stone was laid in 1802 by Nathaniel Heywood of Heywood's Bank, Manchester and it opened in January 1806. It was established as a subscription library for a maximum of four hundred and the first proprietors paid an initial fee of thirteen guineas per share as well as an annual subscription of one guinea.

*29. A View of the Portico Library & Newsroom 1839*

There were already a number of libraries in Manchester: Chetham's, founded in 1657; The Old Manchester Circulating Library, in 1765; The Manchester New Circulating Library in 1792; the Manchester Literary and Philosophical Society in 1781, and the Manchester Reading Society, 1792.[40]

The need for a new library appeared to have arisen for two key reasons. The first was the massive increase of Manchester's population between 1770 and 1801 and the second, the apparent disquiet of some of the 'educated classes' at the effect that radicalism was having on the existing libraries. The difference with this proposed library was its concept of an institution 'that afforded a common ground, free of the political, professional or religious affiliations'. The members were 'drawn from a variety of middle class occupations and Protestant sects'.[41] It was this middle class that dominated the politics of the Town. The aims of the new library and newsroom were:

> to keep pace with the increasing population of the town and to gratify this thirst for knowledge, which is now so prevalent...promote a greater degree of intercourse amongst the inhabitants.[42]

The middle class members comprised a variety of occupations which were listed with the members' names in the minutes of the first committee of 1806. The chairman was Dr John Ferriar, a physician; the secretary, Dr Peter Mark Roget, a physician and author of the first thesaurus; and the treasurer, Nathaniel Heywood, a banker. The list of membership included the following occupations: Physicians, bankers, druggists, merchants, manufacturers, cotton spinners, one attorney and one dry-salter, cotton manufacturers, fustian and check manufacturers, one vicar, calico printers, small-ware manufacturers and merchants.

Besides the library, with its extensive catalogue, the newsroom contained forty different weeklies and periodicals. Members were able to purchase tea, coffee and soup in the newsroom but no alcohol was provided in the building. Members had the opportunity to play backgammon, draughts, chess and whist. The Portico was open from 8 a.m. to 10 p.m. in the winter but in the other seasons of the year it opened at 7 a.m. These hours suggest that most members lived nearby as did Rowland Broomhead a few streets away.

The Rev Edward Kenyon, who at that time was priest in charge at St Mary's Mulberry Street, had joined the library, 18 September 1807, and held share number 275 and transferred his ownership 8

March 1817. Rowland Broomhead was the second of the Catholic priests from the Manchester Mission to become a proprietor of the Newsroom and Library. On 14 April 1809 he became a subscription member under share number 221 which had been originally the share of Sir Robert Peel (1788–1850) when he was still a young man.

It is somewhat ironic that Broomhead should hold the share of a man who was later to be known as 'Orange Peel' because he displayed such anti-Catholic views. Other clergy of the Manchester Mission also joined the library, following the example of Kenyon and Broomhead. The Rev Thomas Lupton became a proprietor under share number 243, 9 June 1810, when he was curate to Broomhead. His share was transferred 6th September 1822, when he moved from Manchester to the chaplain's house at Hollin Hey, close to Old Garswood where he served the hall until his death 29 April 1843. It was his brother John who was a great benefactor to the Presentation Convent at Manchester, where his daughter was one of the nuns and Thomas was buried in the cemetery there.

The Rev Richard Rimmer, one of the executors of the will of Rev Rowland Broomhead, transferred the latter's share number 221, to the use of Rev John Ashhurst 19 January 1821. The Rev Joseph Curr, who was a witness to the previous transfer, and an assistant priest to Broomhead, became a member, 26 March 1818, under share number 370.

It was considered that 'not to be a member of the Portico was to be regarded as being outside the circle of Manchester cultural society'. Membership gave the Manchester priests a place where they could read the latest newspapers and also access books. It also gave Broomhead a chance to meet with the key gentlemen of the Town which was useful both in his charitable work and also the organisation of committees to deal with ongoing problems in the Town especially poverty and epidemics.

*30. The Interior of the Portico Library & Newsroom*

# Notes

1   M. Gaffey, *A Panegyric of the late Rev Rowland Broomhead, Forty-two years a Catholic Priest at Manchester* (Manchester, printed and published by J. A. Robinson, 1822) MCL: 922.2 B31).

2   Broomhead, A member of the Board 19 February 1787 (MI/B).

3   Anonymous writer transposed articles from the Manchester Exchange-Herald in Brief memoirs of the late Rev. Rowland Broomhead (Manchester, printed and sold by Joseph Aston,1820), p. 7–8.

4   Schedule of Deeds 1805–1809 (MI/QB).

5   The efficacy of port-wine 25 April 1796 (MI/B).

6   J. Blackburne, Minister at the Treasury, extract from his letter 25 April 1796 (MI/B).

7   A meeting for the appointment of a new physician 2 April 1812 (MI/B).

8   Rules and regulations 20 February1791 (MI/B).

9   Disorderly people accessing the Infirmary grounds, 31 October 1791 (MI/B).

10  Thanks to the officers 16 January 1792 (MI/B).

11  Thanks to Broomhead for his attentive and obliging behaviour 17 June 1819 (MI.B).

12  J. W. Bride, *A Short History of St Mary's Hospital, Manchester and the Honorary Medical Staff from the Foundation in 1790 to 1922* (Manchester, 1922).

13  See Appendix Eight: The Structure of the New Lying-in Hospital.

14  Weekly Board Book of the Lying-in-Hospital, October 1804 to August 1819 (MLH).

15  Broomhead, one of three trustees who prepared the annual report, 20 May 1806 (MLH).

16  Broomhead, received a subscription from Mr Gibson and Mr Leaf for the hospital, 15 August 1806 (MLH).

17  Letter to the clergy of Manchester asking them to preach a sermon to raise money for the Lying-in Hospital, 26 December 1806 (MLH)

18  Broomhead was a deputy treasurer and donated a guinea a year 1815–1820(MLH)

19  Meeting to establish a House of Recovery, 7 January 1796 (Minutes of the Manchester Board of Health 1796 to 1804) MCL: MC/614.0942 M13) p. 1.

20  Objects of the Board of Health (MBHM 7 January 1796), p. 3.

21  Dr Percival, White washing and cleaning (MBHM 17 January 1796).

22  MBHM, 7 January 1796, p. 6.

23  Stopping the spreading of diseases by contagion (MBHM 7 January 1796), p. 6.

24  Who should be in charge? (MBHM 7 January 1796), p. 7.

25  Description of cellar homes (MBHM 7 January 1796), pp. 12–13.

26  Small houses at public expense (MBHM 7 January 1796), p. 17.

27  The practice of smoking (MBHM 7 January 1796) p. 20.

28  P. A. Gregg, *A Social and Economic History of Britain 1760–1950* (London, George G. Harrap & Co.Ltd., 1950), p. 55.

29  F. A. Renaud, *Short History of the "House of Recovery" or Fever Hospital in Manchester* (Manchester, 1885).

30  Preface to the Proceedings of the Manchester Board of Health, 6 March 1805 (CMUH).

31  Manchester & Salford Lock Hospital & Asylum September 1818 (MSLHA).

32  Set up a committee (MSLHA 19 October 1818).

33  An address to the public (MSLHA 30 November 1818).

34  Thanks of meeting to Broomhead (MSLHA 16 April 1819).

35  Acquisition of furniture (MSLHA 23 April 1819).

36  Houses in Cumberland Street (MSLHA 12 July 1819).

37  J. Pigot, *A New Plan of Manchester and Salford* (Manchester, J. Pigot publisher, 1819), MCL: 25607).

38  Last meeting of Broomhead (MSLHA 20 May 1820).

39  Appointment of Rev Mr Lupton (MSLHA 22 May 1820).

40  A. Brooks & B. Haworth, *The Portico Library* (Manchester, Carnegie Publishing, 2000).

41  A. Kidd & K. Roberts, *City, Class and Culture* (Manchester, Manchester University Press, 1985), p.11.

42  Letter from Michael Ward, 25 January 1808, a founder member of the Public Library & Newsroom (Cowdray's Manchester Gazette).

# 10 BROOMHEAD 'THE POOR MAN'S FRIEND'

BROOMHEAD WAS NOT a lone figure in the care of the poor, for the needs of the poor had exercised the minds of previous generations. Every quarter of the year, the Overseers of the Poor would pay out to those in need. For example the quarter year, 27 June to 26 September 1812, paid out £559. 1s. 0d to three hundred and fifty seven persons called 'regular poor'; £2,541. 6s. 10d to one thousand two hundred and sixty persons called 'casual poor' and £1,404. 2s. 0d to five hundred and thirty-nine 'Irish poor'.[1]

The years 1778 to 1820 were years influenced by war. The wars that affected Britain were the War of American Independence from 1775 till 1783, the French Revolutionary wars of 1793 to 1802 and the Napoleonic wars, from 1803 until 1815. All of these wars involved Manchester soldiers and their families in great suffering. The inhabitants of Manchester in 1782 'raised a corps of 150 volunteers to serve during the war in America'.

The demands from a growing population, for housing, food, clothing and employment, within a dramatically changing town made life in Manchester very difficult. The growing population that came to work in the centre of this trading town and in the outer areas of the town, in the huge mills, brought with them demands for housing and much of it was substandard. A growing population needed more food, and supply was affected by weather and war and many vital commodities were often in short supply.

The movement from cottage industries to mechanised factories was not an easy change for people who did not welcome the changes or resisted the use of new machinery. Just a year after Broomhead arrived in the Town, 'serious riots broke out in Manchester and throughout Lancashire in 1779, because of the introduction of factories and machinery in place of the old handcraft'.[2]

Lack of food often gave rise to social tension. As a result of the failure of the harvests of 1794 and 1795 there were riots in Manchester in the July of 1795. As a result an order was issued closing all public houses at 7 p.m. and making all private persons give an account of themselves if found in the streets after 9 p.m.[3]

Affluent Manchester people would often subscribe funds to support the poor of the Town and they responded in August, following the riots of July 1795. The *Manchester Mercury*, 11 August 1795, recorded a meeting that was held at Manchester, 5 August 1795:

> At the meeting of the Subscribers to raise a generous amount for the Relief of the Poor of the Town of Manchester during the present Scarcity, held this Day at eleven o'clock, at the Bull's Head agreeably to public advertisement.[4]

The meeting supported seven resolutions:

1) That the money to be now subscribed, be applied to the Relief of the Poor, in the Town of Manchester, during the Scarcity and High Prices of Grain, Flour, and Oatmeal.
2) That a Committee of Eleven Subscribers be chosen to appropriate the Money subscribed for the above Purposes, and for defraying the necessary expenses incurred by the Committee
3) That Mr James Ackers be appointed Treasurer of this Fund; and that the Subscribers be asked to pay their Subscriptions, as early as possible, as the Money will be immediately wanted.
4) That it be recommended to the Committee, to offer Premiums to Persons bringing, betwixt this Day, and the first of

October next, the greatest quantities of Fish, Potatoes, and other Vegetables, to Retail in the Manchester Markets.

5) That two or more Gentlemen in each District be appointed by the Committee to collect subscriptions from House to House, within their several Districts.

6) That the Thanks of this Meeting be given to the Officers and Privates of the twenty-eighth Regiment of Dragoons, in the Barracks at Manchester, for their ready assistance given to the Civil Power during the late Riots; and that the Chairman be requested to communicate this Resolution to them.

7) That the Proceedings of this Meeting be signed by the Chairman, and published in Hand Bills and in both the Manchester Papers, and that the List of the Subscribers be also published in both Manchester Papers.

Broomhead, subscribed £2. 2. 0., to this charity, 18 August 1795, and became a committee member. Once the above resolutions were acted upon, subscriptions began to be taken up, and the premium system, which encouraged suppliers to stock the Manchester market, began to bring the food into the Town and the marketeers began to serve the poor. Premiums were suspended whenever there was an adequate supply of a particular item.

The Committee for the Relief of the Poor ordered, 16 January 1796:

> that potatoes shall be sold at Four Pounds a Penny, at the Market-Hall, every Tuesday, Thursday, and Saturday, from Nine to Twelve o'clock in the Forenoon, and from Two to Five in the Afternoon.[5]

In December 1796 the working classes were already on the verge of starvation and the gentry, clergy and tradesmen pledged themselves, in a series of resolutions, advertised in the newspapers, to reduce their use of wheat flour, at least one-third and pies and puddings ceased to appear on the tables of some of the middle classes.[6]

As a response to the food riots of 1799 in Manchester, 'Soup Shops' were set up to help feed the poor. The Soup Committee met, 13 November 1799, to request the collection of subscriptions; to thank Mr Yates for his gift of a 'Digester'; to agree the opening of a 'Soup Shop' at Copperas-street; and to agree the need for another 'Soup Shop' at Jackson's Row. They also ordered: 'that two thousand tickets be immediately printed, and given out in the proportion of twenty for every Guinea subscribed'. An invitation was made 'to Gentlemen in the country who have gardens, to send what vegetables they can spare to the Soup House, or give notice...that they may send a person to gather them'. Broomhead donated one guinea, which gave him twenty tickets to distribute to the poor.[7]

About four weeks later, Tuesday 10 December 1799, there was another meeting of the Inhabitants of Manchester, convened by the Boroughreeve, for the relief of the poor. The committee, approved by the previous meeting, dated 27 November 1799, agreed the following resolutions:

- That a large quantity of Potatoes be immediately purchased, and resold to the poor at a moderate price
- That a quantity of Meal be purchased, and resold to the poor at a moderate price.
- That encouragement be given for the more plentiful supply of the market, by granting premiums ... to such persons as shall bring the quantity of Meal or Wheat Flour to the Manchester market for sale, during the months of December and January ... these premiums to commence on the 14th of December instant. No premiums will be allowed to any person bringing less than six loads of Meal or wheat flour.

- That a quantity of Coals be immediately contracted for, to be deposited in convenient situations for retailing to the poor at reduced prices.
- That a Committee be appointed to carry the above Resolutions into effect; and that such Committee be composed of the following Gentlemen: The Magistrates of the Division of Manchester; The Boroughreeve and Constables of Manchester, The Churchwardens and Overseers of the Poor and twenty-two named Gentlemen (including Rev Rowland Broomhead). Any three of them were empowered to act.

At the same meeting, Manchester was divided into fourteen districts, and gentlemen were appointed to solicit subscriptions in their allocated district. Broomhead paid a second subscription of 10s. 6d to the 'Soup Shops', 31 December 1799.[8] The Manchester Mercury, also recorded a subscription of one guinea from him for the 'Soup Shops', 11 March 1800.

A further subscription of one guinea from Broomhead was recorded at a meeting held on Friday, 18 July 1800, at the Police Office and notice was given at that meeting, that the 'Soup Shops' would open the following Wednesday.[9] The main business of the meeting was to inspect the Treasurer's Accounts and to 'consult on the expedience and means of continuing of the Distribution of Soup to the poor inhabitants of this Town'. A special Committee was set up to audit the Treasurer's Accounts and Broomhead was elected to serve on it. A decision was made 'that no tickets would be delivered to Subscribers, but that every poor person, be served with soup for one penny per quart'.

The poor relied on receiving one of the tickets for relief from one of the benefactors of the Town, so if they did not manage to get a ticket they would have received no help. So the decision of the meeting of 18 July 1800 to cancel the ticket system and give access to all the poor persons, removed this possible discrimination.

Broomhead, as one of the Committee responsible for buying some of the goods for the Relief of the Poor, was one of those who were appointed at the meeting, 18 November 1800, held at the Police Office to purchase rice and coals.

A further meeting of the Committee for the Relief of the Poor, 27 November 1800, passed further resolutions:

- That straw beds and bedding, with different necessary articles of wearing apparel shall be provided for the use of the sick and destitute Poor.
- That Rice shall be bought and retailed to the Poor in general, at a reduced price, with a view not only to furnish a wholesome substitute for bread-corn, but likewise to induce the Poor to make a more general use of nutritious and palatable an article of food.
- That Coals be immediately purchased and laid up for the use of the Poor, during the most severe part of the Winter, at which time they may be retailed out to proper objects, in small quantities, and at an inferior price.
- That a Committee be appointed for the general management of all matters connected with this Charity... [10]

The Clergy of all Denominations in Manchester were appointed to the Committee, along with the civil authorities, the Manchester Infirmary staff, and fifty-three Gentlemen. [11]

The following letter, to the Inhabitants of Manchester, was printed in the Manchester Mercury, 2 December 1800, with the intention of encouraging further subscriptions for the poor. The first paragraph recognized the contribution of the wealthy of the town and the gratitude of the poor:

> During the pressure of last winter, when the increased price
> of corn deprived many of the labouring Poor of the power
> to support their families with food, the wealthy part of the

Inhabitants of this Town came forward with laudable alacrity, and subscribed most liberally, to relieve the wants of their indigent neighbours. The Poor received all donations with gratitude; and by their quiet and orderly behaviour have evinced their sense of the favours then bestowed upon them; and also their dependence upon the wisdom of the Legislature, joined with the beneficence of their richer neighbours for the alleviation of their present (—-) calamities. The Public have already been generally informed of the situation of the necessitous and sick Poor of the Town of Manchester. After a minute and diligent enquiry into the nature and extent of the present distress, a plan to afford prompt and efficacious relief has been maturely considered; but it is deemed necessary to introduce this Plan by a few observations on the necessity for its speedy adoption.

The second reflected on the problem of those with fever:

It appears that upwards of 288 Home Patients, chiefly labouring under Fever, are at this time entered on the Books of the Physicians belonging to the Infirmary. The Out-Patients amount to, at least, double that number; and although the wants of the latter, may not be so urgent as those of the former, yet, in general, the Out-Patients are incapable of earning more than a small portion for their subsistence.

The third emphasised the very real problems of extreme poverty:

To the pressure of sickness, extreme poverty is added; several of these miserable sufferers are compelled, from want of beds, to lie upon straw or filthy rags, spread on the damp floor of a cellar. The want of proper clothing among the Poor is universal. To support life, the scanty necessaries in their possession, have been sold for food: and in some instances, the only bed of the family has been disposed of in the morning, to furnish bread for the day!

The fourth concerned the financial situation and the lack of everyday needs:

> It is also manifested from the high price of all the necessaries of life, that the exertions of the healthy and industrious poor are inadequate to maintain a young family of an average number. The relief therefore of such individuals as are struggling with penury, and ready to fall into disease from the want of comfortable clothing, forms an indispensable part of the present plan; for by these means, the timely prevention of many maladies, (especially fever) may reasonably be expected.

The fifth referred to people who endured much and complained little:

> There is another class of Poor who have likewise claims to the sympathy of their opulent neighbours; such for example, who endure much but complain little; who are resolved to accommodate their wants to their narrow means: to such meritorious persons, rice and coals, at reduced prices, will furnish considerable aid. Besides, the partial substitution, of a wholesome and palatable article of food, for bread-corn, will be encouraged; and thus the liberality of the Public, will aid the wise intentions of the Legislature.

The last paragraph recognized the benevolence of the wealthy and the reason why it was more than just duty:

> The cause of the sick and distressed has always been benevolently cherished by the Inhabitants of this wealthy, commercial Town. In a season, therefore, of peculiar calamity, like the present, the exercise of their generous feelings may be indulged to their own gratification—to the rescue of the poor from want and disease, and to the Support of civil society, which is always exposed to violent shocks, from the pressure of temporary scarcity. And let it be remembered

that it is not only the duty and (...) interest of every one possessing the means, to contribute to the necessities of the sick and needy; but also with respect to future prospects we have the highest assurance, that 'He that giveth to the Poor lendeth to the Lord; and that by so doing he shall layup treasures in Heaven, and his reward be everlasting'.[12]

A Proclamation by King George III issued 10 December was printed in the *Manchester Mercury* 13 December 1800:

Whereas an Address has been presented to Us by Our two Houses of Parliament, requesting Us to issue Our Royal Proclamation recommending to all such persons as have the means of procuring other articles of food the greatest economy and frugality in the use of every specimen of grain. We, having taken the said Address, into consideration, and being persuaded that the prevention of all unnecessary consumption of corn will furnish, out of the forest and assert effectual means of alleviating the present pressure and of providing for the necessary demands of the year, have, therefore, in pursuance of the said Address and out of Our tender concern for the welfare of Our people, thought fit (with the advice of Our Privy Council) to issue this Our Royal Proclamation, most earnestly exhorting and charging all these of Our Loyal Subjects who have the means of procuring other articles of food than corn, as they tender their own immediate interests and feel for the want of others to practise the greatest economy and frugality in the use of every species of grain; and We do, for this purpose: more particularly exhort and charge all masters of families to reduce the consumption of bread in their respective families, by at least one third of the quantity consumed in ordinary times and in no case to suffer the same to exclude one quarter loaf for each person in each week; to abstain from the use of flour in pastry, and, measure, carefully to restrict the use thereof in all other articles than bread: and do also, in like manner, exhort and charge all persons who keep horses, especially horses for pleasure, as far as their respective circumstances will admit, carefully to restrict the consumption of oats and other grain for the subsistence of the farm. And we do hereby further charge and command every minister in his respective parish church or chapel, within the Kingdom of Great Britain, to read, or cause to be read Our said Proclamation, on the Lord's Day, for two successive weeks after receiving the said Proclamation. Given at Our Court of St James, the third day of December one thousand eight hundred, in the forty-first year of Our reign. God Save the King.

We, whose Names are hereunto subscribed highly approving of His Majesty's Proclamation, do hereby pledge ourselves to promote the objects of it to the utmost of our power.

Manchester, December 10, 1800.

Broomhead was one of the signatories and read the proclamation of the King to his community at Rook Street. A list of subscribers in the *Manchester Mercury*, 13 January 1801, recorded another donation from Rowland Broomhead of one guinea.

At a further meeting of the Soup Committee at the Police Office, 26 February 1801, it was resolved:

That the following Gentlemen be requested to take upon themselves the trouble of collecting Subscriptions for the support of the Soup Charity in their respective Districts; and that the Secretaries inform each of them by letter, of such nomination, which the Committee hopes they will accept, and compleat their collections as soon as possible, paying the same to Mr Nathaniel Gould, Treasurer. Districts eight and ten collectors, five in number, were: Samuel Smith, Rowland Broomhead, Richard Potter, William Starkie and Robert Peel, Junior.[13]

The 'Manchester Mercury', 14 April 1801, recorded the subscription collected from Districts Eight and Ten, by three of the collectors namely, Broomhead, Potter and Starkie, but Robert Peel, Junior, and Samuel Smith did not collect. The total of the Subscriptions collected were £1,330. 0. 0. Rowland Broomhead donated one guinea.[14]

On the 20 December of the same year, the 'Manchester Mercury' recorded, that Rowland Broomhead was one of the Committee for the Relief of the Poor.

The Boroughreeve and Constables posted a notice, dated 9 December 1808, which was printed in the 'Manchester Mercury' 13 December 1808, appointing a public meeting of the inhabitants of Manchester at the Police Office on the following Wednesday, the 14th at eleven o'clock in the forenoon. The purpose of the meeting was outlined as follows:

> On the re-establishment of Soup Shops in Manchester would be a species of Benevolence well applied to the relief of the Poor, at this season; and, under that impression, We beg you will be pleased to appoint an early Meeting of the Inhabitants for the consideration of the subject, as well as any other measure which may be calculated to relieve the necessitous.[15]

The public meeting, 14 December 1808, was convened 'for the purpose of determining the most eligible means of giving RELIEF to the NECESSITOUS POOR, during the WINTER MONTHS'. They resolved:

- That it appears to this meeting, that the Establishment of SOUP SHOPS is the best mode of administering Relief to the Poor.
- That a Subscription, at once proportioned to the exigency of the times, be immediately entered into
- That four or more Gentlemen be appointed in each District, to solicit Subscriptions.

- That a Committee be appointed...the Committee meet every Monday and Friday Evenings, at six o'clock precisely, and that three members be competent to act.
- That the attention of the Committee be particularly directed to have the Soup made good; and that one or more of its Members shall purchase the materials, superintend the making, to be present during the time of serving it out to the Poor.
- That the Soup be delivered out every Monday, Wednesday, and Friday, between the hours of eleven and one o'clock, at one penny per quart.
- For the convenience of the Poor, it is recommended, that Soup Shops be opened in three different parts of the Town.[16]

Broomhead was elected to this committee and in January 1809 was also a collector for Districts 8 and 10.[17]

According to the *Manchester Mercury*, 16 January 1812, Broomhead subscribed two guineas for the Relief of the Necessitous Poor. He was once again nominated to the committee 29 April 1812 and became a collector in Districts 8 and 10.[18]

A meeting of the inhabitants of Manchester was held at the Police Office, Thursday 14 November 1816: 'to take into consideration the best methods of relieving the Necessitous Poor'. The Committee, of which Broomhead was a member, resolved to take up subscriptions and to re-establish the distribution of soup which had been found a very reasonable relief.[19] Once again he became a collector for districts 8 and 10. The Manchester Mercury, 10 December 1816, recorded his subscription of two guineas to the fund.

In the Manchester Mercury, Tuesday 5 August 1817, there was a report of a meeting, at the Police Office, 30 July 1817, for the Committee for the Relief of the Poor of Manchester. The Rev Rowland Broomhead was in the Chair. The auditors reported 'that they had examined the Treasurer's Accounts, and the Accounts of the different 'Soup Shops' and 'Coal Wharfs', and that they had found the same to be correct'.[20]

After building the two churches of St Mary's and St Augustine's, Broomhead:

> still adhered to his own peculiar flock in Rook-street-which was in a very great degree composed of the poor, to whose necessities, temporal, as well as spiritual, he was a never ceasing benefactor. The poor he deemed more particularly his children, and he would not forsake them.[21]

Broomhead was responsible for carrying out the wishes of two benefactors, Mr William Moorhouse and Mr John Casey. He gave an account of money received and spent on account of the Poor Catholics of Manchester left by the late Mr William Moorhouse. William. was a butcher by trade and was entered in the Returns of the Papists 1767, which recorded him as resident for the previous seventeen years. When a gallery was being erected in the old chapel in Rook Street, the money ran short and Charles Houghton and Rowland Broomhead, both incumbents of that mission, were obliged to borrow money to complete the job. Forty pounds was borrowed from the Senior Catholic Sick Club, which debt was paid off by the two incumbents. Another forty pounds was borrowed from William Moorhouse. Broomhead recorded the repayment of most of the £40 but kept £10 which he left as a debt on the gallery of Rook Street till it could be paid off either by himself or another incumbent, but in the meantime paying ten shillings per annum interest to be paid to the poor.

William. Moorhouse died on or about eighteenth day of October 1795, and in his will of 10 February 1795, which was proved 13 March 1798, he bequeathed between £1,000 and £2,000 to his relations. His will recorded the following:

> It is my will that ten pounds be given to the Catholick
> Chapill (sic) for the use of the poor Catholicks (sic) in
> Manchester.[22]

According to Broomhead he received the sum of £10 for the poor,
24 June 1796 and paid interest of £3 for the period 1797 to 1802
through Rev R. Thompson to the poor and likewise £2 for the
period 1803 to 1806, through Mr Lupton.

The ten pound debt was divided and paid to the following poor
of the Mission: William Mitchell, George Warburton, Laurence
Fegan, Dorothy Carey, Mrs. Maini, William Yates, Betty Rider, Ellen
Rothwell and Cecily Flood each received a guinea and Elizabeth
Carty eleven shillings which brought this account to a close.[23]

John Casey, an Irish linen merchant, lived in Manchester for
many years and having retired from business in the Town relocated
to Chester where he lived independently and died 13 September
1792. The introduction to his will read:

> In the name of the most Holy and undivided Trinity the
> Father, the Son and the Holy Spirit, three divine persons
> yet one only God. Amen.
>
> I, John Casey of Manchester in the County of Lancashire
> Merchant being weak in health but of sound and disposing
> Mind memory and Understanding do make this my last Will
> and Testament in Writing in manner following that is to say
> I give to God my Soul hoping for Mercy through the Merits
> of my Lord and Saviour Jesus Christ And my Body I desire
> may be committed to the Earth in a plain coffin without any
> Plates or ornaments as privately as may be.

In his last will and testament he left a sum of money for the Poor
Catholics of Manchester which terms were clearly indicated:

> after the payments of his just debts and some few legacies the
> remainder and residue of his Personal property to Trustees

that they should place out this money on Mortgage, or Government security that the Interest of it might be forever hereafter applied to the relief of the Poor Catholics of this Town; not by the Priests except they be Trustees, but by their direction and appointment as expressed in his will.

An extract from his will expressed how the distribution of monies should take place:

And in order that the Monies left for that purpose [viz poor] may be applied properly I desire & it is my wish & Will that the sole disposal of the Yearly Interest of the Sum or Sums left for this purpose may always be disposed of by the Clergy the Catholic Incumbents in Manchester in the manner following that is to say— That when they visit the sick, or know any of their Respective Congregations to be in distress, they shall give them an Order for as much as they are of opinion is necessary for their immediate relief; & this order shall be directed to the Executor or Trustee who collect the rents & interests of the Monies so arising for that Charity, who they immediately on receipt thereof pay such sum as ordered by the Clergyman aforesaid—But the Clergymen Incumbents of Manchester aforesaid distributing this Charity, shall not at any time have the Interest of the Monies arising from this Charity given to them, but shall like good pastors order the distribution as directed above.[24]

The three trustees were Rev Rowland Broomhead, Richard Hope Price and Thomas Harold Gorman. The first named executor was Broomhead but he was also the incumbent of the Manchester Mission and, on the bankruptcy of Mr H. R. Price was then the sole trustee so he found himself in a dilemma, which he addressed as follows:

Now as I was the first named Executor to the late Mr Casey's Will & the first named Trustee to his effects & at this present time ever since Mr R. H. Price's Bankruptcy The only acting Trustee for Mr Casey I am therefore to Collect the Interest of this Money altho' an Incumbent & have to dispose of any part I may think necessary the same as any other Incumbent. This is going as near the Will as circumstances will permit. I, therefore (without giving a written ticket to myself ordering myself to relieve such a sick person) immediately that I see an object give him or her, what I judge necessary & place it to account. In like manner with respect to the other two Incumbents serving the Catholicks of Manchester, I do not require tickets, as it would employ too much of my time to wait in the house to receive such tickets & would be a very great inconvenience to many sick families (who are chiefly in immediate want of relief) to send such tickets I therefore get each Incumbent to put down in his pocket Book what he advances to the poor & on presenting me with a list with each person's name & the sum given him I repay him the amount. This, tho' perhaps not exactly agreeable to the words, yet is agreeable to the sense & meaning of the Will: for all he seems to aim at in his Will is, that the Incumbents or Priests shall not claim the interest in the bulk; & then say, they have given it away, without any one poor object's name being expressed, or, any other account given where or when such money was distributed.

After all debts and legacies were paid the residue of Casey's personal property amounted to £540. A further £300 was referred to in a codicil to his will. This money was to be given to his son John Casey if 'he became steady and likely to do well' but if the Trustees thought otherwise they were ordered to pay him the interest of it during his lifetime and at his death to let the capital be added to the Fund for the Poor.

The Trustees considered that as there never appeared the least prospect of his entering into any trade to do himself (sic) any good, they would withhold the capital and pay him the interest for life. Unfortunately, he perished in a shipwreck on the banks of Newfoundland, during the month of October 1795. As a consequence of John Casey's untimely death the £300 became part of the Fund for the Poor.

A short time before his death in 1820, Broomhead requested Benjamin Sanford, George Gibson and John Leeming to become trustees for the property which John Casey senior had bequeathed to the poor of Manchester. The trust deed that they signed consisted of the sum of £840, which was mortgaged on St Mary's Chapel, Mulberry Street; £300 that arose, with accumulated interest, out of the personal property of Mr Casey and was mortgaged against the chapel of St Augustine's Granby Row, Manchester.

In the death notices of the *Manchester Mercury*, 17 October 1820, the following statement was recorded by the paper:

> On Thursday, the Rev Rowland Broomhead, of this town; a Catholic Minister whose virtues and whose disinterested benevolence will be referred to with respect and veneration by all who knew him; to the Poor he was a kind and unsparing benefactor.[25]

Even in death, Broomhead remembered the poor:

> I order and direct my clothes and wearing apparel of every description and also such money as may arise from my debts owing to me by persons resident in Manchester unto and amongst such poor sick aged or infirm persons of the Catholic persuasion in Manchester and Salford or either of them and in such shares and proportions as my said executors or the survivor of them shall in their of his discretion think fit and proper

and I do give and bequeath the same and every part
thereof accordingly.[26]

The evidence of newspapers and letters, and by the witness, not just
of the thousands of his congregation, but the evidence of people of
other religions in the Town of Manchester, who called Broomhead
'The Poor Man's Friend', underpins the writings of Michael Gaffey:

> The poor who knew him knew it was his joy
> To cherish them, and all their wants supply;
> To hide their faults, to make their virtues known,
> And bear their sorrows as they were his own.
> To him they look'd as to a saint come down
> From the celestial city to their town
> To sweeten bondage, make their sorrows light,
> Remove their fears and fill them with delight.
> Thousands were, at his hospitable board,
> With food celestial and terrestr'al stored;
> Nor did he lack the means, for God had sent
> Sufficient to make him and them content –
> He was so—but the poor would oft abuse
> His generosity, and make bad use
> Of what he gave them, which to remedy
> He must refuse, or suffer poverty-
> The last he chose, and, to supply their need,
> Would often on the coarsest victuals feed.
> Others he clothed, tho' he himself oft wore
> The clothes he had worn threadbare long before:
> Nor can the muse (unless she soars above
> To search the book of life) compute his love,
> Such great solicitude was manifest
> In all he did to comfort the distrest[27]

The image that we get, from this poem is that of a person walking
with the needy and deeply involved in the traumas of the lives of
the poor and offering ways to comfort them in their distress.

Broomhead 'bears their sorrows as they were his own' and cherishes the poor with joy. There is no hypocrisy in his treatment of them. He gives with generosity from his own monies, wears threadbare clothes and would 'often on the coarsest victuals feed'.

Michael Gaffey emphasised Broomhead's charity:

His charity shone high above the rest
Of all his virtues, and was thought the best;
It had no limits-boundless, unrestrain'd,
In his pure breast this prince of virtues reign'd
Triumphant, and without the least controul.
Proud to inhabit such a god-like soul.

## Notes

[1]   *Publication of the accounts of the Overseers of the Poor 6 October 1812* (Manchester Mercury) CLM.

[2]   T. H. G. Stevens, *Manchester of Yesterday* (Altrincham, 1958), p. 74.

[3]   *Ibid.* pp. 81–82.

[4]   Manchester Mercury 11 August 1795.

[5]   MM. 2 February 1796.

[6]   Stevens, *Manchester of Yesterday*, p. 82.

[7]   MM. 19 November 1799.

[8]   MM. 31 November 1799.

[9]   MM. 22 July 1800.

[10]   MM. 27 November 1800.

[11]   MM. 9 December 1800.

[12]   MM. 2 December 1800.

[13]   MM. 3 March 1801.

[14]   MM. 14 April 1801.

[15]   MM. 13 December 1808.

[16]   MM. 20 December 1808.

[17]   MM. 10 January 1809.

[18]   MM. 5 May 1812.

[19]   MM. 19 November 1816.

[20]   MM. 5 August 1817.

[21]   Manchester Exchange Herald, 1820 (MCL).

[22]   *The last Will and Testament of William Moorhouse 3 March 1798* (LRO: WCW/3 March 1798).

[23]   *The William Moorhouse & John Casey Charities 1794–1847* (The Account Book of Casey's Charity Trustees of Manchester & Lancashire FHS 2004 (SDA).

[24]   *The last will and testament of John Casey* (LRO: WCW 17 September 1792).

[25]   MM. 17 October 1820.

[26]   *The last will and testament of Rev Rowland Broomhead* (LRO: WCW 1821).

[27]   Gaffey, *A Panegyric of the late Rev Rowland Broomhead.*

# 11 SUNDAY SCHOOLS AND FREE SCHOOL

THE DRIVING FORCE to overcome the illiteracy of the working classes mainly came from the churches. The 'idea of the Sunday school, as a direct adjunct of each congregation was first put into practice by Robert Raikes at Gloucester in 1780'.[1] His aim was to teach the children to read, to know the catechism, and to see that they went to church. The Sunday schools:

> seemed to the mind of the time to be a new Revelation of how crime could be prevented … The magistrates were not thinking of Sunday schools as religious institutions, branches of church organisation, fields for devoted personal Christian service. They were thinking in practical terms of the schools as rescue agencies, as a means of reforming the lives and characters of the uneducated classes—the main source of crime and threats to property.[2]

The various parties involved in the debate, traded bitter arguments, but the key fear underlying this acrimonious debate was that the children of the poor would be educated and would then want to remove themselves from their station in life which would undermine trade and manufacturing:

> The charity school is another universal nursery of idleness; nor is it easy to conceive or invent anything more destructive to the interests and very foundation principles of a nation entirely dependent on its trade and manufactures than the giving an education to the

children of the lowest class of her people that will make
them contemn (to treat as of small value) those drudg-
eries for which they were born.[3]

Sunday schools were first introduced into Manchester in 1784 by
Thomas Fildes and the first one was started at Gun Street in
Ancoats, in the cellar of a shoemaker. Within a short time two
others were established, one in a garret and the second in a purpose
built room in proximity to London Road. The success and popu-
larity of this new system encouraged people to demand further
Sunday schools and a public meeting was called for Friday, 24
September 1784, at the Bull's Head, in Manchester.

The Manchester Sunday School movement was formally initiated
in an advertisement which appeared in the Manchester Mercury, 10
August 1784, entitled 'An Address to the Public on Sunday Schools':

> The neglect of it (education) is one principal Cause of the
> Misery of Families, Cities and Nations: Ignorance, Vice and
> Misery, being constant Companions. The hardest Heart
> must melt at the Melancholy Sight of such a Multitude of
> Children, both Male and Female, in this Town, who live in
> gross Ignorance, Infidelity, and habitual Profanation of the
> Lord's Day. What Crowds fill the Streets! Tempting each
> other to Idleness, Play, Lewdness, and every other Species of
> Wickedness ... To attempt a remedy is laudable and divine.[4]

A subscription book was opened at the Exchange Coffee Shop and
by 21 September 1784 there were twenty-five schools attended by
1,800 children.[5]

It was agreed that the Sunday schools would be non-denominational. The Roman Catholics took part in the new arrangements.
The incumbent of Rook Street Chapel was Rev Charles Houghton
since 1778 and Rev Rowland Broomhead was his assistant. It was
Charles Houghton who represented the Roman Catholics in this

Sunday school movement in the early years from 1784 until Broomhead took over from him in 1787.

The members of the Committee came from the Tory and Whig parties and representatives of the churches. The rules and orders for the governance of the Sunday schools were drawn up.[6] The arrangements for Manchester closely followed those used in Leeds, where they had divided the town into seven divisions; set the time for attendance as 1pm till evening; masters instructed the children in reading, writing and the principles of Christianity; a form of prayer was used; the masters conducted the children to the church at some time in the afternoon; inquisitors were appointed to visit schools; funds were raised by house to house collection; the teachers were paid 2s., 1s. 6d or 1s. Per Sunday according to their qualifications, and rooms and houses were hired for 30s. 21s. or 15s., on a yearly basis.

The town of Manchester was divided into five separate districts called: Christ Church; St Mary's; St John's; St Ann's & St Paul's, after the five Anglican churches. The buildings that housed the Sunday schools were rooms in houses, warehouses or factories.

Children under the age of six could not attend. Those who were eligible had to get a subscriber's recommendation, but children whose parents were considered able to send their children to a private school were not eligible. Annual subscriptions and collections taken up at the churches funded the Sunday schools and sometimes collectors went, door to door, to request donations. Sermons were preached in the Anglican churches, the Dissenters' chapels and the Roman Catholic chapel at Rook Street, and after 1795 at St Mary's Mulberry Street as well.

The hours of attendance were 'October to February, 9 to 12 and 1 to 4; March to September, 9 to 12, 2 to 5'.[7] In the case of Dissenters, which included the Roman Catholics, they could choose to attend a school, which was run by a master of their religious persuasion; otherwise they had to attend the nearest school to their home in the district. School visitors exercised control over the schools and reported to the Committee, and they were also responsible for 'the time and mode of attendance at divine service'. The masters were paid 1s. 6d. a day and the under-masters and mistresses 1s. Pupils who swore, lied or profaned were expelled.

The school opened and closed with prayer. All children were expected to be taught the catechism of their particular faith so Roman Catholics would have used the Catechisms for the use of the Northern District, called the 'Little Catechism' and their prayer books would have been specifically Catholic, such as 'The Daily Companion', which contained a preparation for the sacraments. Prizes of books were given for regular attendance and proficiency and these were chosen for their Catholicity.

Charles Houghton was one of the eight gentlemen 'deputed to examine the qualifications of the Masters for the Christ Church District' 6 November 1784 and on 6 December 1784; he was also charged with the role of visitor to Parsonage Lane School in St Mary's District.

In a resolution 6 June 1785, the secretary was requested to send a circular letter to the Clergymen of the different Churches requesting their assistance in catechising the Scholars of their respective districts. A further resolution, 1 August 1785, requested:

> that the Clergymen of the different Churches, preach an annual sermon for the Sunday school charity, on different Sundays in the month of September and that notification of the sermon should be given in the public papers of the preceding week, so that all the children belonging to the district of that particular Church, where the sermon was preached, together with as many from other schools, as can be conveniently accommodated with room, should attend on that occasion.

The Bishop of Chester, Beilby Porteus, wrote to Thomas B. Bayley, chairman of the Sunday School Charity, 11 August 1785, which appears to have been written after the chairman, had sent the Bishop certain papers regarding the charity:

> The Institution of the Sunday Schools, I have always considered as one of the most probable means of diffusing sentiments of virtue and Religion amongst the common people. They are more especially necessary in such populous manufacturing towns as Manchester, where the children are, during the week days, generally employed in work, and on the Sunday are too apt to be idle, mischievous and vitious. It is, therefore, with peculiar satisfaction I see this matter taken up, by such respectable Gentlemen at Manchester, and carried on with so much vigour and success.

The list of the different churches of 5 September 1785, where sermons were to be given, did not include Roman Catholics. The resolution of the Committee, 3 October 1785, and that of, 7 November 1785, suggests that a problem had arisen regarding the Roman Catholic School in Black Friars. Robert and Mary Turner, teachers at the school, at their own request, had asked for the school to be discontinued and that their salary be paid up to the 20 September last, and the resolution had been carried. However, on 7 November 1785, on representation to the Committee, that the discontinuance of the Roman Catholic School was a mistake, it was resolved:

> that the same school should be continued at the desire of that people under its present form and that the Rev Mr Houghton, Mr Newham and Mr Thomas Philips be nominated as visitors.

This suggests that the Turners had rescinded their decision to leave the school. The Committee referred to the Sunday school as a Roman Catholic school, which might suggest that all the Sunday schools were defined by the religious affiliation of their occupants.

In a resolution, 2 January 1786, the committee decided to rescind a previous resolution which limited the number of children to be instructed for the year 1786, to 3,000, and allow that entire offer to be admitted. From 3 April 1786 children were ordered to come to School in the afternoons, at half-past one and be dismissed at five. In the same year, 2 October 1786, it was resolved 'that a sermon be preached at the Romish Chapel on 1st November', which was St Chad's, Rook Street.

In August 1786, in the face of a recent crime wave in the Salford Hundred, the magistrates acclaimed the work of the Sunday schools and requested that more of these schools should be opened:

> That where Sunday schools have been opened, their good effects have been plainly perceived in the orderly and decent Comportment of the Youth who are instructed therein: That it is therefore most earnestly to be wished that those virtuous Citizens who have begun this good work, would continue their efforts to forward it, with that Zeal and Perseverance that its great Importance requires; and that if these Institutions should become established throughout the Kingdom, there is good reason to hope they will produce an happy change in the general Morals of the People, and thereby render the Severities of Justice less frequently necessary.[8]

In 1786 the Committee resolved 'that no teacher shall be permitted to instruct any children belonging to the Sunday schools in writing on the Lord's Day'.[9]

There was a record made 2 April 1787 that the Rev Mr Houghton was on the visitors committee, and at the same meeting it was resolved to hold meetings, from then on, at the Spread Eagle in Hanging Ditch. The Committee was concerned that having children working on a Sunday stopped them attending school which defeated the aim of the Sunday schools. They resolved 2 July 1787:

> that an address to the Public be drawn up against the growing
> evil of working on Sundays a practice which has so obvious
> a tendency to defeat the good affects of this Institution.

Mr Houghton left the Manchester Mission 1787 and in the light of the appointment of Broomhead to be the senior priest at Rook Street it is clear that the Catholic Sunday Schools would have needed a leader from the Mission to take charge immediately and we can presume that Broomhead took up this role for he was mentioned later as a committee member.

In 1788, it was decided by the Committee, that they should open one school in each of the five districts to give instruction for grown up persons. This was a significant decision and probably the first evidence that the Sunday school movement was moving to introduce adult education which would have had the potential to raise the hackles of people who resented progress for the lower classes.

The Committee 6 July 1789 agreed that the annual sermon should be given at the 'Romish chapel'. There is no record of monies raised. On 2 August 1790, the preaching of the annual sermon was once again allocated to the Roman Catholic Chapel and an entry for, 31 October, recorded a sum of £36. 15. 0 collected for the charity. At the July meeting the Committee was trying to decrease the number of teachers by increasing class sizes:

> Resolved that the Visitors be requested to examine the state
> of their respective Schools and see if they cannot reduce the
> number of teachers, allowing forty children to each teacher.

Rowland Broomhead was appointed 4 April 1791, as one of the vice-presidents of the Charity and it is the first mention of him in the charity minutes. At a meeting of the Sunday School Committee 4 July of the same year he was in the chair and also took the chairmanship 1 August 1791. A sermon was given by Broomhead

13 November 1791, at the Catholic Chapel, Rook Street, which raised £30.

Not everybody of Roman Catholic persuasion was happy about the introduction of non-denominational Sunday schools for on the 9 December 1791, George W. Coombes wrote a letter from Bath, to William Gibson, Vicar Apostolic of the Northern District an extract of which read as follows:

> A paragraph appears lately in the papers that a collection had been made at the R. [Roman] Cath [Catholic] Chapel in Manchester for the support of the Sunday Schools. I suppose it was inserted without any foundation in truth … [10]

Coombes was a Roman Catholic priest, theologian and writer but despite this letter, William Gibson continued to allow the clergy to be involved in the Sunday school movement.

The Charity minutes, 2 January 1792 recorded:

> that in the future it would be presumed that every school would be provided with a Book, in which would be entered the names of all the children who attended that school, and marked every Sunday, whether present or absent: This Book had to be produced to the Overseers (of the Poor) once or twice in every month. All parents receiving pay from the town and neglecting to send their children regularly to the Sunday school would, by this means, be strictly noted.

A meeting of the Committee, 6 February 1792, decided:

> that the general visitors be requested to wait on the Visitors of the School in Angel Meadow and recommend to them the letting of the School Room for the weekdays as a School for the benefit of this Charity.

This was an important change, for the first time the Committee were supporting the development of day schools. A further advance in educational opportunity came, 3 December 1792, when the Committee:

> Resolved that a School be opened for the purpose of instructing grown up young women and another for young men in Manchester & two others for the like purpose in Salford.

Political bias appeared in the meeting of 7 January 1793, which stated:

> that every visitor be requested to discharge any teacher or assistant who shall prove to be disaffected to the present Government. (This would have been the administration of Pitt the Younger, often referred to as a Tory who called himself an 'independent Whig').

From the meeting of 1 July 1793 it was clear that the teachers were responsible for cleaning the schools and providing the cleaning materials, for the committee, resolved:

> that no allowance shall be made to any Teacher for Brooms, brushes or other implements used for cleaning the Schools.

Spelling was an important part of the curriculum and the committee 2 September 1793 resolved:

> that Mr Walker be requested to purchase Three Dozens of bound Spelling Books for the use of the Catholick School No. 3.

The Sunday school movement continued to expand for the committee, 7 April 1794, agreed that the Rev M. Cheek's motion 'for a Sunday School at the New Bayley be complied with and that Rev M. Cheek be appointed visitor'.

The use of the Sunday school rooms for other educational work continued afoot for the committee, 7 July 1794, agreed:

> That school no. 31 in Ancoats Lane be allowed to teach writing to the Sunday Scholars on Wednesday evenings; and that the sum of Four pounds & Ten Shillings be allowed

the Visitors of that school to provide desks to write on &
also ink stands. All other expenses attending this business
are to be paid for by the Visitors themselves.

Mr Hall was asked by the General Committee, 7 December 1795,
to write 'to the two Romish Ministers to preach a Sermon at their
respective Chapels for the benefit of the Sunday schools'. The first
chapel was that of Broomhead's at Rook Street and the second was
that of the Rev Edward Kenyon at Mulberry Lane. The sermon at
Mulberry Street was the first given at that chapel.

The Trustees of the Sunday Schools, meeting 4 April 1796, made
Rev Rowland Broomhead a Vice-President. In the same year, 5
September, they resolved that 'every child hereafter to be admitted in
a Sunday school must have a recommendation signed by a subscriber'.

Broomhead, in his capacity of a vice-president, was present at
the committee meeting, 3 July 1797 and 8 October 1798.

There was now a growing concern about Sunday schools teaching on the Sabbath which was articulated by the parson of Mellor
Church near Stockport:

> Those Sunday schools are direct violations of the law
> of the Sabbath (1) where any kind of learning is taught
> during the season of public worship and made to serve
> instead of it, and (2) where any instructions are given,
> on any part of the day, which relate only to this world,
> and not immediately to the soul. In all such cases, both
> the teachers and the taught are employed in profaning
> the Lord's day, instead of keeping it holy, and improv-
> ing it for the soul's spiritual advantage.[11]

In response, Joseph Mayer, a teacher from Stockport:

> contended that as the children had to go in relays to church,
> since there were so many of them, it was better to occupy
> them in writing than to turn them loose.

Discord broke out among the members of the Manchester Sunday School Committee for the Anglicans, as against the Methodists and Dissenters which included the Roman Catholics, did not usually accept the teaching of writing in their Sunday schools.

The first signs of dissension within the Sunday school movement in Manchester came to light at a meeting held, 3 December 1798, when the committee:

> Resolved that the Rev Mr Clowes, Mr William. Wright and Mr Richard Barlow be requested to wait upon Dr Bayley to desire that he will preach a Sermon this year, in order to do away the Report that he has some serious objection to this Establishment.

At the meeting, 4 February 1799, no answer was received from Mr Bayley respecting his preaching for the Charity. This was a serious matter, for Dr Thomas Bayley had been the chairman of the Charity since its inception.

Broomhead was present at the Board 4 March 1799, which 'resolved that as many Children as can conveniently be accommodated shall be brought once every Sunday to their respective places of worship'. This was a new directive and suggests that pressure was coming from a majority to make sure the children of each denomination separated once a week, rather than once a month, and attended at their own places of worship.

Meanwhile there was a financial problem concerning Catholic School No. 3. The general Board, 1 April 1799:

Resolved that the Quarter due to the Catholic School No. 3 is not to be paid for the present, Rev Mr Broomhead promises to preach a sermon before Whitsunday for the benefit of the Sunday Schools. He wishes that the state of his school may be calculated from the beginning to determine how the account really stands.

Broomhead was unclear about how the accounts had been kept for School No. 3, since its inception. It is quite clear from this passage that he was the key Catholic representative on the Committee. At the same meeting of the Board, Rev C. P. Middleton declared that he would, that very night, resign his office of Secretary. This was the beginning of the breakup of the Non-Denominational Sunday school movement in Manchester.

On 3 June 1799 the committee resolved:

> that Mr A. Place & Mr Wm. Wright be delegated by this committee to wait on the Rev Dr Bayley & the Rev Mr Middleton, to show them the old rules, from which the Committee have agreed this evening not to depart & to request them to preach for the support of the Charity & to catechize the Children belonging to it. The Rev Gentlemen are further requested to return their answer in writing to the Committee adjourned to the 17th June for the purpose of receiving the same.

At the adjourned meeting of 17 June 1799, they revisited the rules and resolved:

> that the 14th rule (Children of all Protestant Dissenters, shall if possible have Masters provided for them of their own persuasion) be interpreted as relating to all the Children of this Charity who are thereby ordered to attend Divine Service in their respective places of worship.

This resolution took away choice and demanded that a scholar attend the church of his place of worship and the school of the same faith. The original constitution of 1784 was at this point under attack. The committee decided to find out whether there was still support for the original constitution and resolved, 1 July 1799:

> that the Clergy be applied to, to know whether they be willing to support the Institution according to its original plan as set forth in the present Rules ... that a select committee be appointed to consider of the best plans calculated to

allay the present Dissensions, & settle the Institution upon
solid ground.

The meeting of the select committee took place, 12 July 1799, and
resolved:

- that the management & direction of the seminaries shall be
  vested in a committee consisting of subscribers of one guinea
  each & that all the Clergy in the Towns of Manchester &
  Salford shall be considered as Members of the Committee
- that it is the opinion of this Committee that the Institution of
  the Sunday School in Manchester & Salford, on the broad basis
  on which they were first established & conducted according to
  the Rules which were originally & have been since agreed upon,
  has been attended with the most beneficial consequences &
  therefore deserves every support & encouragement.
- that it is the opinion of this Committee that the abuses lately
  complained of in regard to the attendance of the children at
  their respective Places of Public Worship are such as the present
  Rules of the Institution, if rightly enforced would sufficiently
  obviate & that therefore nothing is wanting towards the Regu-
  lation of such abuses, but to enforce the present Rules.
- that it be earnestly recommended to the general Committee &
  to the Visitors of the Particular Schools, as a means of correcting
  the abuses complained of, to attend especially to the Observance of the Rule which requires that the Children be taken
  regularly every Lord's day to their respective places of Public
  Worship, from the consideration & under the Persuasion, that
  the Principal use of the Institution of the Sunday schools is to
  habituate the children to a pious & orderly Observance of the
  Sabbath Day, & of the duties to which it points; & that whatever
  advantages may be derived from learning to read, it is a benefit
  of far higher Importance & more essential concern, to impress

on young minds a devout sense of Duty towards God & their Neighbour, by introducing them early into the habits of public & private Worship, & thereby forming them to the Love & Practice of all Christian Virtues.

It was clear that the select committee did not feel that any changes were necessary and deserved every support and encouragement, for the charity had been attended with the most beneficial consequences. There may well have been abuses with regard to the rule of, 17 June 1799, but they recommended that the children were regularly taken to their churches.

By the second of December the committee had decided that the following should be inserted in the rules:

> that the Children shall attend regularly their respective Places of Public Worship, as weather & other circumstances will admit, & that the Visitors shall determine the Rotation in which the Children shall attend.

At the same meeting they decided to transmit a copy of the new rule to:

> Dr Bayley & Mr Middleton, attended with a note from the Secretary, to signify, that if they do not declare Waiting to the Committee at their next Monthly Meeting their intention to preach, as soon as ever they can make it convenient for the Benefit of the Institution, they shall be considered as excluding themselves from being members of the Committee.

At the meeting of the committee, 6 January 1800, it was resolved unanimously:

> that the Rev Dr Bayley & the Rev P.P. Myddletton (sic), having expressed their Disapprobation of the present Rules for the Management of the Sunday Schools, & their unwillingness to preach or subscribe for the Benefit of the Institu-

tion, be considered as excluding themselves from being Members of the Committee, according to the first Rule.

This brought about the secession of the Church of England Sunday schools from the union of all the churches, involved in the original agreement of 1784. On 10 March 1800, Bayley and Middleton, in what appeared to be an attempt at compromise, proposed:

> That the scholars, attendant upon any Church, shall be sent one Sunday in four to attend Divine Service, considering four Schools as attendant upon that Church

The meeting answered, that the Rule already left discretion to the Visitors.

A preamble, at the meeting, 5 May 1800, described the events of those last few months which had brought disunity into the open and had materially affected the Charity:

> Much Dissatisfaction giving for sometime prevailed in the minds of many Persons well affected to the Institution of Sunday Schools respecting the management of such school in this Town & the Funds having in consequence materially suffered in order to obviate every cause of complaint & restore that good Understanding & mutual co-operation which formerly prevailed amongst the Members of the Committee & eventually to re-establish the Funds.

Three propositions were recommended 'unanimously by the Clergy to their approbation'. They were as follows:

- That a certain Number of Schools, bearing an adequate Proportion to the Contributions made by Members of the Church of England, shall be set apart & assigned to the sole Government of the Clergy & their friends to be called School under the Establishment or Church-of-England Schools
- That the Schools so set apart shall as heretofore derive their support, as to all necessary expences (sic), from the Funds of

the General Committee; the Clergy contributing their best assistance towards maintaining & improving such Funds

• As the Committee must be expected to disdain all Interference in the future Management & regulations of Schools under the Establishment the Clergy shall engage to renounce all Authority over the remaining Schools.

It was the meeting of 5 May 1800 that marked the break of the Anglicans and the Dissenters, the latter of which included the Roman Catholics. The Anglicans divided the parish of Manchester into ten districts each under a parish clergyman. The Dissenters continued as a group and called themselves the 'Sunday School of All Denominations' but within a short time some Dissenters, including the Roman Catholics, elected to leave.

When the Catholics opted out is unclear but in a letter from Rowland Broomhead to Bishop William Gibson 31 August 1804, it suggests that the 'Catholic Sunday Schools' may have been an entity of their own at that time for Broomhead used a title, 'The Poor Children of the Catholic Sunday Schools' rather than a title which included the other members of the 'Sunday School of All Denominations':

> The Poor Children of the Catholic Sunday Schools (who work in the Cotton Factories from 5 o'clock in the Morning to 8 at night) and they worked Saturdays and some were being forced to work on a Sunday as we have already seen. This amounts to 15 hours per day and 75 hours for a five-day week.

According to the same letter, the children had also subscribed a half penny a week to buy religious books: 'This has also given them another good resolution of each subscribing a half penny a Week to be spent in Religious Books'. In the non-denominational Sunday schools the books would have been provided from the funds which suggest that the Manchester Catholic mission were in need of funds for their Sunday school necessities as they were now on their own.

The Catholic Board, of which the clergy were ex officio members, was certainly in existence in 1813 and was set up to provide day schooling for the Catholics of Manchester and Salford and also had a remit to oversee the Catholic Sunday schools.[12] Statistics recorded that in 1816 there were three Catholic Sunday schools in Manchester and Salford with 1,674 scholars.[13]

In a letter from Rev Thomas Lupton, assistant to Broomhead at Manchester, to Bishop William Gibson, 24 December 1816, he raised the subject of:

> Bishop Hay's *Pious Christian* published at Dublin from which it appears that a society has been formed of pious lay persons throughout the different parishes of Ireland, with the consent and approbation of the bishops for the purpose of instructing the ignorant in the principles of religion and the Christian doctrine; and in order to stimulate and encourage them in this pious undertaking the late Pope Pius 6th thought proper to annex certain indulgences to the performance of so meritorious a work.

Thomas Lupton told the Bishop:

> I should wish much to see a similar society established among us with your Lordship's approbation being fully persuaded that the benefits arising from such an institution here, would be almost incalculable, particularly to the Children of our Sunday Schools who amount to nearly a thousand besides numberless others, who would by this means be initiated in the principles and duties of their religion. Will your Lordship therefore allow us to form a similar society, adopting exactly the same rules and regulations as mentioned above and which have been approved of by the Bishops in Ireland, allowing at the same time the

members of the society here the same indulgences granted
by the late Pope Pius 6th.

There is no evidence to show whether the bishop agreed or not but
the former is more likely as he would have had permission from
Broomhead to approach the bishop.

In a letter dated 31 August 1804, from Broomhead to William
Gibson, he referred to the raising of funds for Ushaw College, but
in a short phrase about the amount of money that might be raised
he obviously had the education of boys on his mind:

> If anything was raised more than necessary for the
> Building, it might be appropriate for establishing funds
> for the education of Boys, for which every well wisher
> to Religion must be very anxious.[14]

Michael Gaffey described Broomhead's aims for establishing a free
school for poor illiterate children in Manchester:

> ... a free-school prov'd his next concern,
> That poor illiterate children might learn
> The rudiments of useful knowledge, and
> Have every word in scripture at command,
> Be taught their faith, practice each principle
> Defend the same with proofs invincible
> Against it's enemies, espouse the cause
> Of loyalty, and vindicate the laws.

A letter from Rev Rowland Broomhead, Rev Mr Kenyon and the
Rev Thomas Lupton addressed to the Right Rev Dr William
Gibson, Old Elvet, Durham, dated 25 March 1813, informed him
that a fund had been set up at Manchester for the education of the
poor children of the Catholic congregation and emphasised the
need for donations:

> The inclosed will inform you of the Resolutions entered into
> by the well disposed Catholics of this Town to proceed

without delay in establishing a fund for educating the numerous poor children of our Congregation. On a calculation of the necessary expenses attendant on this Institution we find ourselves forced to look round for pecuniary assistance; & therefore take the liberty of requesting your Charitable attention in promoting so desirable an attainment, your donations will be thankfully received by your humble servants.[15]

The letter also included a printed statement about Catholic Schools which emphasised the importance of day schools, which had been established in Manchester by those of other religions and that it was timely for the Catholics of the town to replicate that system of education, where the Catholic poor could be taught reading, writing and accounts:

Taking in to consideration the very great advantages arising from the institution of day Schools, in which indigent parents may have their children regularly taught Reading, Writing, and Accounts; benefits which the Established church, and other denominations, liberally bestow on the children of their respective congregations; it would be a reflection, no ways creditable to the better circumstanced CATHOLICS of this town, to withhold any longer their charitable aid towards founding and supporting a similar institution, for the poor children of their own communion.

The letter asked for donations, which would allow donors who subscribed one guinea or more, to recommend two children per one guinea:

It is therefore proposed, without delay, to solicit annual subscriptions for this. The better to promote their liberality, it is also proposed that an annual subscriber of one guinea, shall be empowered to recommend two children; a subscriber of two guineas, four, and so in proportion.

Broomhead and his fellow clergy sent this letter to the Bishop on the very day of the institution of the school:

> This Institution is to take date from March 25, 1813; and at the expiration of each year, every subscriber will be furnished with a printed Report of the Receipts and Disbursements, properly audited, together with the sums subscribed by each individual.

According to Michael Gaffey it was Broomhead and his friends who were responsible for the success of establishing the free school:

> This holy father and his friends did raise
> A house of learning, for the public good,
> That all might sacred wisdom gain who would.
> Thus did the worthy hero of my tale
> Gainst satan, sin, and ignorance prevail
> For many a year, with wonderful success,
> None more belov'd than he, none hated less.

When Rowland Broomhead built St Augustine's Church in Granby Row Manchester in 1820, he made provision for the children of the mission to be educated, in a vast schoolroom underneath the church, which was built to hold a thousand pupils. Michael Gaffey described it:

> Beneath the floor a school, of vast extent.
> (For upwards of a thousand scholars meant)
> Lies coextensive with the church, and shews
> Sixteen cast iron pillars, set in rows,
> Which, to support the same, their tresses rear,
> Proud of the sacred burthen which they bear;
> There will the rising generation be
> Instructed in true faith and piety;
> Taught to adore the only living God,
> And learn to tread the paths their Saviour trod.

# Notes

1    N. J. Frangopulo, *Rich Inheritance, a Guide to the History of Manchester* (Manchester, Richmond Press Ltd., Wilmslow, 1962), pp. 37 & 74.

2    A. P. Wadsworth, *The First Manchester Sunday School* (Manchester, Manchester University Press, reprinted from the Bulletin of the John Ryland's Library March 1951), vol. 33, no. 2, p. 299.

3    E. S. Furniss, *The Position of the Labourer in a System of Nationalism* (New York, 1920) reprinted *Considerations on the Fatal Effects to a Trading Nation of the Present Excess of Public Charity* (1763), pp.148–149.

4    MM. 10 August 1784.

5    MM. 21 September 1784

6    *Rules and orders for the government of the Sunday schools* (Manchester, Harrop's, 1784) CLM.

7    Wadsworth, *The First Manchester Sunday School,* vol. 33, No. 2, p. 299.

8    MM. 8 August 1786.

9    Wadsworth, *The First Manchester Sunday School,* p. 313.

10    G. W. Coombes, *Letter to W. Gibson 9 December 1791* (LDA: WG 84, pp. 1–2).

11    Wadsworth, *The First Manchester Sunday School,* p. 313.

12    D. Lannon, *Bishop Turner and Educational Provision within the Salford Diocesan Area 1840—1870* (University of Hull, unpublished thesis, 1994).

13    Wadsworth, *Statistics from the Minutes of the Select Committee on Children in Manufactories* (Manchester, printed in The Cotton Trade and Industrial Lancashire, 1816), p. 326.

14    Broomhead, *Letter to W. Gibson 31 August 1804* (WG. 497).

15    Broomhead, Kenyon & Lupton, *Letter to W. Gibson 25 March 1813* (LDA: WG. 805).

# 12 DANGERS & DIFFICULTIES

## 1. Broomhead and the Notables of the Town

**B**ROOMHEAD CAME FROM a minor gentry family, and as such would have been regarded as a gentleman and would have automatically positioned himself with the 'notables' of Manchester, and any attempt to show allegiance to any other class would have made him a pariah in the town. His own position as a Roman Catholic priest, brought up in the secrecy of a half-world, becoming a leader of an emerging, growing, Roman Catholic community, recently relieved from some of the disabilities under the law, and looked upon by many as an interloper, was formidable and challenging. He reached out to those in need, but while he was not one of them, he was one with them.

By the latter part of the eighteenth century there were few influential gentry left in the neighbourhood of Manchester; those still there were the Trafford, Mosley, Wilton, and Egerton families. It was the merchants and manufacturers who then dominated Manchester. The industrial and commercial leaders, however, were divided by their religious denominations into Tory/Anglican and Liberal/Non-conformists. The former belonged to the county society, whereas the latter were defined by their Non-conformity, which under the law barred most of its members from accessing universities or professions. There was much bitterness between these two groups, both political and religious. The Liberals, were also known as Whig Dissenters, while the Tory/Anglicans as the 'Church and King Club'. The evidence proves that Broomhead supported any attestation of loyalty in support of King and Country for he signed and donated and encouraged his congregation to follow his example.

Broomhead was soon accepted by the influential figures of Manchester, for by 1787 he had been elected to the committee of the Manchester Infirmary and went on to be accepted on the committees of all the major hospitals and also as a member of the influential Portico Library and Newsroom. He was also a dominant member of the Board of Health and the Committee for the Relief of the Poor.

## 2. The French Revolution and Émigrés Priests

The last two years of Broomhead's studies at the English College and the three years spent in Sheffield prior to his arrival in Manchester in 1778 were coterminous with the Boston Tea Party (1773); the declaration of American independence (1776); French and Spanish support for the American revolutionaries against Britain (1776); the Spanish siege of Gibraltar (1777); the threat of French invasion of England (1778) and in Ireland, malcontents agitated for reform, both for trade barriers and constitutional restrictions.

The inhabitants of Manchester had raised a corps of one hundred and fifty volunteers, to fight in America, and these were supported financially by the Town, through subscriptions. It took till 1783 for England, France and Spain to sign the Treaty of Versailles.

In 1789, with the fall of the Bastille, the French Revolution was launched. The French passed a law of the Civil Constitution, 12 July 1790, which required the priests of France to take the so-called 'Civil Oath' by which they professed themselves 'servants of the State'.[1] Pope Pius VI confirmed its unlawfulness. A further law, 27 November 1791, deprived all priests of their offices and benefices, if they refused to take the oath. Few were prepared to take the oath and priests and bishops began to leave France secretly for many of their colleagues by 1792 had already been executed. Those who came to England were largely from Normandy, Brittany, Picardy and Paris. The English people:

as soon as they understood the true meaning of the events which were happening on the other side of the Channel, and recognized that the refugees who arrived in such vast numbers were in truth the victims of religious persecution, they rose as one man, irrespective of religion or party, and joined together in making a supreme effort to help the exiles.[2]

In the *Manchester Mercury* 16 October 1792, there was an entry requesting subscriptions for the relief of the Clergy and others of France, refugees in England. It did not carry the name of a sponsor:

> The destitute circumstances of numbers of CLERGY and others of France, who have fled into this kingdom as an Asylum to the unfortunate, calling for our assistance as Men and as Christians; and the Inhabitants of the Towns and Neighbourhood of Manchester and Salford, being distinguished for their charitable contributions and liberality to the distressed—it is proposed, that a Subscription be opened, for the purpose of affording them immediate relief. Those who are disposed to contribute their mite towards forwarding so laudable a design, are requested to leave their Subscriptions at Mr Harrop's shop, in the Market-place, Manchester; which will, from time to time, be remitted to the Committee in London, who have undertaken the distribution of this Charity.[3]

The Manchester Mercury, 23 October 1792, contained a list of only fifteen subscribers, which included Broomhead's donation of one guinea.

Most of these émigré priests were found accommodation in the south of England, but some came into the Northern District. A letter of Bishop Milner of the Midland District to Bishop William Gibson, Vicar Apostolic of the Northern District, at Hexham, dated 31 August 1796, gives us some idea of the difficulty of dealing with the large number of émigré priests and how the Government moved them around the country:

> My good friends in the French Clergy, who to the number of 900, inhabit the King's House in this City (Wickham/Winchester), exclusive of 200, who live in private lodgings have received orders to quit that comfortable situation which is to be made into barracks for 4,000 soldiers. Two small houses are prepared for some at Reading & at T——. The rest, with two or three thousand of them from Jersey, are required to disperse themselves over the Kingdom. Several have mentioned to me their intention of going to York and other places in the north, exclusive of those whom Government have already landed in the District. In answer to your Lordship's inquiring, whether there are any amongst them who are well-acquainted with our language & who are qualified to serve the Mission, I think I can safely say I know several, particularly a Monsieur Mensis who has been these two years chaplain to the Benedictines here, and Confessor to a few of them, a Monsieur Fleury who serves a small English congregation at Wickham. & a Monsieur Prevost who occasionally officiates to the Catholics at Ramsey, who a few months back, was in the point of setting out to York, in quest of employment, merely from his own ideas ... [4]

William Gibson wrote to Thomas Eyre in York, 5 January 1794: 'I have 7 or 8 French priests employed in some shape'.[5] In a further letter dated December 1796, from William Gibson to the Bishop of Arras, sympathy was expressed over the French Bishop's exile and it records that almost 600 clergy from the Arras Diocese were in the Northern District.[6]

In correspondence, 12 February 1807, Broomhead, wrote to William Gibson, referring to a number of French émigré priests working in Manchester:

> You had given faculties formerly to Rev Mr Boulenger not only to say Mass & give Confessions at Mass & hear Confessions of Foreigners, but also to church Women. When I last got faculties for all the French Clergy of this Town together the last grant of Churching of Women was not expressed; and Mr Kenyon (at whose Chapel he says prayers) being engaged in the Confessional desired him, as usual, to church one or more Women, who were waiting for that purpose, which he did. He has since had some doubts whether your last faculties allowed him this power, nor do I recollect the words myself; but as the faculties were for all the French Clergy I expect not...[7]

There was also an émigré priest, Fr Joseph Barbe, working at Glossop.

### 3. The French Wars 1793–1802

The French Wars began soon after the execution of Louis XVI of France, in January 1793, with a declaration of war by France on Britain and Holland. The mutual hatred of the Tories in Britain for the Jacobins in France, and the partial occupation of the Netherlands by the French, was the main cause of the war. Jacobins were members of a French political club established in 1789, at Paris, in the old convent of the Dominican friars, who in France were called Jacobins, to maintain and propagate the principles of extreme democracy and absolute equality.[8] Their political philosophy was a long distance away from that of the Tory party and Pitt refused to 'recognize the French Republic and to treat with her officially'.[9] From 1793 to 1815, with occasional periods of peace, Britain was preoccupied with defeating the French and Napoleon, and securing its hold in Europe. The danger hanging over them was described by the historian Trevelyan:

In 1797–8, with heavy taxation, distress and discour-
agement in England, with the navy mutiny at Nore, the
rebellion in Ireland, the desertion of our allies, the
enforced abandonment of the Mediterranean by our
fleets, and the star of Bonaparte rising, the situation was
gloomy enough to bring out Pitt's higher qualities of
stubborn will and inflexible courage.[10]

The British were deeply concerned about the possibility of invasion
and this fear was felt in every town and village in the country,
including Manchester, which raised many battalions in support of
the war. The Manchester Mercury, 6 March 1798, recorded a
meeting at The Bull's Head Inn, Manchester, of inhabitants of the
Town and neighbourhood of Manchester and Salford, for the
purpose of entering into a voluntary contribution towards supplying the exigencies of the State at the present juncture. They
unanimously resolved the following:

> That in the present state of public Affairs when the envied
> Establishments of Britons, their Liberties, their Laws, their
> Commerce, their Property, their very Happiness, and eve-
> rything dear and valuable to Society, are openly menaced
> with the Subversion, Havock (sic) and Inhumanity of
> French Invasion, all (...) Descriptions of his Majesty's
> Subjects are called upon to unite with Zeal and Effect in
> defeating their hostile Intentions.

> That for the Defence of the Country, on this important
> Occasion, a Voluntary Contribution be immediately
> entered into, and afterwards transmitted to the Bank of
> England, under the Direction of a Committee to be
> appointed by this Meeting, and that the Gentlemen present,
> be desired to put down their Names, with the form they
> intend to subscribe, in the Books now produced.

That it is the bounden Duty of every Individual, whatever may be his Situation in Life, to use his best endeavours, in promoting the contributory Aid now resolved upon.

It was recorded in the Manchester Mercury and Harrop's General Advertiser of Tuesday, 13 March 1798, that the Rev Rowland Broomhead subscribed one guinea, and a collection taken up at the Catholic Chapel (Rook Street) had subscribed twenty three pounds, two shillings.

## 4. The Danger Hanging Over the Clergy 1798

The Vicar Apostolic of the London District, John Douglass, wrote to his counterpart, William Gibson of the Northern District, 27 April 1798, an extract of which follows:

> The danger hanging over us must induce us to beseech Heaven most fervently to be our refuge & protection. The News Papers tell the state of the nation, & the grounds there are for being alarmed. If we consider only the strength, & ways & means of offence & deference provided by men we have nothing to fear. But alas there is no wisdom, there is no counsel against the Lord & we know not what he has appointed or what may be permitted by his ever adorable Providence.[11]

Bishop Douglass shared his deep concern for the dangers of a French invasion and called for prayers at that difficult time.

It seems, from the next extract of the same letter, that there were very serious concerns amongst the clergy about their personal safety and that this safety might be compromised as a result of events in Ireland, as well as in England:

> In Ireland the sword is drawn & the scabbard thrown away. If it should become necessary to fly from London into the North, I beg you will give me full powers for my clergy if any of them should be compelled to fly thither. I grant to you full powers for your clergy, should you & any of them be

driven into the London District. We are credibly informed
that the conspirators at Manchester designed to murder Mr
Broomhead, as well as the Boroughreeve & etc. It appears
clear that the Revolutionists look upon us and our Clergy
as the most hostile of all men, to their views & works of
irreligion. It strikes one with horror that they should think
of resorting to fire & poison our new river & the Waterworks
are well guarded.

The Boroughreeve was the governor or the chief municipal officer,
and Broomhead the leader of the Catholic community in Manchester and an indigenous English Catholic priest who supported the
leaders of the Town. The murder of both these men would have
been an important boost for the Irish revolutionaries who were in
cahoots with the French, who had landed in Ireland to support the
Irish cause for freedom. The Bishop also underlined the anti-
clericalism of the Revolutionaries.

Two important newspaper accounts from Manchester April
1798 are pertinent to our understanding of the background to this
letter. The first is dated, Tuesday 17 April 1798, and was entered
under 'The Manchester Overseers Weekly Report' in the *Manchester Mercury*, and it referred to events in the town the previous
Wednesday 11 April:

> A considerable bustle was caused on Wednesday morning
> in this town, by the arrival of several King's Messengers and
> Bow Street Officers, with warrants against some of the
> residents, on a charge of treasonable practices. The business
> was so managed, that, in a very short time, ten persons were
> taken into custody. The charge against them is High Trea-
> son, and they were served by the authority of warrants from
> the Secretary of State. About noon they were taken in
> carriages, accompanied by the officers on their route to
> London, escorted by our corps of cavalry, a part of whom
> went with them a little beyond Newcastle (under-Lyne)

> when the cavalry corps of that town took the duty. It appears
> at present, that there was a plan forming systematically; and
> that the town is indebted to the active and unremitting
> vigilance of our Magistrates for its direction ... [12]

The warrants against some of the residents on a charge of treason-
able practice was about as serious as one could imagine, for not only
did these ten persons face capital punishment if found guilty, but
the Habeas Corpus Act had been suspended since 1794, which
meant that they could be held without trial and incommunicado.
This report did not list any names. It did not indicate who these
people were and what organisation they might have belonged to,
but the only groups who had links with the French were the United
Irishmen and United Englishmen. The second newspaper account
was dated, Tuesday 24 April 1798:

> The persons who were taken up in this town, as stated in
> our last, for treasonable practices, have been repeatedly
> examined by the Privy Council. The result of these exami-
> nations cannot be laid before the public. The discovery,
> however, of the Conspiracy in this town, is far more impor-
> tant to the public than anything that was likely to arise from
> the flight of the prisoners at Maidstone to France. The
> enemy to land on our shores; whereas the Manchester Plot
> was formed to excite a Rebellion in the heart of the country
> and to set fire to different places, in order to take advantage
> of the general confusion. [13]

The reference to Maidstone, referred to a trial for High Treason,
held there in 1798. On trial were five Irishmen: James Quigley,
Arthur O'Connor, John Binns, John Allen and Jeremiah Leary. The
State trial began, 12 April 1798, and following on the arrangements
for their defence, the indictment was read on 18 April, and in short
they were charged with:

conspiring compassing the King's death; aiding and com-
forting the King's enemies and compassing, imagining,
inventing, devising and intending to move and stir certain
foreigners and strangers, that is to say, the persons exercising
the powers of Government in France under the government
of the said persons, with force to invade this realm'.[14]

The miscreants, involved in this trial, were Irishmen working in
conjunction with the French, to bring about the invasion of England.
The arrests of John Quigley and Arthur O'Connor en route to France,
left the radicals around Manchester in constant fear of arrest'.[15] Some
of the United Irishmen in Manchester escaped to Ireland, but ten of
them appear to have been arrested in the early morning raid of 11
April 1789. There is evidence, which concludes, that in Lancashire,
United Irishmen and United Englishmen could have combined to
result in something approaching a revolution through its secret-cell
organization, republican aims, and French backing.[16]

After the success of the English in putting down the rebellion in
Ireland, Pitt wanted to settle the Irish Question, by uniting the two
countries in their legislature. It was the view shared by Cornwallis
(viceroy in Dublin), Castlereagh and Pitt that, 'until the Catholics
are admitted into a general participation of rights (which when
incorporated with the British Government they cannot abuse)
there will be no peace or safety in Ireland'.[17] In August 1800, the
Act of Union was passed and Ireland merged with England and the
Parliament in Dublin was abolished. Pitt, a supporter of Catholic
Emancipation, resigned in February 1801, because of the refusal of
George III to permit its introduction.

As far as the war with France was concerned, it took till March
1802 for the Peace of Amiens to be signed. Unfortunately, by May
1803, the war with France had resumed.

## 5. Increasing Numbers of Irish Migrants in Manchester

There was a long history of economic and commercial links of the Irish with Manchester, reaching back into the early years of the sixteenth century, when they exported commodities such as Irish yarns and wool, and later cheese, eggs, and fish to Smithfield Market, in the early nineteenth century.[18] There were groups who also seasonally helped with the harvest. Some of these agricultural workers became 'an integral part of the British agricultural scene well into the twentieth century'.[19]

In the Manchester and Salford, Papist Returns, for 1767, there were a number of entries of Irish migrants, which can be deduced from their registered names. There are thirteen who stand out, all of whom were weavers:

> Charles Connelly, aged sixty four, married to Dorothy, had arrived in Manchester in 1727; Patrick Carty, aged sixty, married to Johanna, had been resident for thirty years, arrived in the Town in 1737; Joseph Falkner, aged sixty, a widower, had been resident since 1738, had one son Joseph, aged thirty-two, who had been resident only nine years, and was also a weaver; Patrick Linch, aged eighty-seven, who arrived in Manchester in 1742, had no family listed; Timothy Collinge, aged fifty, arrived in the Town in 1745, and had no family entry; Patrick Tully, aged forty-eight, was resident in Manchester in 1747, and was a widower, with four children; James Fitzpatrick, aged forty-eight, and John Bourne, aged forty, settled in Manchester in 1753 and neither had family registered; John Brone, aged thirty-five, arrived in 1758, and there was no family registered; Hugh Cary, aged thirty-five, and Dorothy his wife settled in Manchester in 1760; Patrick Oak, aged forty-five, and his wife Margaret, and Joseph Catrill, aged twenty-seven, had no relations recorded, and resided in Manchester from 1763.

These statistics support the view that early in the eighteenth century, Roman Catholic Irish men and women had settled in Manchester as early as 1727. By the late 1780s the number of migrant Irish was growing significantly for 'by 1787 it was believed that there were over 5,000 Irish born' in the Town.[20] Growing numbers of Irish migrants, certainly by the nineteenth century, were settling down within the area of the Manchester Mission.[21]A further estimate, in 1804, of the Irish population was 'at somewhere between 10,000 and 15,000'.[22] Most of the Irish migrants came from 'the predominantly Catholic north-western counties of Roscommon, Sligo, and Leitrim'.[23]

The causes of unrest in Ireland had always been linked to poverty. It did not have the natural resources of coal, iron and wood so necessary for industrial development. Its only resources were 'land, linen and cheap labour'.[24] The discontent and regular disorder of the people did not encourage investment from mainly absentee landowners, who used their land to raise income, which often was taken out of the country, and they gave little support for the introduction of improvements that had begun to revolutionise agriculture in England. They concentrated on increasing their potato crops which brought about an increase of population who lived 'near subsistence level and resistant to change.' This was the picture for all of Ireland except Ulster. Irish society had three main parties:

The Roman Catholic majority who were aliens in their own country, deprived of all political rights and, in theory, of the rights of property and education as well.

In Ulster, a Presbyterian population was also excluded, like the dissenters in England, from political influence, though exempt from the harsher religious laws affecting the papists.

Both these sections regarded the established church as the club of a small minority in whose hands all power was lodged. These parliamentary Anglicans were traditionally grouped in interests and sold their support to the lord-lieutenant. They were pro-English, only so long as their services were rewarded.[25]

The revolutionary successes of both the Americans and then the French heightened their demands for constitutional changes. Henry Grattan, one of their leaders, explored the relationship of the Crown and his countrymen:

> The King has no other title to his Crown than that which you have to your liberty; both are founded, the throne and your freedom, upon the right vested in the subject to resist by force of arms, notwithstanding their oath of allegiance, any authority attempting to impose acts of power as laws, whether that authority be one man or a host, the second James or the British Parliament.[26]

Three important concessions were made: In 1778 an act was passed to allow Catholics to take leases on land for life or up to 999 years; also to inherit or bequeath land on the same terms as Protestants; in 1779 the Irish were permitted to trade with British settlements in Africa and America, on the same terms as the rest of the British Isles; and lastly on 6 April 1782 a resolution for independence was passed unanimously and in 1783, confirmed the complete legislative and judicial independence of Ireland.

Grattan believed that the Irish could increase their independence and said 'The Irish Protestant can never be free until the Irish Catholic has ceased to be a slave'. Irish radicals in Ulster, October 1791, stimulated by the ideals of the French Revolution, formed the United Irishmen, which included Catholics, Protestants and Dissenters. They were led by Wolfe Tone, a lawyer, Henry McCracken, a cotton manufacturer and William Drennan, a physician and poet and the son of a Presbyterian minister. Their aim was to unite into a single movement, to fight for independence. Wolfe Tone left Ireland in 1795, to try to get support from America and France.

Few regarded the Irish Parliament as a relevant institution and consequently turned to more physical means to achieve their aims. The United Irishmen turned into a militant society and were close in ideals to the principles of the French revolutionists. As a result many Presbyterians in Ulster left its ranks, but the Society of United Irishmen continued to influence the other provinces of Ireland.

Wolfe Tone succeeded in getting support from the French who were already planning to invade England. The failure of the French invasion in Pembrokeshire in 1797 made the British more aware of the need to increase their sea defences, both in Ireland and England. The new lord-lieutenant, Lord Camden, sent General Lake to disarm Ulster and it was to this action that the United Irishmen responded, but not in tune with the French, whose help was on its way. The plot to capture Dublin in February 1798 failed, but the revolutionaries attacked Naas, Carlow, Wexford and Enniscorthy, but Wexford was retaken by the government forces at Vinegar Hill, 21 June 1798. The French force, under the command of General Humbert finally arrived 21 June 1798 with Wolfe Tone, landing at Killala in County Mayo. Cornwallis forced the French to surrender at Ballinamuck, 8 September 1798, and Wolfe Tone and the other Irish revolutionists were executed.

The increase in the migrant Irish population of Manchester in the period of 1778 to 1820 was due to the huge increase of the population in Ireland and the difficulty of feeding them; less favourable employment opportunities in Ireland than in England; the shortage of hand-loom weavers in Manchester and the series of bad harvests in 1801 and 1816 to 1818. Some of the members of the United Irishmen fled to England following the failure of their insurrection. Others emigrated because of the repressive powers of the Insurrection Act of 1796. A large number of these migrants were Roman Catholics and as such they brought their needs and fears to bear on Broomhead and his fellow priests.

Arriving in Manchester, Irish migrants were faced with some very real problems. Deep antagonism towards the Irish, and since the majority were Catholic, deep suspicion, born of anti-Catholicism, that had been part of the culture of Lancashire for generations. Most of the indigenous English saw the arrival of the Irish with some trepidation, fearing a possible threat to their jobs, for they 'believed that the Irish undercut the wages of all working people'. This was not without some foundation for employers faced with strikes, sometimes sent to Ireland for workers who would break a strike. The Commons Select Committee of 1836, surveying the influx of Irish migrants, took evidence from some manufacturers testifying 'that the first wave into Lancashire occurred when they had invited Irish weavers over, to replace native workers turned out during the strikes of 1799'.[27]

The Irish Rebellion of 1798, reinforced the Loyalism of the so-called 'notables' of Manchester and this was expressed through anti-Catholicism. There were a number of factors which gave rise to the increase of anti-Catholicism: that local militia had put their lives on the line in Ireland and resented the arrival of those who had been their enemies; the extent of Irish migration into Lancashire which included both United Irishmen, and Protestant and Catholic Irish; the fear that they would take the jobs away from indigenous locals, and the predilection of the magistrates to suspect any Irish person of wrong-doing.

An influential group of these Protestant exiles were members of the Orange movement, and they coalesced into the existing 'Church and King Club' reinforcing the anti-Catholicism in the Town. Consequently, Orangemen were often found work by sympathetic industrialists, but the latter were wary of Catholic Irish, so for them, getting jobs was difficult.

The Manchester Militia, recruited from the Manchester area, had helped to put down the rebellion in Ireland in 1798, which success boosted the government of the day, and the returning troops were expected to be on hand to put down any insurrection in their home town. That they had fought in Ireland and were then mixing with Irish immigrants, held the possibility of the militia settling a few scores of their own.

Fear of insurrection had been expressed by the merchant-manufacturers and the magistrates who saw in the machinations of the United Irishmen an attempt 'to stir up the working classes'.[28] The power of the United Irishmen and the United Englishmen was feared by the Manchester magistrates, who believed they had the power to disrupt society, but it was the failure of these two groups to overcome their own internal differences that made their aims impossible to realise. They worked in conjunction with one another, but it was religious differences and distrust, that were the roots of their failure.

During the food riots of 1799 to 1801, the mobs were encouraged by the United Irishmen and this action reinforced the exclusion of Irish people in the community, and during the Napoleonic wars, Irishmen were often the suspects of the spy system set up by the Home Office.

The introduction of the Union with Ireland in 1800 and the subsequent demands for Catholic Emancipation, all gave further impetus to anti-Catholicism and during the 1800s sectarianism was also causing problems in Manchester. The Catholic Relief Bills of 1807 and 1813 also encouraged an increase in anti-Catholic activity; the reason for the Bills failing to become law.

The Irish settled in the poorest areas of the Town and initially they would have had mainly indigenous English alongside them, but as the numbers increased three areas were dominated by the Irish. These were: Irish Town by the River Irk; Angel Meadow, off Rochdale Road, and Ancoats. These were the areas where Broomhead mainly lived out his work, visiting the sick and needy and preparing the dying with the last rites. The close proximity of friends and relations from Ireland would have helped them to develop community, even though it encouraged isolationism from the other people living in the town. Most of the witnesses to the Commons Select Committee of 1836 'had strong anti-Irish prejudices, stereotyping the immigrants as drunken, unwilling to work, and prone to crime, disease, and violence'.

Broomhead's role as priest to a largely immigrant community, which had so often experienced difficult times and had expressed deep hatred for the English, required sensitivity to their needs, both physical and spiritual, and his success can be supported by the evidence of the acclamation of the whole of his community at the end of his life. They called him 'Good Father Broomhead'. However, he would not have supported any action that would have undermined the peace of the Town and would have chastised people who joined in any insurrection. There is no doubt that the threat on his life, and that of the Boroughreeve in 1798, came from Irish revolutionaries who did not like what he preached.

These large Irish population increases were bound to bring more Catholics into the Manchester mission and therefore there was a need for more chapels. It was not just the space that was needed, but priests to deal with the increase in religious needs. The increasing numbers of Catholic Irish, boosted the numbers attending Rook Street Chapel, which then led to the building of St Mary's Mulberry Street and by 1820 the erection St Augustine's Granby Row. These were difficult times for Broomhead and his fellow clergy in trying to raise money to be able to build, but nowhere is there any evidence that the clergy were anything but positive. They worked long hours and were true to their vocation.

## 6. Continuation of the French Wars 1803–1815

During the French wars, the people of Manchester continued to offer help to those who were affected. Following a request for subscriptions, for the benefit of disabled and wounded, and of the widows and children of those who fell in the late memorable action under Lord Nelson, Broomhead took a collection at Rook Street Chapel 17 December 1805, which raised ten pounds for the charity.[29]

Between 1806 and 1812 the effect of the war on trade gave serious cause for concern in Manchester. Napoleon issued the 'Berlin Decrees', closing all ports to British shipping. In retaliation, Britain issued 'Orders in Council' from January to November 1807, ordering all neutral ships trading with Europe, to proceed to British ports and pay duties on their way to Europe. Napoleon responded in November 1807, with the issue of the 'Milan Decrees' which ordered the confiscation of all neutral shipping, calling at British ports. In 1808, in retaliation to the 'Orders in Council', which were causing great hardship, the people of Manchester sent a petition against them, signed by 50,000 of the people of the Town. There were widespread petitions from across the country against 'Orders in Council' of March 1812, and in May the Orders were revoked. Following the defeat of Napoleon at Waterloo, the Peace of Vienna brought hostilities to an end, June 1815.

The Waterloo Collection, for Manchester, Salford, and neighbourhood was organized by a committee that met under the chairmanship of Nathaniel Gould at the Police Office in King Street, Manchester, 9 August 1815. The decisions of the committee were as follows:

> In consequence of the subjoined humane letter of his Royal Highness the Prince Regent, the committee appointed to promote and conduct the subscription in the towns of Manchester, Salford, and neighbourhood, for the relief and benefit of the families of the brave men killed, and the

wounded sufferers, in the battle of Waterloo, and in the several battles, which have been and may be fought in the present campaign, take this opportunity of informing the public, that books have been opened at all the Banking-houses, Public News-rooms, and at Mr Gibson's office, Marsden Square, Manchester, and others in the different districts, for the purpose of collecting from the inhabitants, such sums as they may individually be inclined to contribute. They therefore suggest the propriety of a co-operation of the Wardens of each Church, with the Gentlemen of the districts, with whom the books are left, as the most effectual means of securing a general subscription.

Rowland Broomhead was appointed as one of the collectors for districts eight and ten, and subscribed one guinea himself.

## 7. Radicalism in the Manchester Area

The example of the American and French revolutionaries and the philosophy expounded by Thomas Paine's 'Rights of Man', underpinned the thinking of the Manchester radicals in their response to the internal social and economic crises and the external problems arising out of the French wars and Irish problems. Radicalism was soon to come face to face with the Manchester controlled Tory authorities.

In October 1790, the Manchester Constitutional Society was established by Whig Dissenters, supported by the newly published 'Manchester Herald', the voice of reform. Its leader Thomas Walker and his fellow reformists espoused the revolutionary philosophies of the day. The response of the 'Church and King 'club was to encourage riots in December 1792, in defence of tradition:

Manchester's Tory controlled authorities (magistrates and constables) stood by as a drunken mob attacked dissenters' chapel, wrecked the Herald's offices and for three successive

nights besieged Thomas Walker and other radicals in their
homes, breaking windows and threatening bodily harm to
the occupants.[30]

The suppression of the Manchester Constitutional Society in 1792
put a stop to radicalism in Manchester, which was not revived till
1807, when, at a meeting at Ardwick Green, Manchester, to
celebrate George III's birthday:

> toasts by independent candidates marked the public begin-
> nings of the anti-corruption campaign that Sir Francis
> Burdett had revived in Westminster and was becoming
> popular across the country. The toasts subverted ownership
> over the concept of Loyalism.[31]

Broomhead was not disinterested in the developing problems
arising from the growth of radicalism, and took a part, with his peers
in encouraging peace in the Town.

The Manchester Mercury recorded a meeting, chaired by the
Boroughreeve of Manchester, Joseph Green, which had met 13
January 1817, to adopt additional measures for the maintenance of
the public peace. The following resolutions and declarations were
unanimously agreed to:

- That incessant efforts are now used by designing and mischie-
  vous individuals throughout the Kingdom, and more especially
  in this and other populous Districts, to produce insubordina-
  tion and tumult amongst the labouring classes, and cannot be
  contemplated without serious alarm.
- That his Majesty's faithful Subjects owe it to the Constitution
  under which they live, as well as to themselves and their
  Families, to adopt the most effectual means for the maintenance of public peace at this important juncture; and that in
  the Towns and Neighbourhood of Manchester and Salford, it
  is becoming highly expedient to strengthen the Civil Power.

- That the Boroughreeves of Manchester and Salford be requested to apply for the appointment of additional Constables, to act in these Towns and such part of the Vicinity as the Magistrates may direct.
- That it is also needful to submit to the Magistrates the necessity of the early enforcement of the powers of the Watch and Ward Act, in such parts of the District as may not be effectually relieved by the proposed addition of Constables, and that the Boroughreeves and Constables of Manchester and Salford be desired to confer with the Magistrates thereon.
- That the paper now produced and read, is declaratory of the sentiments of this Meeting on the present occasion, and that the same be signed by the Gentlemen present, and such others as the Committee to be appointed, as in hereafter mentioned may apply for that purpose. And also that this Declaration be published (after being numerously signed) at the time and in the manner such Committee may think fit …

The paper referred to their detestation of attempts to excite a spirit of disaffection; the circulation of seditious tracts; inflammatory speeches that suggested to the labouring classes that Government was responsible for their present problems and may be removed by universal suffrage and the use of secret meetings and collections for the dissemination of pamphlets, which mislead and irritate the public mind and assemblies of people intent on disorder:

> We the undersigned, Magistrates for the Division of Manchester, the Boroughreeves of Manchester and Salford and other Inhabitants of these Towns and their Neighbourhood, being at all times sensible of the many blessings of the Constitution under which we live, feel ourselves called upon at this moment to express our firm attachment to its Laws, as well as our utter detestation of these mischievous attempts which are now pursued with incessant diligence

and ardour, to excite a general spirit of disaffection. We especially deprecate the circulation of seditious tracts, and the adoption of inflammatory speeches, to produce an impression amongst the labouring classes, that the present distresses and privations are attributable to the corruption and misconduct of Government; and may be removed by a system of Representation, embracing almost universal suffrage, annual Parliaments, the unqualified exclusion of all persons deriving emolument from the public, and consequently of his Majesty's Ministers.

The numerous Meetings held for these purposes, both publicly and secretly, the organised system of Committees, Delegates and Missionaries, the contributions levied, particularly for disseminating pamphlets, calculated to mislead and irritate the public mind, the indecorous and highly unconstitutional reflections upon the exalted Personage now exercising the Regal Authority, the marked disparagement of the most extensive charitable relief in seasons of unavoidable pressure, the language of intimidation not merely hinted, but plainly expressed,—the appointment of popular assemblies in various parts of the Kingdom on one and the same day, after the meeting of Parliament, and the previous assembling of Deputies in London; all these circumstances afford strong manifestation of meditated Disorder and tumult, and bear no analogy whatever to the fair and legitimate exercise of that constitutional Liberty, which is emphatically the birth-right and security of Englishmen'.

With these decided sentiments, it is our duty, to unite in supporting the Laws and Constitution against those wicked efforts, which we are convinced, must be regarded with equal abhorrence by the great majority of his Majesty's Subjects in every class and condition of society. We therefore severally pledge ourselves to contribute, by the most effectual means our situations may allow, to the maintenance of the peace and tranquillity of these Towns and their Neighbourhood, from the unlawful and nefarious designs of those who are seeking to involve us in riot and confusion; and we earnestly solicit the co-operation of all Friends to social Order and good Government.

The *Manchester Mercury* and Harrop's *General Advertiser* dated Tuesday October 19, 1819 issued the following:

> To His Royal Highness the Prince Regent
>
> We the undersigned Clergy, Gentry, Merchants and Manufacturers and other Inhabitants of the Town of Manchester and Salford and their immediate vicinity feel it our indispensable duty in the present eventful crisis to convey to your ROYAL HIGHNESS the full assurance of our steadfast and unfailing attachment to His Majesty's Royal Person and Government, and of our solemn determination to support and defend, in every emergency, the Laws and the Constitution of our land.

This document was signed by one thousand and eighteen gentlemen including Rev Thomas Lupton and Rev Rowland Broomhead.

## Notes

[1] P. Kennedy Ed., *The Catholic Church in England and Wales 1500–2000* (Keighley, PBK Publishing Ltd., 2001), p. 161.

[2] Kennedy, *The Catholic Church in England and Wales 1500–2000*, p. 161.

[3] *Subscription for émigré priests 16 October 1792*(MM).

[4] Milner, *Letter to W. Gibson 31 August 1796* (LDA: WG. 220).

[5] W. Gibson, *Letter to Eyre 5 January 1794* (LDA: WG. 155).

[6] W. Gibson, *Letter to the Bishop of Arras December 1796* (LDA: WG. 227a).

[7] Broomhead, *Letter to W. Gibson 12 February 1807* (LDA: WG. 553A).

[8] Shorter Oxford Dictionary, 1964.

[9] G. M. Trevelyan, *British History in the Nineteenth Century 1782–1901* (London, Longmans, Green and Co. 1922), p. 80.

10   *Ibid,* p. 83.

11   J. Douglass, *Letter to W. Gibson 27 April 1798* (LDA: WG. 263).

12   MM: Tuesday 17 April 1798.

13   MM: Tuesday 24 April 1798.

14   Maidstone *Oracle & Public Advertiser, 19 April 1798.*

15   K. Navickas, *Loyalism and Radicalism in Lancashire 1798–1815* (Oxford, Oxford University Press Historical Monograph, 2009), p.141.

16   M. Elliot, *Partners in Revolution: the United Irishmen and France* (New Haven, 1982) & R. Wells *Insurrection: the British Experience, 1795–1803* (Gloucester, 1983), p. 235.

17   J. S. Watson, *The Reign of King George III, 1760–1815* (Oxford, Clarendon Press, 1992), Oxford History of England Vol. xii. p. 399.

18   R. Scola, W. A. Armstrong & P. Scola, *Feeding the Victorian City: the Food Supply of Manchester 1770–1870* (Manchester, Manchester University Press, 1992).

19   T. W. Cook, *Notes of a Tour in the Manufacturing Districts in a series of Letters to His Grace the Archbishop of Dublin* (London, Duncan & Malcolm, 1842), p. 72.

20   J. Holt, *General View of the Agriculture of the County of Lancashire and Observations on the Means of Improvement* (Manchester, Nicoll, 1795), p.213.

21   M. Busteed, *The Irish in Nineteenth Century Manchester* (Manchester, Irish Studies No. 18, Spring, 1997).

22   Aston, *The Manchester Guide* (Manchester, 1804), p. 123n.

23   Navickas, *Loyalism and Radicalism in Lancashire 1798–1815,* p. 115.

24   Watson, *The Reign of George III,* p. 387.

25   *Ibid.,* p. 388.

26   *Ibid.,* p. 389.

27   Navickas, *Loyalism and Radicalism in Lancashire 1798–181 5 ,* p. 113

28   *Ibid.,* p. 51.

29   MM. 17 December 1805.

30   Kidd, *Manchester a History,* p. 61.

31   Navickas, *Loyalism and Radicalism in Lancashire 1798–1815,* p. 208.

# 13 THE FINAL YEAR

## 1. St Augustine's Granby Row Manchester

THE HIGH POINT of Broomhead's life was the building of St Augustine's Chapel. Rook Street Chapel, where he lived from 1778 to his death in 1820, was addressed by correspondents as the 'Great Catholic Chapel' and this epithet probably had something to do with his position as dean of Lancashire but he did not use that epithet for he signed his letters with 'R. Broomhead, Rook Street, Manchester'. Both St Chad's Rook Street and St Mary's Mulberry Street were designated 'chapels'.

As early as 1806, Broomhead was aware of the need for another chapel in Manchester, and expressed this need in a letter to Brian Marsh, a student for the priesthood, at Crook Hall, near Gateshead, 27 February 1806:

> We are much in want of another Chapel here as the 2 we have are insufficient for the Congregation.[1]

Twelve months later, Broomhead addressed a letter to William Gibson at Old Elvet, Durham, 12 February 1807:

> We are much in want of a very large Chapel & I mean to set about it, as soon as a favourable opportunity offers: trade is now so bad, that I fear little or no Subscriptions could be raised. Our 2 Chapels at present will not hold our Congregation by many thousands. [2]

He may have wished to build the new chapel in 1807 but he was realistic enough to recognise that subscriptions would not be forthcoming unless trade was improved. He knew the economic problems in Manchester and the rest of the country. From 1793 the country at first had been involved in the Revolutionary Wars and by 1807 they were still at war with Napoleon. When peace came in 1815 and the armies returned, 'false and bloated prosperity' (Cobbett) gave way to a harsh period of suffering.

The following entry recorded the purchase of the land in Granby Row:

> The Land occupied by the Chapel, House and Cemetery situated on the westwardly side of Granby Row, and containing 4,317 square yards, was purchased in 1818 subject to a yearly rent of £17. 19. 9. Payable half yearly, viz. 24th June and 25th December.[3]

In this same record the following was entered:

> The conveyance to this Land is made to the Rev R. Thompson (Grand Vicar), Rev R. Broomhead; Rev Thos. Lupton; Rev M. Ashhurst and Rev Josh. Curr as trustees of the same

The land in Granby Row, sometimes known as Granby Terrace consisted of:

> A range of good houses occupying one side of the present street, with fine gardens at the back reaching down to the Medlock, then a clear bright stream on its way to fall into the Irwell in the vicinity of Knott Mill. The entrance to this pile of houses from London Road was by great white gates, and the locality was regarded as a fitting abode of some leading citizens of Manchester. Opposite them were fields with scarcely a single dwelling upon them. A fine plot of land was fixed upon and purchased at one penny chief rent per annum, on which to erect the new chapel.[4]

Mr John Palmer, a Catholic architect of Manchester, was chosen by Broomhead and the building committee, to become the architect for the new church to be built in the name of St Augustine. The building commenced 1818 and was completed in 1820.

*31. St Augustine's Chapel Granby Row exterior*

It is quite clear from the accounts for the building of the new Catholic Chapel at Granby Row that Broomhead signed for most of the payments made to the various tradesmen. Thomas Lupton's name appears in the accounts and he assisted in overseeing them with Broomhead.

John Palmer 'drew plans, elevations and working drawings and superintended the chapel'.[5] There was an account dated 20 October 1819 which was signed for payment by Rowland Broomhead which read: '3 Barrels of Beer for workmen £1. 16. 0'.[6]

*32. St Augustine's Chapel, Granby Row, Interior*

In 1837 to 1838 a book was published, which included a description
of the Church of St Augustine:

> In 1820, the Catholics erected another chapel in Granby
> Row now called St Augustine's which for beauty of con-
> struction leaves all the rest in the rear as it may justly rank

among the architectural ornaments of the town. Mr John
Palmer was the architect, and the sum expended was not
less than £10,000, although the front only is composed of
stone. This is an extremely elegant specimen of the enriched
Lancet style, and the windows have inserted in their arches
a billet moulding. There are two entrances at each extreme
with a single window above, whilst the centre consists of
three ranged together, and in the point of the gable the same
are repeated on a smaller scale. The body of the interior
which appears to be free is divided from the aisles by a long
row of clustered shafts of narrow circumference which
support arches of equal elegance: the roof is finely ribbed.
The altar piece which was brought from Italy is of very fine
Greek & Italian marble and the orderly arrangement of this
part alone is worth a visit.[7]

A 'Catholic Layman' addressed a letter to the *Manchester Gazette*:

Sir, I hope a short description of the opening of Saint
Augustine's Chapel, Granby Row, will meet your approbation, and prove acceptable to the numerous readers of your
valuable paper. On Wednesday the 27th of September,
although the weather was unfavourable, numbers of genteel
persons crowded the front of that noble edifice. The constituted authorities of the town had kindly offered the attendance of the beadles, to maintain order, which offer was
thankfully received. They therefore attended with the insig-
nia of their office, and by their exertions proved singularly
useful amidst the great concourse of people assembled on
this memorable occasion. The doors of the chapel being
opened, ladies and gentlemen of the first respectability
entered. Those walls, which had been consecrated the
preceding evening by his Lordship, the Catholic Bishop Dr
Smith, attended by the Clergy, contained a more numerous
and respectable congregation of all religious persuasions,
that ever sat down together on such an occasion in this part

of the country. This is a practical proof; if any were wanting, of the universal esteem and respect all good men show our much revered pastor Mr Broomhead. This is a convincing argument to every reflecting mind, that the dark clouds of bigotry and religious animosity are gradually dissipating, to be succeeded by the refulgent rays and benign influence of paternal charity and universal benevolence.

Scenes of this kind but rarely occur to behold multitudes of all religious bow their heads, and with one accord supplicate the omnipotent God of all. Every feeling heart must with the regret that it is not often the case, for me I am persuaded that we need but intimately to know one another to create mutual respect, to banish prejudice, to give the lie to calumnies, to increase charity, in a word to promote our temporal and eternal happiness. Our most grateful acknowledgements are due to our fellow townsmen of all denominations, who have most liberally assisted us in the erection of an edifice honourable to its founders, and a proud monument of the united efforts of all religious persuasions, I have, however, in common with many others of our congregation to regret, that several individuals of rank, were but ill-accommodated with seats, who, if they had been recognized by the persons in attendance, would have had more eligible seats assigned them. My feeble pen cannot sufficiently extol, nor the universal grateful feeling of our congregation make a suitable return for the liberality of our benefactors: that almighty power alone, who has promised that a cup of water shall not go unrewarded, he alone, I say, can appreciate the worth, and remunerate the gift. The candles being lighted on the altar, the procession, consisting of the Right Rev Dr Smith, attended by thirty priests, preceded by the censer bearer, and two youths with lighted candles, proceeded from the vestry, along the side aisle to the bottom end of the Chapel, and up the middle aisle to the foot of the altar. This procession had a very imposing effect. The sound of music awfully grand—the slow majestic pace and humble deportment of so many Reverend gentlemen attendant on his Lordship will never be obliterated from my remembrance. On approaching the altar his Lordship, assisted by his Grand Vicar, the Rev Mr Thompson, of Weld Bank, the Rev Mr Bury of Ince, as Deacon; the Rev Mr Glover of Crosby, as Sub-Deacon, commenced High Mass, the most awful and solemn part of our Church service, with such becoming dignity and exemplary devotion, as must greatly edify the Catholic, and raise the admiration of our dissenting brethren. Mr Glover chanted the Epistle, and Mr Bury the Gospel, in an audible and distinct tone of voice. The singing and stately deportment of Bishop Smith—the rites and ceremonies of our august sacrifice—the responses of the numerous clergy—the melodious vocal and instrumental music of the choir, composed a most pleasing and admirable variety, which baffles all description.

At the conclusion of High Mass, the Rev Mr Curr, of Mulberry Street, delivered an appropriate and most impressive discourse, from the '8th chapter of Kings 1st verse' in justification of the sumptuousness of our places of worship, proved the sanctity of the place, and advocated our religious rites and ceremonies. He eulogised the Catholic for his liberality towards the erection of the Chapel, though he admitted that personal convenience might in some degree influence his donations; but he extolled the munificence of our dissenting brethren in our regard, as absolutely disinterested, and emanating from the pure fountain of charity and impartial benevolence.

At the conclusion he most pathetically addressed the Rev Mr Broomhead, tendered him the grateful acknowledgement of the Catholic congregation, for his unwearied exertions to raise this magnificent structure and informed him that nothing cast a gloom on the joy of this day, but the approaching dissolution of their beloved pastor. This address was more than could be borne. Tears bedewed the cheeks of his hearers, particularly of those who had witnessed the indefatigable zeal of Mr Broomhead through life, to promote the honour and glory of his Creator, and the comfort and salvation of his fellow-creatures.[8]

Whilst Rook Street chapel was built on the edge of the town in the middle of industrial buildings and Mulberry Street built by Broomhead, with a less than obvious frontage in order to avoid any ostentation, the building of St. Augustine's Chapel was very different. It was built opposite the houses of well-to-do; it was not hidden away; it was a 'noble edifice'; it had seats for one thousand, and beneath, room for one thousand pupils.

The key parts of this letter encapsulate the very essence of Broomhead's work in the town and there is a sense running through it of a man who had brought his people out from the margins of society, and the building of the 'noble edifice 'of St Augustine's was a statement of the arrival of the Catholic community and it was the apogee of Broomhead's life. This letter written in September 1820 is awe-inspiring and speaks to every generation. It encapsulates the amazing fabric of the chapel but it is the centrality of the work of Broomhead which brought together such a unique group to celebrate the opening of the chapel of St Augustine.

## 2. Death and Burial of Rowland Broomhead

Four important pieces of primary evidence allow us to construct a description of the final few months of Broomhead's life and his death and burial. They are: an anonymous letter written by a Catholic layman to the Manchester Gazette;[9] the funeral discourse of Rev Joseph Curr;[10] the panegyric written in poetic form by Michael Gaffey[11] and the transposition of evidence that had been written in the Manchester 'Exchange-Herald' which was then presented as a brief memoir and funeral elegy. This latter document contains internal references which show that this memoir and elegy was written by a member of the Protestant Church.

Some four months before the completion of the new church of St Augustine, Broomhead's health gave cause for concern and he went into rural retirement and rest in the hope that he would see the opening of the church. According to a letter written by John Gradwell in Preston, dated 30 April 1819, to his brother Robert, rector at the English College in Rome:

> Mr Broomhead and Mr Curr were at Sheffield so we had not the pleasure of seeing them.[12]

This extract suggests that his rural retirement was the family home at Sheffield where his nephew Richard Broomhead lived.

He returned to Manchester to be present at the opening ceremony of St Augustine's, Wednesday 27 September 1820, but he was so frail that he had to be carried into the church in a chair. He was present at Rook Street, for the last time, for divine service on Sunday, 1 October 1820, but then sickness confined him to his bed. According to the anonymous letter of the Catholic layman:

> He was perfectly sensible of his approaching last hour, and with his last words craving a blessing on his flock, resigned his soul into the hands of his Creator.

The Manchester 'Exchange-Herald' recorded that Rowland Broomhead died on Thursday, 12 October 1820, about half-past four in the afternoon at the age of sixty-nine years. The same paper described the period between his death and his burial:

> for several days, his corpse had rested in the Chapel adjoining his house in Rook-street, in order that the crowding thousands (particularly of the poor), might gratify the

feelings of grateful recollection, by approaching the remains of their constant Benefactor, their Father and their Friend.

Michael Gaffey recorded this scene:

> For many days his body lay exposed
> In Rook-street chapel, where his labours closed,
> That all his people might admitted be
> Their pastor, father, and their friend to see,
> And bid a last farewell, ere he was laid
> In that great monument himself had made-
> For this some thousands gather'd round his bier
> Anxious to shed a tributary tear.
> Each read his loss in Broomhead's closed eyes,
> And fill'd the air with murmurings and cries.

On the day of Fr Broomhead's funeral, Wednesday, 18 October 1820, Michael Gaffey caught the mood of the people of Manchester lining the route from Rook Street, along York Street, Mosley Street, London Road and into St Augustine's Church in Granby Row:

> Until the day of burial was known
> Which seem'd an holliday throughout the town-
> Trade for a while lay dormant, all was still,
> And crowding multitudes the street did fill;
> Windows blockaded were with many a head,
> And tops of houses too were overspread
> With people eager to behold the dead.

The Manchester *Exchange-Herald* reported that:

> By eight o'clock on Wednesday morning many hundred persons were assembled in the neighbourhood of Rook-street, eager to witness the Funeral Procession of a man so universally beloved; and before nine, they had increased to thousands, crowding all the streets on the line between the spot where he rested from his labours and Granby-Row.

As the solemn procession moved slowly between the assembled crowds the Church of St Augustine was already full to capacity awaiting the arrival of the hearse and many thousands were unable to watch the obsequies. The church had been made ready for the funeral and was described by the Protestant writer:

> In respect to the memory of the deceased, the Altar was covered with black, as were the steps which approach it. The back part of the Altar was made strikingly funereal by the Deaths' heads, which marked the sad office to be performed; and the six large candles, which form a part of the decorations of a Catholic Altar, seemed to spring from celestial crowns, over which were also pictured the relics of mortality. The Pulpit was also enveloped in black, and from the elegance of its outline, had a picturesque as well as an impressive effect.[13]

On arrival of the horse-drawn hearse the coffin was carried into the church of St Augustine by the eight porters, members of Broomhead's chapel. The officiating priest in the celebration of the rites was, Rev Thomas Lupton, assisted by the Rev John Ashhurst, Deacon and the Rev James Newshome, Sub-Deacon, Rev R. Thompson, of Welbeck; Rev Joseph Shepherd, of Bolton; Rev James Blundell of Stockport; Rev Jones, of Hassop; Rev Edward Kenyon, of Pleasington; Rev T. Sadler, of Trafford; Rev C. Peisnelle, and the Rev Joseph Curr who gave the funeral eulogy.

The officiating clergy put aside their mourning attire and vested for the beginning of the Mass. Eight of the eleven priests carried the pall while they all processed to the Altar accompanying the coffin and singing the 'Miserere mei, Deus'. At the conclusion of the psalm six candles were lit and placed, three on each side of coffin for the duration of the Mass, and the pall was placed over the coffin. The only description of the liturgy was in the document of the Manchester Exchange-Herald:

We shall not pretend to describe the peculiar ceremonies which were observed on this occasion, a part of which was a Solemn Mass, performed with the usual accompaniments of music, &c. To Protestants, unaccustomed as they are to the ceremonies of the Catholic Church, they certainly did appear, in some particular parts, overcharged; but it must be confessed, that the effect produced (objectionable as many of the ceremonies are to the understanding of those who dissent from the faith of the Church of Rome) was imposingly solemn; and, putting the consideration of religious opinions out of the question, and considering it, simply, as productive of dramatic impressions, it was awfully grand.

According to the same source, the Rev Joseph Curr:

delivered a most impressive and feeling Funeral Eulogy. It was eloquent; but it had a better property than eloquence:-it was true...The Reverend Orator did not confine himself to addressing the Lay part of his hearers; for he most solemnly exhorted his Clerical Brethren who were present, to emulate the Piety, the Zeal, and the Virtues, of their departed Brother.

The final prayers were said over the coffin and his remains were sprinkled with holy water as a reminder of his baptism and reverenced with incense which represented the consuming zeal of the Christian, the odour of virtue and the going-up of prayer to God.[14] His remains were buried in a vault below the floor of St Augustine's Church. He was later reinterred at St Joseph's Cemetery, Moston, Manchester, 2 August 1909.[15]

According to the Manchester *Exchange-Herald*:

In the ceremonial of the interment, a few, only actively assisted; but the sacrifice of the heart was universal; and Catholic and Protestant aspirations ascended together to the Throne of Grace. Such a Funeral, Manchester never before witnessed.

# Notes

1    Broomhead, *Letter to Marsh 27 February 1806* (UCA: Eyre correspondence 43).

2    Broomhead, *Letter to W. Gibson 12 February 1807* (LDA: WG. 553A).

3    *Rules & Regulations, agreed upon by the Bishop and Secular Clergy Priests, in the Hundreds of Salford & Macclesfield, for the future care and management of their Funds and Temporal Affairs 1823* (SDA).

4    Croskell, *Traditions Connected with the Revival of the Catholic Faith in Manchester* (SDA, 'The Harvest' SDA, 1896), vol. ix.

5    J. Palmer, *The Construction of St Augustine's Chapel* (LRO: RCMA 2/1/151).

6    Broomhead, *pays for the beer* (LRO: RCMA 2/1/95).

7    R. Loxham, *Illustrations of parish churches: the district churches and chapelries of the town and townships of the collegiate parish of Manchester in the county of Lancaster 1837–1838* (Manchester, 1838) 2 vols.

8    Manchester Gazette, September 1820.

9    An anonymous Catholic Layman *letter to the Printer of the Manchester Gazette dated October 1820* (MCL).

10   Curr, *A Discourse delivered at St Augustine's Chapel, Manchester, 18 October 1820.*

11   Gaffey, *A Panegyric of the late Rev Rowland Broomhead.*

12   J. Gradwell, *Letter to his brother Robert, Rector of the English College, Rome, 30 April 1819* (VEC Scr. 56. 6).

13   *Manchester Exchange-Herald* (MCL).

14   Attwater *The Catholic Encyclopaedic Dictionary*

15   L. C. Casartelli, Bishop of Salford *From Granby Row to Moston*, The Harvest, Vol. XXII, No. 263, August 1909 (SDA): The acquisition by the City of Manchester of the buildings and site of 'old St Augustine's', Granby Row, Manchester, has necessitated the transference of the remains of the many clergy and laity who were interred during the early part of the last century beneath and around the church. Among these are the remains of eleven priests, interred between 1820 and 1845, and who may be reckoned among the pioneers of Catholicity, not only in Manchester and district, but also in many parts of Lancashire and neighbouring counties. It is proposed to honour the memory of these our venerable predecessors in the Ministry by a solemn translation from their former place of sepulture to the Campo

Santo in St Joseph's Cemetery, Moston Lane, on Monday, August 2nd. In order to add solemnity to this public tribute of respect and veneration for those of the workmen of the vineyard, into whose labours we have entered so abundantly, the Bishops of Liverpool, Salford, and Shrewsbury, whose dioceses together formed the old Vicariate Apostolic of Lancashire, will either take part or be officially represented in the function. The eleven priests were listed as follows with a short biography: Rev Rowland Broomhead; Rev John Rickaby; Rev Thomas Parkinson; Rev John Ashurst; Rev James Smith; Rev Thomas Maddocks; Rev Henry Gillow; Rev John Laytham; Rev John Parsons; Rev John Ward and Rev John Billington. The programme for the service: 9–30. Hearses leave old St Augustine's for St Joseph's Cemetery; 10–45. Hymns at Campo Santo by Choir of Children of Mary; (a) Pontifical Requiem Mass at the Campo Santo, by the Bishop of Shrewsbury (b) Sermon after Mass by the Bishop of Salford (c) The Absolutions by the Bishop of Salford (d) Interment of the eleven Priests in the Campo Santo Vaults (e) After the Interment, while the Bishops and attendants retire, Hymns by Choir of Children of Mary.

# 14 FORMATION & ACCLAMATION

ROWLAND BROOMHEAD IMBIBED the love of his faith and the deep history of their unbroken recusancy and service to those in the neighbourhood who faithfully kept their Catholic religion alive for generations, at the family chapel. The visitors at their home, both priests and people, through word and example, reinforced his commitment to his faith but the commitment of these people who also faced all the possibilities of the penal laws as his parents did, instilled in him a great respect for their strength of will.

The Broomheads were a minor-gentry family but as recusants with a chapel in their home they entertained priests whose secret work of reading the Mass and providing the sacraments was concealed, by acting as tutors to the children. Fr Christopher Gradwell and Fr John Lodge, both secular priests, served Revell Grange, the former from 1736 to 1758 and the latter from 1758 to 1786, and were party to Broomhead's early education.

The very fact that he only attended school at Sedgley Park for about eight months before being accepted as a student for the priesthood is recognition that in his early years he had been well educated. The influences at Sedgley Park were mainly from secular clergy but Challoner's book *The Garden of the Soul* contained a sound basis for the understanding of the religious life of a Catholic, and was a key foundation to Broomhead's year at the school. There were Jesuit influences in *The Garden of the Soul*. Two sections in the book were, 'Instructions for meditation including the meditations of St Francis de Sales' and 'Instruction and devotion for

confession; an examination of conscience upon the ten command-
ments; a prayer for obtaining contrition; a meditation before
confession; affections and resolutions; the method of confession;
a prayer after confession; a protestation out of St Francis de Sales'.

Broomhead's formation, at the English College in Rome, from
1765 till 1773, was for the most part in the hands of the Jesuits. The
curriculum at the English College combined prayer and penance
with teaching and study. The former was translated into daily
meditation; daily Mass; Confession of Obligation; the spirituals;
the recitation of litanies; daily Benediction and recitation of the
rosary. In his membership of the Sodality of the Blessed Virgin
Mary he agreed to go to daily Mass, weekly Confession, monthly
Communion and daily meditation.

The constitution, of the Society of Jesus, conceived by Ignatius
had four strands: to go on the missions at the Pope's bidding; to
educate the youth of all classes; to instruct the ignorant and the
poor; and to minister to the sick, prisoners etc. All aspects of this
Jesuit constitution were mirrored in Broomhead's life. He took the
missionary oath 'to lead a life befitting the clerical state and declare
his readiness to return at the will of superiors to England and there
labour for the good of souls' which he fulfilled. He supported the
Sunday school movement and the Free School through which he
instructed the ignorant and poor and Broomhead ministered to the
sick and poor and prisoners:

> How oft I've seen the subject of my song
> Trudging with short but hasty steps along
> The streets of Manchester, before the sun
> Could shed his beam's above the horizon;
> From house to house he went, from door to door,
> To see the sick, and to relieve the poor.

Ignatius was also a man of few words but selected those which
would make a deep impression on the mind. Broomhead's

approach was much the same, using only words that could be understood by his entire congregation:

> Thus, in a little chapel of his own,
> The truths of Christianity were sown
> For more than forty years, in words that could
> By every auditor be understood.[1]

The *Spiritual Exercises* of Ignatius influenced Broomhead's *Public Instructions*. In the town of Manchester he responded to the needs of everybody in the wider community by inviting Catholics, lapsed Catholics and those of other faiths or none to his chapel in Rook Street. In just the same way that Ignatius had spent time in preparing for general confession during his own conversion, Broomhead followed that same pattern, when instructing the people who had come forward to convert or return to the practice of their religion. He required that they spent about a week in meditation in preparation for their general confession, before they were received into or back into the church. Broomhead was called 'good Father Broomhead' by his congregation and 'the poor man's friend' by the other people in Manchester; epithets which would have delighted Ignatius.

The words of priests and people acclaiming the life of Rowland Broomhead are a perpetual monument to his memory. The discourse given by Rev Joseph Curr at the funeral on 18 October 1820 was not immediately published, but repeated solicitations for its publication prevailed, for he said:

> he could no longer deny to the memory of his lamented
> brother a tribute which everyone seemed both to
> expect and to claim…He hopes, therefore, for the
> indulgence of his readers, and particularly of those
> among them who from a longer and closer acquaint-
> ance with the deceased must on many points feel that

he has done inadequate justice to his extraordinary merits...the memory of Father Broomhead will be handed down with glory to the latest posterity'.[2]

*33. Painting of Rowland Broomhead*

These 'extraordinary merits' can be extracted from this discourse. He asked this 'large and unusual concourse' a rhetorical question; why they were sorrowful and his response was:

Ah! The Christian has lost his brother, the Catholic has lost his father, a dear and respected father, and the child of poverty has lost his best, his most constant and unwearied friend. Yes, your brother, your father, and your friend, is now no more … You have indeed lost your brother, your father, and your benefactor, but let the well-grounded hope that he is in peace, set bounds to your grief; for certainly the same virtues, which have so long endeared him to you, must have endeared him to heaven also. Permit me, therefore, on this day of mourning, to console you with an eulogium of departed virtue, by giving you, not indeed an exact portrait, (for that is only to be found in the book of life) but a faint outline of the qualities, which for more than forty years have raised this great man … so far above the level of the associates in his sacred functions, and to so exalted a rank in universal estimation as a member of society … my only apprehension is, that, as so many are present who have had a much longer and more intimate acquaintance with him than myself, I shall, in their estimation, fail in the attempt to do justice to his merits.

Joseph Curr presented an overview of Rowland Broomhead's priestly ministry:

With reference to the duties of his sacred ministry, truly may he be called a faithful and prudent servant, whom the Lord placed over his family. Numerous, important, and difficult were the charges entrusted to him, but he always went through them with unwearied diligence and perseverance.

He then turned to Broomhead's work, in overcoming the problems of life-destroying ignorance, through education:

What shall I say of the solicitude, which he ever manifested, or how shall I extol the efforts he made, to destroy the baneful effects of ignorance? Convinced that a want of religious knowledge was one of the most fertile sources of vice, he conceived in his vast and judicious mind, a plan of imparting that knowledge to his flock, the effect of which, in every individual among them, could be frustrated by nothing but obstinate perversity. You know how, from your earliest years, he was careful to gather you around the precincts of the sanctuary. You have heard him, in language which spoke to every understanding, and with emphasis which came home to every heart, develop the mysteries, and inculcate the precepts of our holy religion. His success is the astonishment of those who witnessed it, and to those who know it only by report it is almost incredible... Had, however, his plans extended no farther than could have been realized by his own individual exertions, they had been less complete than they are. I allude principally to that invaluable establishment, where upwards of a thousand children are weekly taught the rudiments of useful knowledge, and are instructed in the principles of religion.

The large extent of the Manchester Mission and Broomhead's involvement in the early years of his ministry in those outlying areas and the extent of his work were the next part of his discourse:

Like a good shepherd, he thought no hour unseasonable, no place too distant to go in quest of the wandering sheep. In the days of his vigour, when he had a smaller field for his labours at home, he had gathered together congregations in several of the neighbouring towns and villages, which he regularly visited at stated times. But, as his attention became more required at home, and the advances of old age rendered him less able to bestow his paternal solicitude upon them, he procured the appointment of resident pastors, being convinced that the utmost care he could bestow, particularly as their numbers increased, was less than their spiritual necessities required.

He then celebrated Broomhead's regard for the sick and infirm:

His constant attention to another important branch of a pastor's duty, I mean that of assisting at the bed-side of infirmity and sickness, I cannot pass unnoticed…Did ever one of his flock, whilst reclining on the bed of sickness, however far he might have erred from the path of righteousness, intimate a desire of his assistance, to whom he did not hasten with parental solicitude? Night and day, distance and proximity, poverty and respectability were equally indifferent to his pious zeal. With emphatic language, the unfeigned effusions of his own charitable and affected soul, would he endeavour to rouse the courage of the desponding, to impress on the heart of the death-bed penitent a sincere detestation of his past sinful life, and to animate all with the most lively sentiments of faith, hope, charity, and resignation? That you may form some idea of the extent of his charity in this particular, pass over, if possible, in your minds the days and nights of forty long and successive years; figure to yourselves, if you can, the endless scenes of sickness and misery which during those years have existed among the different families under his spiritual care; and then take a view of this man of God performing among them the daily circuit of his charity, and often too disturbed whilst giving to wearied nature its necessary repose.

Curr then turned to what he called his particular notice; the increase in numbers in the mission and how Broomhead responded:

When first he entered upon his pastoral duties in this town, one small chapel contained his people; when their numbers became considerably increased, the erection of another chapel, on a much enlarged scale, was undertaken and completed. But, both at length became inadequate to contain them, you all know, and have seen, how the last years of his life, which ought to have been dedicated to retirement and repose, were clouded with anxiety and labour by his endeavours to accomplish still more extensive projects. He did, indeed, accomplish them, but it was with the last effort of exhausted nature ... Doubtless, my brethren, you had anticipated almost with impatience the delight of hearing in this house the voice of your beloved Pastor, and of thus witnessing the triumph of his zeal and labours. The day would truly have been to you a day of rejoicing. But your fond hopes have failed, and no other satisfaction remains than to convert into his monument the place which you hoped would have been the theatre of his glory.

He then portrayed the reasons for Broomhead's exaltation:

You will not suffer me to conclude this eulogium without attempting to delineate the pleasing picture of that universal charity and benevolence which raised your Pastor as a man to so exalted a rank in your estimation, which endeared him so much to the poor and indigent, and procured him (I fear no contradiction in what I am going to assert) the unrivalled esteem and regard of all ranks of society.

He asked the congregation in what way they should remember Fr Broomhead:

We shall admit that his name and his virtues ought to be engraven on a monument that will transmit their memory with glory to succeeding ages. But how shall this be effected? Shall they be recorded on one of those perishable monuments raised by the hands of men? No: rather let us who have survived him in his ministry, study to copy his virtues, and thus hand their memory to posterity. And as for a monument to record his name, it shall neither be of marble nor of brass: his name shall be written on the hearts of all to whom Christianity is dear, and parents, when they are teaching their little ones to lisp the principles of religion, shall add that they received them from ... Father Broomhead.

An elegy was printed as follows:

To relieve the wretched was his pride
And e'en his failings lean'd to virtues side:
But in his duty prompt at every call
He watch'd and wept, and pray'd and felt for all
And as a bird each fond endearment tries
To tempt her new fledged offspring to the skies,
He tried each art, reprov'd each dull delay
Allur'd to brighter worlds and led the way.
Beside the bed where parting life was laid
And sorrow, guilt, and pain, by turns, dismay'd,
The reverend champion stood. At his control,
Despair and anguish fled the struggling soul;
Comfort came down the trembling wretch to raise,
And his last faltering accents whisper'd praise[3].

The *Exchange-Herald* supported the discourse of Joseph Curr:

> The latter gentleman, in the course of the service, ascended
> the pulpit, and delivered a most impressive and feeling
> Funeral Eulogy. It was eloquent, but it had a better property
> than eloquence:-it was true. Every trait of character portrayed
> of the good man, whose shell, at the moment, rested beneath
> the eyes of the Reverend Orator, was at once recognized by
> the whole of his attentive, though promiscuous auditory;
> their hearts bearing involuntary testimony of the accuracy
> with which the picture of so much Virtue and Benevolence
> was drawn; while the references to the zeal and piety, which
> marked his professional life, and the allusions made by the
> preacher to the close connexion he had with many present,
> in the performance of the duties of his sacred function,
> vibrated, which responded in melancholy harmony...

An anonymous Catholic layman wrote a letter to the Manchester
Gazette on the death and funeral of Rowland Broomhead:

> Any attempt of mine to enumerate the virtues that shone so
> conspicuous in this great and good man, would be like an

effort to number the sands of the ocean, or give an adequate description to one who has been always blind of the glory of the sun in its meridian splendour. Nor is it necessary, for the number and respectability of those who attended on this melancholy occasion, and the silent eloquence of their tears, speaks more than words can possibly express. About nine o'clock the funeral procession moved from Rook-street, along York-street, Mosley-street, and London Road, to St. Augustine's Chapel, Granby Row, through an immense concourse of spectators of all classes of society. This scene was truly affecting and honourable, both to the deceased and the living, the first commanding respect, and the latter paying a just tribute to the memory of departed worth. The opulent mourned the loss of a worthy associate in their extensive charities; the clergy's zealous fellow labourer in the Lord's vineyard; the poor a father, and all a useful member of society. If any man may be said to have no enemies, he was certainly that man... But my Catholic brethren, the most effectual way of honouring him, the most pleasing to the Almighty, the most useful to society, the most beneficial to ourselves, is to imitate his virtues. The lessons he has so emphatically taught and implanted in our hearts, will, by being often called to remembrance, take deep root, flourish, and produce happy fruits, when he who cultivated them is mouldering in the grave.

## Notes

[1]    Gaffey, *A Panegyric of the late Rev Rowland Broomhead*.

[2]    Curr, *A Discourse delivered at St Augustine's Chapel*, Manchester, 1820.

[3]    *Brief Memoirs of the late Rev Rowland Broomhead of Manchester with an Account of his Funeral and Funeral Elegy* (Manchester, printed and sold by Joseph Aston of St. Ann's Street Manchester based on writings in the 'Exchange-Herald', 1820. The approbation bestowed on the following Brief

memoirs of a most estimable Character, the memory of whose virtues will long be dear to his friends, his flock and his fellow townsmen, has induced the Author to transpose it from the columns of the 'Exchange-Herald in which it originally appeared, and publish it in a separate form, with the addition of a Funeral Elegy, written for the occasion.

# APPENDIX ONE

## *Rowland Broomhead's Family Pedigree*

### BROOMHEAD
#### GENERATION SIX
#### RICHARD OF THORNSETT

Born c. 1548 and married Emote the daughter of John Tomson of Thornsett, yeoman, 10 September 1570, at Bradfield. She and her sister Ann were coheirs to their Father's estate. Richard died 1 January 1625.

#### GENERATION FIVE
#### RICHARD OF NETHER BRADFIELD
#### (1)

Married Beatrice daughter of Thomas Bromhead son and heir apparent in 1620. Had issue 1638. Died 8 March 1638.

#### GENERATION FOUR
#### RICHARD OF NETHER BRADFIELD

Born 7 November 1646 at Nether Bradfield and marriage circa 1665. Had three sisters: Anne, Gertrude and Eleanor.

### REVELL
#### GENERATION SEVEN
#### THOMAS

Living in 1 Edw.VI [1547–48] when he surrendered a Mess[uage], etc in Stannington to the use of Gregory his son and heir, then about to marry Elizabeth, daughter of Thomas Barber

#### GENERATION SIX
#### GREGORY

Gregory of Stannington born about 1530. Married Elizabeth daughter of Thomas Barber 1 Ed.VI [1547/48] Burial 23 March 1588/89 at Bradfield. [?] Will 15th October 1588. Elizabeth died 1st July, 1606. Later married Alice?

#### GENERATION FIVE
#### RICHARD

Richard of Stannington born about 1560. He married Margret Revell 29 October, 1581.

## BROOMHEAD

### GENERATION THREE
### RICHARD OF NETHER BRADFIELD

Born 21 March 1666 at Nether Bradfield married Ann Stead of Onesacre 22 June 1710 at Bradfield chapel. Died 31 October 1749 at Nether Bradfield.

### GENERATION TWO
### RICHARD OF NETHER BRADFIELD

Born 26 December 1718 at Bradfield near Sheffield. Married Ann Revell 10 November 1742 at St. Nicholas Chapel, Bradfield. Died 17 August 1778 buried at Bradfield chapel.

### GENERATION ONE
### ROWLAND

Born 16 August 1751 at Revell Grange, Stannington, in the chapelry of Bradfield in the parish of Ecclesfield near Sheffield. Son of Richard Broomhead and Ann née Revell. Died October 1820 in Manchester.

## REVELL

### GENERATION FOUR
### ROWLAND

Rowland Revel of Stannington. Second son. Married Elizabeth daughter of Francis Percy of Scotton & Stubs Walden & Frances daughter of Ralph Vavasour of Hazelwood. Will date 12 April, 1644. Proved at York 3 Sept 1646. Rowland and Elizabeth were recusants. She was buried in 1682.

### GENERATION THREE
### RICHARD

Born 5 February 1639 at Nethergate Hall and married Hannah Hippon and died 23 April 1679 at Nethergate Hall, and was buried at Bradfield chapel.

### GENERATION TWO
### ROWLAND & THOMAS

Rowland born 1 April 1669 died without issue 23 May 1742

Thomas born January 1675 at Bingley Lane, Stannington. Married Elizabeth Houseman of Eckington 16 April 1703. Inherited estate 23 May 1742. Died at Revell Grange, Bingley Lane, Stannington, 15 November 1744.

### GENERATION ONE
### ANN

Born 20 September 1713 at Nethergate Hall, Stannington. Married Richard Broomhead 10 November 1742. Inherited her Father's estate 15 November 1744. Died 27 May 1792 and buried at Bradfield chapel.

# APPENDIX TWO

## *Various documents*

### Part 1

*Documents Concerning Church Street & Rook Street Chapel, Manchester Trustees 29 December 1784; Old Trust as to Rook Street Chapel. Declaration of Trust & Rules and Regulations written by Rev Rowland Broomhead and accepted and signed by Bishop William Gibson 7 May 1790.*

We whose names are hereunto subscribed, being the Trustees at the time of signing this declaration, for the Catholick Chapel in Rook Street & sundry dwelling houses and sundry other buildings in Church Street Manchester, as well as sundry sums of money now out at interest; do hereby acknowledge & declare to the Right Rev. d Father in God Matthew Gibson that the said Chapel Dwelling Houses & other buildings as well as said sum or sums of Money out at Interest, thereunto belonging; are held by not as Property pertaining or belonging to us or anyone else their executors administrators assigns, but in trust, solely and only towards supplying the said Town & vicinity with one or more priests to chose & appoint out of the Secular Clergy, as shall seem requisite & proper to the said Right Rev Father in God Matthew Gibson & a successor by choice (—-) Bishop for the Northern District of the old secular Clergy & not of any of the Religious orders, monks, Ex-Jesuits, friars &c: and in case such succeeding Bishop is chose out of any of the aforesaid Religious Orders, then the appointment of a Priest or

Priests is vested in the Vicar General or Chief Superior of the old secular Clergy (for the time being) in the County of Lancaster who said Priest or Priests are to be appointed by him or them only for the purpose of serving the said Chapel occupying the house annexed to it, enjoying the annual rents of the benches therein, the rents of Buildings &c: in Church Street belonging to the same and the lawful interest of any sum or sums of money which are or may be committed in trust to us or any of us for such use and purpose. It being well understood & agreed and agreed upon between the said Right Rev Father in God Matthew Gibson (in instalments) as Head of the Old Secular Clergy conscious that it is not in their power so to do. Such Premises &c; being vested in Trust in their hands for the above entered purposes & which must be carefully transmitted to all succeeding trustees Regularly chose agreeable to Regulations & Rules this day agreed upon by the Right Rev Father in God Matthew Gibson & said Trustees. In witness whereof we have hereunto put our hands this day, December 29th 1784, in the year of our Lord one thousand seven hundred & eighty-four.

Matthew Gibson Comanen VA, Charles Houghton, Rowland Broomhead, John Cook, William Moorhouse, William Walton, Benjamin Wildsmith, Richard Kaye, James Ormston, John Cowling & B. Gomutis ...

# Part 2

## *Rules & Regulations, agreed upon by the Bishop and Secular Clergy Priests, in the Hundreds of Salford & Macclesfield, for the future care and management of their Funds and Temporal Affairs 1823 (SDA).*

### Rule 1st.

That said Catholick (sic) Chapel in Rook Street Manchester, shall always be served from out of and by the Old Secular Clergy appointed by the Bishop of the Northern District if said Bishop is of the secular Clergy, but in case said Bishop is of any of the Religious Orders, Ex-Jesuits, Friars, &c: then the appointment is vested in the Vicar General or superior of the Old Secular Clergy in the County of Lancaster; it being well known to and understood by all the subscribing Parties always were the intention of all the (…) and subscribers to said Chapel, other Buildings & monies thereunto belonging.

### Rule 2nd.

No person whatever to be permitted under any pretence whatever to kneel within the aisles or at Rails of said Chapel unless during the time of Communion.

### Rule 3rd.

Whenever it shall be judged necessary and advantageous by the Bishop, Incumbents & Trustees that any seat or seats shall then be sold; such seat or seats shall then be sold by a majority of the trustees provided Purchaser or Purchasers are agreeable to said Bishop Incumbents and trustees; in case not agreeable to all the said parties any one of them may negate said sale or sales.

### Rule 4th.

On the Sunday following each Quarter day all renters of seats are to pay their respective Rents to Persons appointed by the Incumbents, each Persons will always duly attend to receive & collect said Rents on the Sundays next following the 25 of March, the 24 of June, the 19th of September & the 25th of December in each succeeding year.

### Rule 5th.

All Renters of seats refusing to pay their Rents till three quarters are due, shall forfeit the said seats for the length of the Incumbents & if it should be thought proper that the said seat should be sold again then and in that case the money which the Incumbents may have lost by none payment of Rents shall be refunded to them out of the Money arising from said purchases.

### Rule 6th.

No alterations or repair to be made at the expence of the Incumbent to, either in the Chapel or Premises in Rook Street or in the houses in Church Street, without their express consent or that of the Bishop, being first obtained, but if disputes should arise respecting any such alterations or repairs in that case the Trustees shall appoint one referee on their part & the Incumbents shall appoint another referee on their part to settle said Dispute & if these two referees cannot settle & fix what ought to be done; in that case said two referees shall chose a third person to act as umpire in the Business; if these said three Referees cannot settle said business in that case it shall be determined by the Bishop of the Northern District & of the Old secular Clergy; but if there is no such Bishop then by the Superior of the Old Secular Clergy in Lancashire who shall finally determine what ought and is to be necessary to be done.

**Rule 7<sup>th</sup>.**

The Trustees shall not withhold any part of the Income belonging to the Incumbent on any pretext whatever without the express approbation of the Bishop for the time being.

**Rule 8<sup>th</sup>.**

Any purchaser of seat or seats may dispose of the same to any person approved of by the Incumbents or Trustees

**Rule 9<sup>th</sup>.**

Each seat has its original rent fixed to it from which there can be no deviation without the express convent (sic) of the Bishop for the time being if all the Secular Clergy & the Rents of the Benches in the Gallery shall not be fixed without the Bishop's approbation.

**Rule 10<sup>th</sup>.**

If any Trustee shall become obnoxious to the Incumbent or Trustees such Trustee may be expelled by a majority of their votes.

**Rule 11<sup>th</sup>.**

At the Resignation or Death of any Trustee his successor shall not be appointed without the Mutual approbation of the Bishop Incumbents & Trustees, and it is likewise clearly understood& agreed upon by the three aforesaid parties concerned herein viz. The Bishop Incumbents & Trustees, that no person whatever although nominated as a Trustee shall be esteemed duly elected & Qualified to act as a Trustee in future, until he has agreed to the Declaration of Trust & the Rules are now signed and agreed upon by the present Bishop Incumbent & Trustees & have actually signed his name thereunto an acknowledgement that he agrees the said declaration and Rules.

**Rule 12th.**

That the Bishop of the Old secular Clergy shall inspect copies of the Deeds, writings and accounts whenever he shall please to call for them.

**Rule 13th.**

That neither the present Trustees nor future Trustees have any right or power to sell all or any part of the Premises or Properties which they may at present or hereafter hold in trust, without the consent of the Bishop & Incumbents being first obtained.

**Rule 14th.**

As unforeseen casualties may happen requiring an additional rule or rules such may be added by or with the consent of the Bishop Incumbents & Trustees.

Matthew Gibson, Comanen VA
Charles Houghton, Rowland Broomhead
John Cook, William Moorhouse,
William Walton, Benjamin Wildsmith,
Richard Kaye, James Ormston

Manchester
December 29th 1784

## Part 3

### Indenture of 30 November 1808 (Extract)

Grant and Release of a yearly rent out of £54 issuing and arising out of land and buildings in Manchester in the County of Lancashire.

Mr William Walton to the Rev Rowland Broomhead and others.

A yearly Rent Charge issued out of:

All those two messuages or dwellinghouses standing and being in and fronting a certain street in Manchester called Church Street some time in the tenure or occupation of Anthony Jobling and Edward Helme afterwards in the tenure or occupation of Mr Meadow and Widow Slater and later in the tenure or occupation of Mr Cooper and Mr Medhurst more recently in the tenure or occupation of Colonel Herbert Marshall Finch and now in the tenure or occupation of Mr William Rowley Sutton, Estate Agent, Manchester.

And also all that other messuage or dwelling house standing and being at the back of the last mentioned messuages or dwelling-houses some time ago in the tenure or occupation of Thomas Johnson afterwards in the tenure or occupation of Mary Cunney and later in the tenure or occupation of Mr Greenhalgh and now or lately in the tenure or occupation of the said William Rowley Sutton and also all that other edifice or building standing also on the back of the two first above mentioned messuages or dwelling-houses thereby granted and released formerly used as a Chapel but later as a School and in the tenure or occupation of the said William. Medhurst. The said Yearly Rent Charge was by a Release dated the Thirtieth day of November One Thousand Eight Hundred and Eight conveyed by William Walton, Thomas Whitgreave and Richard Kaye to the Reverend Rowland Broomhead the Reverend Thomas Lupton the Reverend Richard Thompson the Reverend James Blundell and the Reverend Edward Kenyon.

# APPENDIX THREE

## *Statistical Charts*

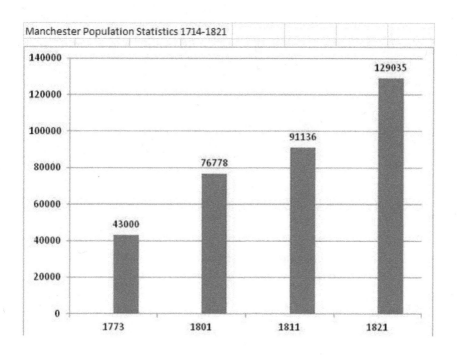

Manchester Population Statistics 1714-1821

*34. Chart of Manchester Population Statistics 1714–1821*

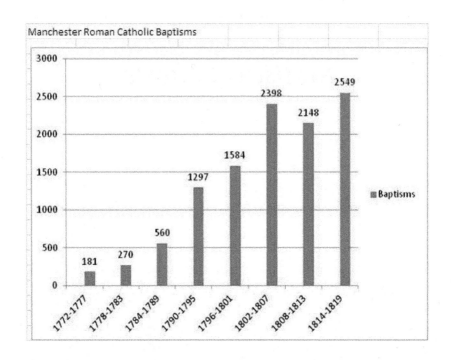

*35. Chart of Manchester Roman Catholic Baptisms 1772–1819*

## 36. Chart: Annual Baptismal Returns for Rook St & Mulberry St Chapels 1772–1819

| DATE | ROOK STREET | MULBERRY STREET | TOTAL |
|------|-------------|-----------------|-------|
| 1772 | 22 | | 22 |
| 1773 | 33 | | 33 |
| 1774 | 31 | | 31 |
| 1775 | 32 | | 32 |
| 1776 | 28 | | 28 |
| 1777 | 35 | | 35 |
| 1778 | 52 | | 52 |
| 1779 | 52 | | 52 |
| 1780 | 29 | | 29 |
| 1781 | 55 | | 55 |
| 1782 | 39 | | 39 |
| 1783 | 43 | | 43 |
| 1784 | 66 | | 66 |
| 1785 | 78 | | 78 |
| 1786 | 93 | | 93 |
| 1787 | 98 | | 98 |
| 1788 | 117 | | 117 |
| 1789 | 108 | | 108 |
| 1790 | 152 | | 152 |
| 1791 | 211 | | 211 |
| 1792 | 251 | | 251 |
| 1793 | 254 | | 254 |
| 1794 | 210 | 2 | 212 |
| 1795 | 135 | 84 | 219 |
| 1796 | 163 | 72 | 235 |
| 1797 | 167 | 107 | 274 |
| 1798 | 211 | 86 | 297 |
| 1799 | 192 | 79 | 271 |
| 1800 | 193 | 77 | 270 |

*36. Chart: Annual Baptismal Returns for Rook St & Mulberry St Chapels*
*1772–1819 (continued)*

| DATE | ROOK STREET | MULBERRY STREET | TOTAL |
|------|-------------|-----------------|-------|
| 1801 | 176 | 61 | 237 |
| 1802 | 215 | 121 | 336 |
| 1803 | 242 | 175 | 417 |
| 1804 | 229 | 133? | 362 |
| 1805 | 271 | 160 | 431 |
| 1806 | 261 | 181 | 442 |
| 1807 | 245 | 165 | 410 |
| 1808 | 281 | 164 | 445 |
| 1809 | 241 | 125 | 366 |
| 1810 | 268 new register | 182 | 450 |
| 1811 | 284 | 129 | 413 |
| 1812 | 243 | 0 | 243 |
| 1813 | 231 | - | 231 |
| 1814 | 294 | - | 294 |
| 1815 | 349 | - | 349 |
| 1816 | 311 | 242 | 553 |
| 1817 | 204 | 268 | 472 |
| 1818 | 255 | 282 | 537 |
| 1819 | 344 | | 344 |
| **TOTAL** | **7826** | **2762** | **10989** |

# APPENDIX FOUR

## *Prayer books*

- *A Preparation for Death* by St Alphonsus Liquori
- Single Catechisms
- *Catechisms for the use of the Northern District.* (In 1784, Bishop Matthew Gibson, in conjunction with Rev Thomas Eyre, President of Ushaw College, produced a revised Catechism, written by Rev Henry Tuberville and his companions in 1649. This revised Catechism was known as the 'Little catechism' which came to be known as the 'Penny Catechism'. It carried the approbation of the four Vicars Apostolic).
- *Catechisms* (The catechism produced by Rev Henry Turberville ET alia in 1649).
- *Imitation of Christ*, Written by Thomas A Kempis (One of the most read spiritual books).
- Fénelon's *Reflections* (Full title: *Fénelon's Pious Reflections for Every Day in the Month.* Written by Francois de Salignac de la Mothe-Fénelon 1651–1715).
- *Bouhours Meditations* (Full title: *Christian Thoughts for Every Day of the Month: with a prayer, wherein is represented the nature of unfeigned repentance, and of perfect love towards God.* Written by Dominique Bouhours 1628–1702).
- *Think Well On't* (Full title: *Think Well On't or Reflections on the Great Truths of the Christian Religion for Every Day in the Month.* Written by Bishop Challoner and published at Manchester by Thomas Haydock).

- *Contrite and Humble Heart* (Full title: *The Contrite and the Humble Heart, with Motives and Considerations for Preparing for it*).
- *Spiritual Combat* (Full title: *The Spiritual Combat: to which is added, The Peace of the Soul, and, the Happiness of the Heart which Dies to itself, in order to live to God*. Translated from the work of Lorenzo Scupoli 1530–1610).
- Boudon's *Holy Sacrament of the Altar* (Full title: *The Love of Jesus in the Adorable Sacrament of the Altar*. This was translated from the French by Fr Thomas Penswick, who later became Vicar Apostolic of the Northern District, and published by Thomas Haydock in Manchester).

# APPENDIX FIVE

## *The Protestation of 1789*

1) They declared that contrary to accepted opinion neither the Pope, a General Council, Prelate, Priest, or any Ecclesiastical power can 'Absolve the Subjects of this Realm...from their Allegiance to His Majesty King GEORGE THE THIRD, who is, by Authority of Parliament, the lawful King of the Realm, and all the Dominions there unto belonging'.

2) They denied that the Pope and General Councils could demand implicit obedience of them to subvert the Laws and Liberties of the Country and acknowledged no infallibility in the Pope.

3) They solemnly declared that any ecclesiastic could not absolve or dispense anyone from 'the Obligations of any Compact or Oath'.

4) Contrary to accepted opinion 'We believe that no sin whatever can be forgiven at the Will of any POPE, or of any priest, or of any Person whomsoever; but that a sincere Sorrow for past Sin, a firm Resolution to avoid future Guilt, and every possible Atonement to God and the injured Neighbour, are the previous and indispensable Requisites to establish a well-founded Expectation of Forgiveness.

5) The denial of the accusation that Roman Catholics held a principle 'no Faith is to be kept with Heretics' in other words a government which is not Catholic cannot have any security 'from us for our Allegiance and peaceable Behaviour'.

# APPENDIX SIX

## *Broomhead's Invoices for Milner & Parkinson at the Asylum*

| There were 4 invoices for Rev. Thomas Milner: 1800; 1801; 1809 & 1810 | | | |
|---|---|---|---|
| **1800** | **L** | **s** | **d** |
| To one year's Board and Lodging | 20. | 16. | 0 |
| Mending shoes | 0. | 3. | 0. |
| Snuff | 0. | 6. | 0. |
| 3 new shirts | 1. | 5. | 6. |
| Cloth for a suit of clothes & making | 2. | 15. | 0. |
| A hat | 0. | 6. | 6. |
| A pr. of new shoes | 0. | 9. | 0. |
| Augst 25th 1800 settled by RB | 26. | 1. | 0. |
| | | | |
| **1801** | **L** | **s** | **d** |
| 1800 August 29th Shoemaker's bill | 0. | 12. | 0. |
| 1801 One year's board | 20. | 16. | 0. |
| Settled August 25th 1801 {no signature}. | 21. | 8. | 0. |

| 1809 | L | s | d |
|---|---|---|---|
| April 13th | | | |
| Cloth for a suit of clothes | 1. | 11. | 6. |
| Pocket handkerchief & stockings | 0. | 11. | 6. |
| Linen for shirts & making | 0 | 15. | 6. |
| August 24th | | | |
| Taylor's bill | 1. | 13. | 6. |
| One year's board & lodging at 10s/6d per week | | | |
| from June 24th 1808 to June 24th 1809 | 27. | 6. | 0. |
| Cash advanced by the Hospital for shaving and | | | |
| other necessaries. | 1. | 11. | 0. |
| Physician's fees for 2 years | 2. | 2. | 0. |
| By cash from Rev. Dr. Rigby. Sig.RB | 35. | 11 | 0. |
| | | | |
| **1810** | **L** | **s** | **d** |
| 1809 December 25th. To 6 months Board at 10s/6d | 13. | 13. | 0. |
| 1810 June 24th. To 6 months Board at 10s/6d | 13. | 13. | 0. |
| To cash paid for necessaries | 0. | 18. | 6. |
| Paid August 4th 1810 | 28. | 4. | 6. |
| | | | |
| The other priest at the Manchester Lunatic Asylum was Mr Parkinson {James}. | | | |
| There is only one receipt for him. | | | |
| **1804** | **L** | **s** | **d** |
| June 24th. Cloth and Taylor's bill | 1. | 13. | 6. |
| August 24th. A pair of shoes | 0. | 10. | 0. |
| One year's Board & Lodging | 20. | 19. | 6. |
| By cash August 28th 1804. RB {The addition is incorrect}. | 22. | 19. | 6. |

*37. Broomhead's Invoices for Milner & Parkinson at the Asylum*

# APPENDIX SEVEN

## *Background to the Old Chapter of England*

D URING THE PERIOD, from the break with Rome till 1575, there was no papal ecclesial jurisdiction in England and Wales until Pope Gregory XIII appointed William Allen, the founder of Douai, to be vicar general with jurisdiction for England and Wales. He was made a cardinal in 1587. He did not establish a chapter. Following his death in 1594 there was no replacement till 1599. The Holy See:

> finding that the Catholic clergy in England were much in need of a recognised head, yet unwilling to send a bishop, lest the government should take it as an excuse for fresh cruelties against the Catholics generally chose instead to send an archpriest, whose principal function was, during the illness or absence of the bishop, to replace him in the Church offices.[1]

The Chapter of England appears to have grown out of a need for some supporting structure to those in episcopal authority. The first archpriest was Rev George Blackwell, 1599 to 1608. At the same time as Blackwell was appointed, Rome also 'nominated a consultative body of twelve assistant priests'.[2] The next two archpriests were: Rev George Birkhead, 1608 to 1614, and Rev William. Harrison, 1615–1621, and they both had a consultative body of twelve assistant priests.

In 1623, William Bishop was appointed by Gregory XV, as the first vicar apostolic with the title, Bishop of Chalcedon, with jurisdiction over England and Wales, though he held his powers 'at the pope's good pleasure and subject to the higher authority of the papal nuncio in France acting as ordinary for England'.[3] He was not given the privilege of having twelve assistant priests as had the archpriests.

A vicar apostolic ruled a territory called a 'vicariate apostolic' as a delegate of the Holy See. Vicars apostolic 'had no territorial diocese, cathedral church or chapter of canons'.[4] Despite the restrictions of his office William Bishop went ahead and established a chapter of twenty canons, who were geographically located across the country. He also divided England and Wales into six districts. In spite of not being a bishop in ordinary he would appear to have:

> behaved as though he possessed such powers and estab-
> lished a Chapter, not only to advise and assist him and to
> exercise jurisdiction 'sede vacante', but even, according to
> its patent of institution, to elect future bishops.[5]

Rome never confirmed the status of this Chapter but did recognise 'the existence of the Chapter and allowed it to exercise certain jurisdictions'.[6] William Bishop died, after only a year in office.

Richard Smith, a member of the Chapter, was appointed by the Pope, to replace William Bishop, in 1625. Immediately, he set about dividing the provinces of England and Wales:

> into a certain number of vicariates and archdeaconries; consti-
> tuted seven vicars-general, and twenty-three archdeaconries
> (allotting to each vicar-general and archdeacon his proper
> district, and constituting also rural deans under the said arch-
> deacons); and, in 1627, confirmed, by his letters patent, the
> chapter, in a more ample manner; settling first an agent at
> Rome, to treat of the affairs of him and his clergy, and to
> acquaint that see with his proceedings, none of which were in
> the least either opposed or disapproved of by that court.[7]

Richard Smith came into conflict with the regulars, over his claim to be a bishop in ordinary, but Pope Urban VIII supported the regulars' case. Smith spent only six and a half years in England before he escaped to the Continent in 1631, to avoid arrest and subsequently 'resigned his Episcopal title in what appears to have been an ill-judged fit of pique'.[8] In those six and half years he had succeeded in alienating both the regulars, especially the Jesuits, some of the gentry and a significant number of his fellow Chaptermen. He retired to the home of Cardinal Richelieu in Paris. However, he appears to have 'asserted to the end, his authority over the Secular Clergy by means of the Chapter'.[9] The papacy did not appoint a replacement to Smith when he resigned in 1631, and appeared to allow Smith to continue to assert his control over the English Secular Clergy through the Chapter. He died in France in 1655.

After the death of Smith, the Chapter 'ruled' for thirty years, during which time the Chapter men continued to play a large part in the governance of the English and Welsh mission. For twenty-four years of the 'retirement' of Richard and another thirty years without a vicar apostolic, the Chapter in effect administered the mission for a total of fifty-four years.

The agent of the Chapter in Rome informed Pope Innocent X of the death of Smith and 'desired to know his pleasure concerning the state and government of the Catholic Church in England'. His Holiness replied, 'I will not disapprove of your chapter, but will let you alone with your government'.[10] Throughout the period, 1655 to 1685, the English and Welsh missions were without Episcopal governance, but the Chapter appears to have filled this gap corresponding with Rome through their agents and consistently demanding the appointment of a bishop in ordinary and not a vicar apostolic.[11]

In 1685, John Leyburn was appointed vicar apostolic much to the chagrin of the Chapter and James II, who wanted a bishop in ordinary. Leyburn was a chapterman but received instructions from

Rome 'to act independently of the chapter'.[12] From that point on the Chapter's former authority was somewhat curtailed.

On election, members took an oath to preserve the rights of the Chapter. The question arises as to whether the Chapter had a justifiable claim to those rights on legal or moral grounds? The Papacy saw fit to nominate twelve assistant priests, to act as consultants to the archpriests during the seventeenth century; six appointed by the cardinal protector and six by the archpriest himself.[13] For the period 1599 to 1621, there were assistant priests to the archpriest, with limited authority in their specific geographical location. When William Bishop was appointed, in 1623, one of the assistants to the last archpriest, William Harrison, became a member of the new Chapter.[14] There was an obvious need for some kind of network to support the person wielding ecclesiastical authority.

William Bishop, on his arrival in London, set about establishing the structures of episcopal government. There was no church in which he could establish his see; he had no financial support for his chapter, yet he had Catholics to govern and religious duties to perform.[15] Despite the fact that Rome never gave Bishop and the other vicars apostolic, the status of a bishop in 'ordinary', the Chapter always considered that it held 'ordinary' status.[16]

When Bishop John Leyburn, in 1685, took an oath[17] not to recognize the Chapter and then subsequently successfully appealed to Rome for England and Wales to be divided into four districts, with a vicar apostolic for each, the Chapter was insecure about its role when its jurisdiction was suspended. Sergeant's book of 1706 is the 'response of a dedicated chapterman whose views while not dispassionate are useful to identify the importance of the work of the Chapter'.[18]

In 1688, Pope Innocent XI divided England and Wales into four districts: London, Midland, Northern, and Western. Each district was ruled under the jurisdiction of a Vicar Apostolic. From 1688 till 1752 the following were the Vicars Apostolic of the Northern District: James Smith (1688–1711); George Witham (1716 1725); Thomas Dominic Williams O. P. (1726–1740), and Edward Dicconson (1740–1752).

In their general assembly of 1694, the Dean and Chapter were informed, by the four Vicars Apostolic, that they 'will not be allowed, without leave and confirmation from the see apostolic' to erect chapters and further 'that they would promote it, when it should be judged a convenient time'.[19] In the meantime, Leyburn, after a request from the Chapter, to 'declare to us the name and nature of his jurisdiction as to the secular clergy, as also how he would carry himself in order to the chapter', answered 'that he had no commission either to allow or deny the chapter, but that he would carry himself abstractedly towards it'.[20] The Chapter 'ceased to claim or exercise jurisdiction, but they determined not to dissolve, but to keep up their Body with Dean and Canons and Archdeacons, and to hold their regular meetings'.

In a period of interregnum a diocese had a Chapter to rule until a successor was appointed, but in a vicariate this was not so. The Chapter argued:

> that if there was no chapter then there was no one to provide priests for missions; there would be no governance of the clergy; no infliction of censuses; no one to oversee the granting of faculties or the approval of preachers; no one to give leave for a foreign bishop to administer the sacrament of confirmation.[21]

According to Sergeant, the Chapter was governed well by William Bishop and Richard Smith who:

> worthily presided over and directed this Church, and exercised ordinary Episcopal jurisdiction, in the two vacancies of the said bishops, between thirty and forty years; how it ever maintained itself and the rights of the whole secular

clergy ... against all the attacks of its adversaries; how many wholesome provisions have been made by it for the prosperous government of the Church; how many honourable actions it hath done for the advance of the clergy in piety and learning.[22]

Following the Restoration of the Hierarchy in 1850, the Old Chapter discussed the way forward as there was no longer any Episcopal role to play. They changed the name to the 'Old Chapter Trust' in 1853, but in 1862 changed its name to 'The Old Brotherhood of the English Secular Clergy'. It still retains this latter title and continues its charitable work to this day.

## Notes

[1] Addis & Arnold, p. 150.

[2] Addis & Arnold, p. 150.

[3] Questier, p. 403.

[4] Attwater. p. 515.

[5] Williams, vol. 1.

[6] Burton, vol. 1. p. 85.

[7] J. Sergeant *Transactions of the English Secular Clergy 1706*(London, reprinted by William Turnbull, 1853) p. 51–52.

[8] Questier, p. 467

[9] T. A. Birrell *English Catholics without a Bishop 1655–1672* (Recusant History IV, 1958) p. 142.

[10] Sergeant, p. 79.

[11] Burton *'From the year 1655, therefore, until the appointment of a new vicar apostolic thirty years later, the chapter exercised jurisdiction, granting faculties for the administration of the Sacraments and for other spiritual functions, making reports to Rome on the state of the mission, and carrying on correspondence with the Congregation of Propaganda'*(p. 248).

[12] Burton, p. 85.

[13] Questier: *'The archpriest's assistants exercised limited authority under his direction in the various geographical districts of the rudimentary Catholic clerical system of ecclesiastical administration. The cardinal protector nomi-*

nated six of the twelve assistants with the archpriest appointing the other six'
p. 252, also P. Guilday, The English Catholic Refugees on the Continent
1558–1795 (1914), p. 104.

[14] Questier: 'John Colleton, the future dean of the secular clergy's episcopal chapter', p. 323.

[15] Sergeant, *Notes of William Turnbull*, p.49.

[16] Sergeant, Note by William Turnbull: ' *In the sequel of the authors argument, it will be seen, first, that the chapter, as a body, was recognised by the Roman court; secondly that the validity of its powers was acknowledged and approved by the sovereign pontiff; and thirdly, that it continued, under the eye of Rome, and during a space of thirty years, in the constant exercise of its ordinary jurisdiction without once receiving an intimation from its superiors that it was acting improperly', p. 78.*

[17] Sergeant note of William Turnbull: '*On the 6th of September, 1685, Leyburne took an oath at Rome, by which he declares that he does not, and never will, recognise the chapter as a legitimate body; that he will never acknowledge any spiritual power to reside in it; that he will never approve of any act which can either directly or indirectly tend to the allowance of its pretended spiritual jurisdiction; and that, in fine, he does and will condemn any exercise of such jurisdiction as null, void, and of no effect', p. 104.*

[18] A List of the Members of the Old English Chapter founded in 1623 and of its heir, the present Old Brotherhood of the English Secular Clergy, 1979 (AAW: p. 6).

[19] Sergeant, p. 114–115.

[20] Sergeant, p. 104.

[21] Sergeant, p. 118.

[22] Sergeant, p. 119.

# APPENDIX EIGHT

## *The Structure of the Lying-in Hospital*

### 1. Trusteeship and the rights of subscribers:

The government ... be placed in the hands of Trustees; all persons contributing one guinea annually be trustees ... any subscriber, after the expiration of the present year, shall have a vote at any General Board ... all persons contributing Ten Guineas at one time be Trustees for life ... that all the Men-Midwives be Trustees during their attendance on the Charity ... that every Trustee be entitled to recommend any number of women not exceeding six within the year to be attended at their own habitations, or two at the Lying-in-Hospital when erected ... that every annual subscriber of half a guinea, shall be entitled to recommend three women every year to be attended at their own Habitations or one at the Lying-in-Hospital when erected, and so in proportion for larger sums ...

### 2. Governance, laws and rules:

A General Board, which shall consist of seven Trustees at the least, be held quarterly, at the Bridgewater Arms, or such convenient place ... on the first Wednesday in May, August, November and February, at eleven o'clock in the Forenoon ... That all Ladies who are Trustees may send their proxy in writing, mentioning the name of the Trustee who is to vote for them at the Election of any Officer ... That the sole power of making or altering Laws and Rules, and electing in displacing officers, be lodged in the General

Board…That all elections at a General Board shall be determined
by Ballot if required… That there be a Monthly Board of Trustees
which shall consist of seven at least, to meet the first Friday in every
month at eleven o'clock in the forenoon at the Bridgewater Arms,
on every Friday, at the Hospital when erected, to manage the affairs
of the Charity and to examine into any complaints that might come
before them…that a President, Treasurer, and two auditors be
chosen Annually on the first Wednesday in May…

### 3. Staffing of the hospital:

That there shall be only three Men-midwives Extraordinary, and
three Men-Midwives in Ordinary…That when any vacancy shall
happen in the office of Man-Midwife Extraordinary it shall be filled
up, in succession from the Men-Midwives in Ordinary…That such
men-Midwives as are fixed upon to attend this Charity shall remain
in their several departments so long as they continue to discharge
the Duties of their Office…That there shall be midwives appointed
in different parts of the Town to attend the poor Women and deliver
them in common cases and they shall be paid for their trouble; but
upon misbehaviour they may be suspended at a Monthly
Board…That the Midwives shall in all cases of Danger and Difficulty
immediately call in one of the Men-Midwives in Ordinary…That
the Men-Midwives Extraordinary shall attend whenever called upon
by the Men-Midwives in Ordinary…That all the Gentlemen of the
Faculty who have the care of this Charity engage to attend at their
own Houses betwixt the hours of eight and nine o'clock in the
morning to give all necessary advice to the poor women or to the
midwives, and to countersign Recommendations.

### 4. The education and training of staff:

That Lectures or instructions be given, at the expence (sic) of this
Charity, to the practising midwives, belonging to this Institution

and to female Pupils, in order to qualify them in future, to be eligible to that Office, by one of the Men-Midwives to this Charity to be appointed by the Quarterly Board...

## 5. The control of medicines:

That until a Hospital be built, the medicines be purchased at an Apothecary's, or Druggist's Shop, but that no medicines be dispensed without the directions of one of the Men-Midwives Extraordinary or in Ordinary...

## 6. Women who could be admitted and the terms of their relief:

That every Recommendation shall be signed by a Trustee or annual subscriber of half a guinea, and countersigned by one of the Medical Gentlemen of the Charity before it be taken to the secondary in admission; and that no women be permitted to partake of this Charity who is able to pay for attendance... That the midwives attend the Monthly Boards, and should bring with them the poor women who are fit to be discharged and able to attend, to return thanks to the Board... That every women relieved by the Charity shall return thanks to Almighty God at her usual place of public worship, and to the person who recommended her; and upon neglect shall be refused any benefit from the Charity in future... That no person in a Poor House, Prison, or House of Correction, shall partake of the Charity... That as soon as the Society can afford, a few sets of Child-bed Linen shall be provided for those who start much in need of such assistance, for their use during the month of their Confinement...

## 7. The building and the boundaries of the work of the charity:

That as soon as the Society is possessed of £2,000 a house shall be built for the reception of Lying-In Women, which shall be under the care and directives of the same Officers as the other part of the Charity... The Boundaries of this Charity beyond which the Midwives are not to go, are: Strangeways Hall; Red Bank; Angel Meadow; Five Houses in Great Newton Street; Pottery in Ancoats Lane; Ardwick Bridge; Knott Mill; Nether end of Oldfield Lane, Salford; Paradise, Salford.

# BIBLIOGRAPHY

## *Archive Collections*

Birmingham. Archdiocesan Archives

Borthwick Institute York

Chester Record Office

Chetham's Library Manchester

Derbyshire Record Office

Greater Manchester Record office

Lancashire Record Office

Leeds Diocesan Archives

Liverpool Archives of the Archbishop

London, Archives of the English Province of the Society of Jesus

Manchester Central Library

National Archives Kew

North Yorkshire County Council

Sheffield City Library

Ushaw College Library

Venerable English College Rome

Westminster, Archdiocesan Archives

## *Primary Resources*

### Archives of the Archbishop of Liverpool

Letter from Rev John Lingard to Rev John Orrell 26 December 1802
(AAL: Orrell Papers, 18).

## Archives of the Archbishop of Birmingham.

Letter from Rt. Rev John Talbot, Vicar Apostolic of the Midland District to Rt. Rev John Hornyold, Coadjutor, Vicar Apostolic of the Midland District 26 August, 1753 (BAA: Z5/3/89/19/7).

## Borthwick Institute York

Peacock, E. (Ed.) A List of the Roman Catholics in the County of York in 1604 (London, 1872)

Archbishop of York *Visitation Book 1606 to 1628* (BIY: R. vi/B/3 f. 50v).

## Catholic Record Society

Burton, E. H. & Nolan, E. editors *The College Diaries, The Seventh Diary, 1715–1778 preceded by a Summary of Events 1691–1715* (T Wilson & Son Kendal, 1928) CRS publication 28.

Worrall, E. S. ed., Returns of Papists 1767. Vol. 1: Diocese of Chester, Catholic Record Society Occasional Publication, 1(1980)

Worrall, E. S. ed., Returns of Papists 1767. Vol. 2: Diocese of England and Wales, except Chester, Catholic Record Society Occasional Publication, 2 (1989)

## Chester Record office

Chester, Diocese of. *Returns of Papists 1767* (Transcribed under the direction of E. S. Worrall, published by the Catholic Record Society, 1980) p. vii.

## Chetham's Library Manchester

Some of the Clergy of the Diocese Chester *A Description of the State, Civil and Ecclesiastical, of the County of Lancaster about the year 1590* (Printed from the original MS., in the Bodleian. With an introduction by the Rev F. R. Raines, M.A., F.S.A., printed for the Chetham. Society, 1875).

Manchester Cathedral Title Deeds (CLM: Mancath.CE 1/Pars/1/1).

Rules and orders for the government of the Sunday schools, 1784 (Manchester, Harrop's, 1784 (CLM).

Wadsworth A. P. *Statistics from the Minutes of the Select Committee on Children in Manufactories* printed in *The Cotton Trade and Industrial Lancashire* (1816) p. 326.

## Chetham's Library

Manchester *Mercury* and Harrop's *General Advertiser* of these dates

10 August 1784

21 September 1784

8 August 1786

16 October 1792

11 August 1795

2 February 1796

17 April 1798

24 April 1798

19 November 1799

31 November 1799

22 July 1800

22 July 1800

27 November 1800

2 December 1800

9 December 1800

3 March 1801

14 April 1801

17 December 1805

13 December 1808

20 December 1808

10 January 1809:

5 May 1812

6 October 1812

19 November 1816

5 August 1817

17 October 1820

## Derbyshire Record Office

Glossop Accounts 19 July 1739 DRO: D3705/8/55.

Glossop Accounts 10 September 1740 DRO: D3705/8/67.

## Greater Manchester Record Office

Borough Reeve's Records *Manchester Poll Book of 1690* (GMRO: M91/74 & M91/28).

## John Rylands Library

Heywood, O. & Dickenson, T. compilers *Excerpts from Nonconformist Register, of Baptisms, Marriages, and Deaths 1644–1702, 1702–1752*. Generally known as the Northowram. or Coley Register, But comprehending numerous notices of Puritans and Anti-Puritans in Yorkshire, Lancashire, Cheshire, London, & with Lists of Popish Recusants. Ref. R192745

## Lancashire Record Office

### *Lancashire Secular Clergy Fund:*

1672–1782: Book of rules, accounts of legacies and donations and memoranda (LRO: RCCF 5/1

1770: Rules of the Secular Clergy Fund with annotations (LRO: RCCF 3/1).

1736 to 1820: The rules of the secular Clergy who are associated to the general Fund in the Counties of Lancaster, Westmorland, Cumberland and Chester (LRO: DDSC/19/38).

25 August 1795 to 1831: Roman Catholic Clergy Fund. Book containing list of fund members, dates of death, benefactions and dividends (LRO: RCCF 1/2).

1797: Rowland Broomhead listed Cash Account Book (LRO: RCCF 5/9).

1783–1846: Book of rules, accounts of legacies and donations and memoranda (LRO: RCCF 5/2).

1800–1919: Miscellaneous bills, receipts, extracts from accounts and related papers (LRO: RCCF).

25 June 1886: John Canon Worthy, Treasurer of the Lancashire Infirm Secular Fund to George Arnold & Co., Lincoln's Inn, London, sent from Euxton, Chorley (LRO:RCCF 2/4).

Anonymous article *The Lancashire Infirm Secular Clergy Fund* (SDA 'The Harvest', July 1918) ref. 370, vol. xxxi, p. 129–131. Also LRO: RCCF Misc. 4/3.

November/December 1775: Letter from Bishop William Walton to Rev John Chadwick (LRO: RCV 2/5/124).

17 January 1780: Letter from Bishop William. Walton to Rev John Chadwick (LRO: RCV2/5/226).

January/February 1780: Letter from Rev John Chadwick to Bishop William. Walton (LRO: RCV 2/5/129).

8 December 1782: Visitation and Confirmation lists of Vicar Apostolic, Matthew Gibson (LRO: RCV 2/6 transcript).

6 December 1784: Visitations and Confirmations etc., of the Vicars Apostolic of the Northern District (LRO: transcript of Ushaw document, RCV2/6).

1785: Diary records Bishop Matthew visiting Stannington (LRO: transcript, RCV 2/6).

8 January 1787: Letter of Bishop Matthew Gibson to Rome (LRO: transcript, Ref RCV 2/6)

25 July 1791: Rev Rowland Broomhead, Registration of the Chapel at Rochdale, General Quarter Session of the Peace, Manchester (LRO: QDV/7/33).

17 September 1792: The last will and testament of John Casey (LRO: WCW 17 September 1792).

1794 First Register of the Catholic Chapel of SS. Peter & Paul Bolton (LRO: RCBO MF 9/53–57).

21 January 1795: Rev Joseph Shepherd, Registration of the Chapel at Wood Street Bolton, General Quarter Session of the Peace, Manchester (LRO: QOV/7/12).

1796: Baptismal Records for Bolton with attached list of Communicants at Rochdale (LRO: RCBO 1/5).

27 February 1796: Letter from Rev Rowland Broomhead to Brian Marsh a student at Crook Hall (UCA: Eyre Correspondence 43).

1797: Rowland Broomhead listed in Cash Account Book (LRO: RCCF 5/9).

3 March 1798: The last Will and Testament of William. Moorhouse (LRO: WCW/3 March 1798).

1821: The last will and testament of Rev Rowland Broomhead (LRO: WCW 1821).

## Leeds Diocesan Archives

1 August 1775: Faculties granted by Bishop William. Walton (Matthew Gibson, Vicar General) to Rev Rowland Broomhead (LDA: 48/MG).

1780–90 Matthew Gibson's Address Book (LDA: 48/MG).

12 January 1784: Letter from John Chadwick of Weld Bank, Chorley to Matthew Gibson at Headlam., Darlington (LDA: 11/MG).

31 January 1787: Letter from John Chadwick of the Blackburn Incumbency at Weld Bank, Chorley, to Matthew Gibson at Stella Hall near Newcastle-upon-Tyne (LDA: 11/MG).

31 January 1787: Letter from Rev John Chadwick to Bishop Matthew Gibson (LDA. 28/MG).

C. 1790: Letter from the Lancashire Clergy to the Lords and Gentlemen of the Committee of English Catholics (LDA: 46/MG).

May 1791: Accounts of the Northern District, p. 111. (LDA: 57/WG).

9 December 1791: Letter from George Wm. Coombes of Bath to Bishop William Gibson (LDA: 84/1&2/WG).

5 January 1794: Letter from Bishop William Gibson to Rev Thomas Eyre in York (LDA: 155/ WG).

31 August 1796: Letter from Bishop Milner to Bishop William Gibson (LDA: 220/ WG).

December 1796: Letter from Bishop William Gibson to the Bishop of Arras (LDA: 227a/WG).

27 April 1798: Letter from John Douglass, Vicar Apostolic of the London District to William Gibson, Vicar Apostolic of the Northern District (LDA: 263/WG).

28 October 1803: Letter from Rev Rowland Broomhead to Bishop William Gibson (LDA: 478/WG).

31 August 1804: Letter from Rev Rowland Broomhead to Bishop William Gibson (LDA: 497/WG).

8 December 1804: Letter from Rev Anthony Lund of Fernyhalgh to the Right Rev William Gibson, Old Elvet Street, Durham. (LDA: 501/WG).

12 February 1806: Letter from Rev Rowland Broomhead to Rev Thomas Eyre at Ushaw (LDA: 553A). 12February 1807: Letter from Rev, Rowland Broomhead, Rook Street Manchester to Rev, Dr William Gibson, Old Elvet, Durham. (LDA: 553A/WG).

18 March 1811: Letter from Rev Rowland Broomhead to Bishop William Gibson at Durham. (LDA: 690).

23 February 1811: Letter from Rev Thomas Longden, 5 Sunderland Street, Macclesfield to the Right Rev Dr

William Gibson, Old Elvet, Durham. (LDA: 679/WG).

7 July 1811: Letter from Rev Rowland Broomhead, Rook Street, Manchester to the Right Rev Dr William Gibson, Old Elvet, Durham. (LDA: 706/WG).

25 March 1813: Letter from Rev Rowland Broomhead, Rev Mr Kenyon & Rev Thomas Lupton to Bishop William Gibson (LDA: 805/WG).

25 September 1813: *Meeting of the Catholics of Sheffield with a view to building a new chapel* (Sheffield, 1813) LDA: 834.

20 May, 1817: Meeting of the Trustees of Ushaw College (LDA: 999/WG).

20 December 1817: Letter from Rev Richard Thompson to Bishop William Gibson (LDA: 1040/WG).

15 January 1818: Letter from Rev Richard Thompson to Dr William Gibson (LDA: 1044/WG).

12 February 1818: Letter from Rev Richard Thompson to Bishop William Gibson (LDA: 1051/WG).

9 December 1819: Letter from the Rev Richard Thompson to the Right Rev Dr William Gibson (LDA: 1144/WG).

**Manchester Board of Health**

1796–1804: Manchester Board of Health, printed minutes (MCL: MC/614.0942 M13).

**Manchester Central Library**

Curr, J. Rev *A Discourse delivered at St Augustine's Chapel, Manchester, 18 October 1820 at the Funeral of the Rev Rowland Broomhead* (Printed and Published by J. Robinson, Catholic Bookseller, 44, Deansgate, Manchester 1820).

Gaffey, M. *A Panegyric of the late Rev Rowland Broomhead, Forty-two years a Catholic Priest at Manchester* (printed and published by J. A. Robinson, 44, Deansgate, Manchester. February 1822; sold also by Mr A. Cuddon, 62, Crown-street, Finsbury Square, London) MCL: 922.2 B31.

Manchester 'Exchange Herald' anonymous author *Brief Memoirs of the Rev Rowland Broomhead of Manchester with an Account of his Funeral; and a Funeral Elegy,* transposed from the 'Exchange Herald' with the addition of the Elegy (Printed and sold by Joseph Aston, 14, St Ann's-street, price fourpence, Manchester, 1820).

*Plan of Manchester and Salford 1750.* (MCL: 14723).

Green, W. A Plan of Manchester and Salford. Drawn from an actual survey by William. Green. Begun in the year 1787 and completed in 1794

Tinker, T. Junior *A Plan of Manchester and Salford in the County Palatine of Lancaster* (Manchester 1772).

Roman Entry: 23 November 1914: J. & N. Philips & Co. Ltd. Plan of a proposed warehouse to be built alongside Roman Entry. Agreement between Messrs Isaac Thorp and Sons Limited and Messrs R. B. Carr & Co. Ltd., for the lease of a warehouse to be erected in Church Street and Roman Street. MCL: M97/ 21/14.

Roman Entry: Photograph dated 1930. MCL: 913.4273, no originator.

Roman Entry:26 July 1944: Letter from F. S. Fairey, Entwistle & Co. of Yorkshire House, 45 Cross Street, Manchester to J & N Philips, 35 Church Street, Manchester (dimensions of the land at Roman Entry) MCL: M97/10. 22/8.

Roman Entry: Philips J. & N & Co. Ltd. Details of Apportionment Account, £54 payable to the Diocese of Salford, 1951. MCL: M97/10, 26/22.

Wise F. & James I. Vintners Arms, Old Smithy Door (Drawing dated 1825. Demolished 1875) MCL:

## Manchester Central Hospitals Trust Archives

22 August 1763: Decision to erect the Lunatic Ward (MI/SGB:

26 September 1765: management of the Lunatic Ward (MI/QB)

15 July 1779: Plan to set up New baths (MI/QB).

19 February 1787: Rowland Broomhead a member of the Board (MI/B).

20February 1791: Rules and regulations (MI/B)

31 October 1791: Disorderly people accessing the Infirmary grounds (MI/B).

16 January 1792: Thanks to the officers (MI/B).

25 April 1796: The efficacy of port-wine (MI/B)

25 April 1796: Quotation from the letter of J. Blackburne, Minister at the Treasury (MI/B)

1805–1809: Schedule of Deeds (MI/QB).

2 April 1812: A meeting for the appointment of a new physician. (MI/B)

17 June 1819: Thanks to Broomhead for his attentive and obliging behaviour (MI.B).

## Manchester Lying-in Hospital

October 1804 to August 1819 listed in the Weekly Board Book of the Lying-in-Hospital (MLH).

20 May 1806: Broomhead was one of three who prepared the annual report (MLH).

15 August 1806: Broomhead received a subscription from Mr Gibson and Mr Leaf for the hospital (MLH).

## Middlesex County Records

*Middlesex Sessions Rolls 1632* Vol. 3: 1625–67 (1888) pp. 41–49.

## The National Archives Kew

College of Arms *Calendar of the Talbot Papers* Vol. II. Folio 615(Historical Manuscripts Commission, JP7, G. R. Batho. H. M. S. O. 1971).

## Salford Diocesan Archives

1794–1847: The William. Moorhouse & John Casey Charities (The Account Book of Casey's Charity) Trustees of Manchester & Lancashire FHS 2004 (SDA).

Hughes, Fr Philip *St Chad's Manchester 1847–1947* in 'The Harvest', 1947 (magazine of the Diocese of Salford) p.154–5.

Rules & Regulations, agreed upon by the Bishop and Secular Clergy Priests, in the Hundreds of Salford & Macclesfield, for the future care and management of their Funds and Temporal Affairs 1823 (Salford Diocesan Archives).

Handbook to the Catholic Truth Society's Conference, Silver Jubilee 1884–1909. (Published by the Salford Catholic Federation, Bishop's House, Salford, 1909). Contains: The Story of the 'Old Faith' in Manchester by John O'Dea.

## Sheffield City Library

*First Register Roll of the Papists Estates: Lists of registration of papists' estates in Derbyshire 1717* (Sheffield Archives: OD1389).

Hall, T. W. *The City of Sheffield, Descriptive Catalogue of Charters, Copy Court Rolls and Deeds* (Sheffield, J. W. Northend, 1920).

Hunter, J. Rev *Familiae Minorum Gentium.MS.170* compiled by the Rev Joseph Hunter (Sheffield, 1894–6 transcribed by Hunter and printed for the Harlean Society) SCL: ms.170, p. 387—390.

## Ushaw College Archives

1688–1711: The Barton Trust (UCA: III, 27).

16 June 1774: Letter from Right Rev William. Walton to Francis Petre, Vicar Apostolic (UCA: Collection 2/11/ 196c).

5 July 1776: Letter from Rev John Orrell to Bishop William. Walton, Vicar Apostolic of the Northern District, regarding the income of the Manchester incumbency (UCA: 11/473).

5 March 1778: Letter from Bishop William. Walton in York to Rev John Chadwick, Grand Vicar (UCA: Presidents' Archives/C2).

3 February 1783: Letter from Rev John Chadwick to Bishop Matthew Gibson (UCA: 11/129/MG)

31 January 1787: Letter from Rev John Chadwick, Grand Vicar, to Bishop Matthew Gibson (UCA: PA/C20/MG).

17 July 1780: Letter from Bishop Matthew Gibson to Rev John Chadwick (UCA: II/126/MG).

1789: The Declaration and Protestation Signed by the English Catholic Dissenters in 1789 with the NA.M.ES of those who signed it (UCA: 475C; printed in 1791).

I January 1790: Letter signed by fifty-five Lancashire Priests to the Vicar Apostolic William Gibson (Ward, Bernard vol. 1, p. 201–20).

6 March 1791: Letter from Rev Rowland Broomhead to Rev John Chadwick, Grand Vicar (UCA: Presidents' Archives/C20).

30 June 1791: Letter from the Vicar Apostolic to all the faithful, clergy and laity in the Northern District (UCA: X. E. 2. 76/WG).

30 August 1791: Letter from Rowland Broomhead, and twenty-nine other priests, who had signed an address to the three Vicars Apostolic of the districts of London, the Midlands and the North. (UCA: Library: X. E. 2. 7p). 4 September 1797: Rev Rowland Broomhead to Rev Thomas Eyre at Crook Hall (UC: President's Archives 42).

1 November 1802: Letter from Rev Richard Thompson to Rev Thomas Eyre, President of Crook Hall (UCA: Calendar of Eyre Correspondence, vol. 2, p. 381–383).

3 December 1803: Letter from Rev Richard Thompson, Grand Vicar, to Rev Thomas Eyre at Crook Hall (UCA: Calendar of Eyre Correspondence, vol. 2, page 384).

24 April 1804: Letter from Robert Banister to Henry Nutter (UCA: 143).

26 April 1805: Letter from Rev Mr Thompson, Grand Vicar in Lancashire to the Rev Dr William Gibson at Durham. (UCA: 513 WG).

27 April 1804: Letter from Robert Banister to his nephew Henry Nutter (UCA: 142).

27 February 1806: Letter from Rev Rowland Broomhead to Brian Marsh a student at Crook Hall (UCA: Eyre Correspondence, 43).

6 November 1806: Letter from Rev Rowland Broomhead to Rev Thomas Eyre, President of Crook Hall (UCA: Eyre correspondence 47).

20 November 1806: Rowland Broomhead to Rev Thomas Eyre (UCA: Eyre correspondence 47b).

26 February 1807: Letter from Rev Rowland Broomhead to Rev Thomas Eyre, President of Crook Hall (UCA: Eyre correspondence, 49).

7 July 1807: Letter from Rev Rowland Broomhead to Rev Thomas Eyre (UCA: Eyre Papers 50).

28 September 1819: Letter from Rowland Broomhead to Rev Mr Winstanley, rector of the English College Lisbon (UCA: English College Lisbon).

3 May 1820: Letter from Bishop Milner to Rev Rowland Broomhead (UCM: PA/D30).

### Venerable English College

Casemore, W. *The Diary of William. Casemore* (VEC: 1765 to 1775).

Kirk, J. *The Diary of John Kirk 1773–1785* (VEC: Lib. 815).

*The Pilgrim Book:* VEC: Libri. 282, 283, 292 [Parts published in Foley].

*1657 visitation,* (VEC: Liber. 228).

*Liber Ruber* (VEC: CRS 37).

6 September 1775: *Letter of George Halsey to Magnani, Vice-Rector of the English College, Rome 6 September 1775.* (VEC: Scritture 50. 5. 7).

12 March 1818: Letter from John Gradwell to his brother Robert Gradwell (VEC: Scr. 56. 6).

30 April 1819: Letter from John Gradwell to his brother Robert Gradwell, rector of the English College in Rome (VEC: Scr. 56.6).

### West Yorkshire Archives Service

West Riding Quarter Sessions Records Orders, 1611–1642 (Printed by the Yorkshire Archaeological Society, Vol. LIII, preface p. xvi/xvii).

Yorkshire Archaeological Society

*Archbishop Herrings Visitation Returns 1743* (YAS) volumes 71, 72, 75, 77, 79

# *Secondary Resources*

Addis, W. E. & Arnold, T. *A Catholic Dictionary containing some account of the doctrine, discipline, rites, ceremonies, councils, and religious orders of the Catholic Church* (revised with additions by Scannell. T. B., 9th edition, London, 1925).

Amherst, W. H. *The History of Catholic Emancipation and the Progress of the Catholic Church in the British Isles (chiefly in England) from 1771 to 1820* (London, Kegan Paul, Trench & Co, 1886).

Anderson M. S. *Europe in the Eighteenth Century 1713–1783.* (London, 1976)

Anstruther, G. *The Seminary Priests: A Dictionary of the Secular Clergy of England and Wales 1558–1850* (London 1969).

Aston, J. *The Manchester Guide: A Brief Historical Account of the Towns of Manchester and Salford, the Public Buildings and the Charitable & Literary Institutions.* (Manchester, 1804) p. 123n.

Aston, J. A Picture of Manchester (Manchester, 1822).

Attwater, D (Ed). *The Catholic Encyclopaedic Dictionary* (London, 1949).

Aveling, J. C. H. *The Jesuits* (London, 1981).

Axon, W. E. A. (Ed) *The Annals of Manchester, A chronological record from the earliest times to the end of 1885.* (Manchester, 1886).

Birrell, T. A. *English Catholics Without a Bishop 1655–1672* (Recusant History IV, 1958) p. 142.

Birt, H. N. *The Elizabethan Religious Settlement, A Study of Contemporary Documents* (London, George Bell & Sons, 1907)

Bolton, C. A. *Salford Diocese and its Catholic Past* (Manchester, Jas. F. & C. Carter Ltd. 1950).

Bossy, J. *Rome and the Elizabethan Catholics: A Question of Geography.* Historical Journal VII, (1964)

Boudon, H. M. *The Love of Jesus in the Adorable Sacrament of the Altar.* (A New translation from the French, printed by R. & W. Dean and Co. Market-Street Lane for T. Haydock, Manchester, 1801).

Bride, J. W. MD. *A Short History of St Mary's Hospital, Manchester and the Honorary Medical Staff from the Foundation in 1790 to 1922* (Manchester, 1922).

Brooks, A. & B. Haworth, The Portico Library (Manchester, Carnegie Publishing Lancaster, 2000).

Burton, E. H. *The Life and times of Bishop Challoner 1691–1781* (London, Longmans, Green and Co., 1909) vol. 1. p. 85).

Buscot, W. *The History of Cotton College at Sedgley Park, 1763–1873* (London, 1940

Busteed, M. *The Irish in Nineteenth Century Manchester* (Irish Studies No. 18. Spring, 1997).

Callow, J. *James Dymock or Dymock, Roman Catholic priest* (Oxford Dictionary of National Biography).

Challoner, R. et alia *Memoirs of Missionary Priests* (New edition revised and corrected by John Hungerford Pollen S.J. London, 1924).

Chaloner W. H. *The birth of Modern Manchester* contribution 9 to Manchester and its Region: A Survey prepared for The British Association for the Meeting held in Manchester 29 August to 5 September 1962.

Champ, Judith F. *The English Pilgrimage to Rome: A Dwelling for the Soul* (Buckinghamshire, Gracewing Publishing, 2000).

*Commercial & Trade Directory for Rochdale* (Rochdale, 1825).

Cook, T. W. *Notes of a Tour in the Manufacturing Districts in a series of Letters to His Grace the Archbishop of Dublin* (Duncan & Malcolm, 1842).

Croskell, R. *Traditions Connected with the Revival of the Catholic Faith in Manchester* 'The Harvest' Diocese of Salford, Vol. ix. 1896).

Curley, T. *The Catholic History of Oldham.* (East Yorkshire, 1911).

Davies, C. S. (Ed). *A History of Macclesfield* (Macclesfield, 1961).

Dodd's, M. H. & R. *The Pilgrimage of Grace, 1536–1537, and the Exeter Conspiracy 1538,* 2 vols. (Cambridge, 1915).

Duffy, E. The *Stripping of the Altars Traditional Religion in England c. 1400-c. 1580* (New Haven and London, Yale University Press, 1992).

Dymock, J. Rev *The Great Sacrifice of the New Law, Expounded by the Figures of the Old. To which is added The Mass for the Dead With divers other Additions and Alterations* (Printed for Matthew Turner at the Lamb in High Holborn, 1687)

Earwake, J. P. *East Cheshire Past and Present* (London, 1877) p. 93.

Elliot, M. *Partners in Revolution: the United Irishmen and France* (New Haven, 1982). Wells, R. *Insurrection: the British Experience, 1795–1803* (Gloucester, 1983),

Evinson, D. *The Lord's House. A History of Sheffield's Roman Catholic Buildings 1570–1990* (Sheffield, Sheffield Academic Press, 1991).

Fay, C. R. *Great Britain from Adam. Smith to the Present Day, an Economic and Social Survey* (London, 1940).

Finney, Isaac *Macklesfelde in ye Olden Time* (Macclesfield, 1873).

Frangopulo, N. J. Editor *Rich Inheritance, A Guide to the History of Manchester* (Manchester Education Committee, 1962).

Furniss, E. S. *The Position of the Labourer in a System of Nationalism* (1920) reprinted *Considerations on the Fatal Effects to a Trading Nation of the Present Excess of Public Charity* (1763), p. 148–149.

Gandy, M. (Ed). *Catholic Missions and Registers 1700–1880, Volume 5 North West England* (London 1993).

Gasquet, F. A. *A history of the venerable English College, Rome* (London, Longmans, Green and Co., 1920).

Gee, H & W. J. Hardy, W. J. (Ed) *Documents Illustrative of English Church History* (London, Macmillan, 4ᵗʰ ed. 1921).

Gillow, J. *A Literary and Biographical History or Bibliographical Dictionary of the English Catholics from the Breach with Rome in 1534 to the Present Time* (London, Burns & Oates, 5 Vols., 1885–1902).

Gillow, J. *The Haydock Papers: a glimpse into English Catholic life under the shade of persecution and in the dawn of freedom* (London, Burns & Oates, 1888).

Gooch, L. (Ed) *The Catholic Revival in England, the Banister/Rutter Correspondence 1777–1807* (North West Catholic History, 1995) Letter no. 90.

Gregg, P. *A Social and Economic History of Britain 1760–1950* (London, George G. Harrop & Co.Ltd., 1950).

Hadfield, C. *A History of S. Marie's Mission and Church, Norfolk Row, Sheffield* (Sheffield, 1889).

Heywood, T. T. (compiled) *New Annals of Rochdale* (Rochdale, 1931)

Hollingworth, R. *Mancuniensis; or, an history of the towne of Manchester* (Manchester, 1839).

Holt, J. *General View of the Agriculture of the County of Lancashire and Observations on the Means of Improvement* (Nicoll, 1795).

Hughes, P. Rev *The Catholic Question 1688–1829, A Study in Political History* (London, Sheed & Ward, 1929) p. 143.

Hughes, P. Rev *St Chad's Manchester 1847–1947* in 'The Harvest', 1947 (magazine of the Diocese of Salford) p.154–5.

Hughes, p. *The Reformation in England* (London, Hollis & Carter, 1956).

Husenbeth, F. C. *The History of Sedgley Park School* (Staffordshire, 1856).

Husenbeth, F. C. *The Life of the Right Rev John Milner, D. D., Bishop of Castabala, Vicar Apostolic of the Midland District of England* (Dublin & London, 1862).

Jungmann, J. A. *The Mass of the Roman Rite, its Origins and Development Missarum Sollemnia* (London, 1959)

Keir, D. L. *The Constitutional History of Modern Britain 1485–1937* (London, 1943)

Kennedy, P. (Ed) *The Catholic Church in England and Wales 1500–2000* (West Yorkshire, PBK Publishing, 2001) p.165.

Kidd, A. *Manchester a history* (Lancaster, 2008).

Kidd, A & Roberts, K *City, Class and Culture* (Manchester, 1955).

Kirk, J. *Biographies of English Catholics in the eighteenth century, being part of his projected continuation of Dodd's Church history* Edited by John Hungerford Pollen and Edwin Burton (London, Burns & Oates, 1909).

Knowles, D. Dom *The Religious Orders in England Volume III The Tudor Age* (Cambridge, University Press 1961).

Lannon, D. *Rook Street Chapel Manchester* (article in North West Catholic History 1989) vol. 16, p. 10–17.

Locke, J. *An Essay Concerning Human Understanding* (London, 1690).

Loxham., R *Illustrations of parish churches: the district churches and chapelries of the town and townships of the collegiate parish of Manchester in the county of Lancaster 1837–1838* (Manchester, 1838) 2 vols.

Marshall, B. *A History of the Parish of St Paul's Catholic Church, Hyde, 1848–1998.*

Mayer, A. O. *England and the Catholic Church under Queen Elizabeth* (Trubner, Keegan Paul, Trench, 1916).

Navickas, K. *Loyalism and Radicalism in Lancashire 1798–1815*(Oxford, 2009) p.141

Pollen, J. H. *English Post-Reformation Oaths*. The Catholic Encyclopaedia, Vol.11. (New York, Robert Appleton Co., 1911).

Prendergast, P. *Old Catholic Manchester* (Manchester, 1905) JRL: 166830, special collection,

Procter, R. W. *Memorials of Manchester Streets* (Manchester, 1874).

Questier, M. C. *Catholicism and Community in Early Modern England: Politics, Aristocratic Patronage and Religion, c. 1550–1640* (Cambridge, University Press, 2006).

Reilly, J. *The History of Manchester* (Manchester, 1865) p. 259.

Renaud, F. *A Short History of the "House of Recovery" or Fever Hospital in Manchester* (Manchester, 1885).

Rochdale: *Commercial & Trade Directory for Rochdale* (Rochdale, 1825)

Saintsbury, G. *Manchester: A Plan of Manchester and Salford about 1650* Drawn by Edward Weller. (London 1887).

Sergeant, J. *Transactions of the English Secular Clergy* (London, 1706).

Scola, R. *Feeding the Victorian City: the Food Supply of Manchester 1770–1870* (Manchester University Press, 1992).

Shutt, F. J. *The Visitation of 1657* (VEC: May 1947) vol. XIII, no. 2).

Slater, J. *A Catholic History of Eccles and Barton* (Eccles, 1897).

Stebbing, G. *The Story of the Catholic Church.* (London, 1915)

Stevens, T. H. G. Manchester of Yesterday (Altrincham., 1958).

Tate, W. E. *The Parish Chest, A Study of the Records of Parochial Administration in England,* (Cambridge, 1969).

Taylor W. Cook *Notes of a Tour in the Manufacturing Districts in a series of Letters to His Grace the Archbishop of Dublin* (Duncan & Malcolm, 1842).

Thomson, W. H. *History of Manchester to 1852* (Manchester, John Sherratt & Son Ltd., 1967).

Trevelyan, G. M. *British History in the Nineteenth Century 1782–1901* (London, Longmans, Green and Co. 1922).

Ullman, M. J. *St Alban's Macclesfield* (Macclesfield, 1982)

Wadsworth A. P. *The First Manchester Sunday School* (reprinted from the Bulletin of the John Ryland's' Library Manchester) Vol. 33, No. 2, March 1951, p. 299.

Walton, J. K. *Lancashire: A Social History 1558–1939* (Manchester University Press, 1987)

Ward, B. *The Dawn of the Catholic Revival in England 1781 1803*(London, Longmans, Green, and Co., 1909).

Watson, S. J. *The Reign of King George III, 1760–1815* The Oxford History of England XII (Oxford, Clarendon Press, 1992).

Wells, R. *Insurrection: the British Experience, 1795–1803* (Gloucester, 1983) p.235.

William's, J. A. *Catholic Recusancy in Wiltshire 1660–1791* (CRS: 1968 Monograph Series) vol. 1.

William's, M. E. *The Venerable English College Rome: a history 1579–1979* (Associated Catholic Publications for the Venerable English College, Rome, 1979).

Wright, G. & Dove, H. *Our Lady and the Apostles, Stockport, 1799–1999. Two Hundred Years of Witness* (Stockport, 1999).

## Unpublished Theses

Connolly, G. P. Catholicism in Manchester and Salford, 1770–1850 (Unpublished thesis for PhD, Manchester University, 1980) TH10287.

Lannon D. Rev Dr unpublished thesis, *Bishop Turner and Educational Provision within the Salford Diocesan Area 1840—1870,* (University of Hull, 1994).

# INDEX

*Figures in italics indicate a picture, chart, map or other image*